A Discourse Analysis of
First Corinthians

Summer Institute of Linguistics and
The University of Texas at Arlington
Publications in Linguistics

Publication 120

Editor

Donald A. Burquest
University of Texas at Arlington

Consulting Editors

Doris A. Bartholomew
Pamela M. Bendor-Samuel
Desmond C. Derbyshire
Robert A. Dooley
Jerold A. Edmondson

Austin Hale
Robert E. Longacre
Eugene E. Loos
Kenneth L. Pike
Viola G. Waterhouse

A Discourse Analysis of First Corinthians

Ralph Bruce Terry

A Publication of
The Summer Institute of Linguistics
and
The University of Texas at Arlington
1995

©1995 by the Summer Institute of Linguistics, Inc.

Library of Congress Catalog No: 93–61605

ISBN: 0–88312–707–5

ISSN: 1040–0850

The text of the Greek New Testament is taken from the *Greek New Testament*, 3rd edition and 3rd (corrected) edition, © 1966, 1968, 1975, 1983 by the United Bible Societies. Used by permission.

Cover sketch and design by Hazel Shorey

Copies of this and other publications of the Summer Institute of Linguistics may be obtained from

International Academic Bookstore
7500 W. Camp Wisdom Road
Dallas, TX 75236

This book is lovingly dedicated to the five most influential women in my life: my mother, Hazel Terry, who instilled in me a great love for the Scriptures; my wife, Barbara Terry, who supported me throughout my academic journey in countless ways; and my three daughters, Brina, Breta, and Becka, who put up with a father constantly in school.

Contents

List of Tables

Preface

While serving on the Navajo reservation as a missionary, my emphasis in teaching the Bible moved from the word level to the paragraph level. Therefore, it was only natural when I returned to the academic world, that I should pursue discourse studies. My dissertation at the University of Texas at Arlington represented an attempt to combine biblical studies and discourse linguistics.

This book is substantially that dissertation, reproduced here with only minor changes. Thus I would like to express my appreciation to the members of my dissertation committee—Robert E. Longacre (chairman), Joseph W. Bastien, Donald A. Burquest, Kenneth L. Pike, Robert J. Reddick, and Nancy V. Wood—for all their help and encouragement in bringing this study to fruition. Any errors in this work are mine, but many other errors, no longer here, have been removed through their diligence. I would also like to thank Bill Merrifield and the staff at Academic Publications for their ready acceptance of this work for publication. The editors there have made this book better for their work on it; special thanks goes to Laurie Nelson for the care which she took in editing.

The discourse theory upon which this study is based is the tagmemic approach put forward by Robert Longacre and Kenneth Pike. The multiple perspective approach of analyzing a text according to particle, wave, and field and dividing the linguistic analysis into phonological, grammatical, and conceptual hierarchies is based on the work of Pike. The general outline for this book—studying rhetorical situation, macrostructure, macrosegmentation, constituent structure analysis, peak, participant analysis, word order considerations, and quoted material—comes from the methodological approach of Longacre.

This study is one of an increasing number in which the computer is used as an analytical tool. The forces at work in discourse grammar are so complex that only with the help of the rapid analysis provided by the computer can they begin to be identified. Once a database is established, the computer allows the researcher to test hypotheses in minutes that until recently would have taken years.

To the extent that style is defined grammatically, as it often is in biblical studies, this work presents material that complicates the application of source criticism and those disciplines built upon it. It shows that there is a statistically significant stylistic difference between peak and nonpeak sections of 1 Corinthians and between those sections written in response to oral reports and those sections written in response to the Corinthians' letter, even though all scholars agree that the entire letter was written by one person. The premise that a change in style implies a change in authorship must be rejected as too simplistic. Rhetorical situation variations and rhetorical devices for emphasis must be added to change of authorship as possible explanations for a change in style.

This work does not attempt to study all aspects of discourse in the book of 1 Corinthians. The scope of possible studies is extremely wide. Focus here is on grammatical areas, with some attention to conceptual as well. More study can be done in the grammatical areas; much more can be done in the conceptual areas. But this study demonstrates that discourse analysis proves to be an important tool for the study of texts, even ancient texts such as 1 Corinthians.

I would be remiss if I did not express my deep gratitude to my family and friends for their support and encouragement during the time that I was engaged in this study. I know that my children—Brina, Breta, and Becka—had to put up with daddy typing on the word processor all too often. I especially want to thank my wife Barbara, who has provided loving support in more ways than I can count.

My greatest thanks are due to our God for His salvation in our Lord Jesus Christ. May this study be to His glory as we more clearly hear His Spirit speak in His Word.

1

Introduction

1.1 The research problem

In the latter part of the twentieth century, the focus of certain linguists has turned to a study of linguistic features on a level larger than that of the sentence. This focus has carried various labels: textlinguistics, discourse analysis, discourse study, and conversational analysis. In a broader sense it has been interdisciplinary in method, involving scholars from linguistics, literary criticism, sociology, psychology, cognitive science, and artificial intelligence. It has begun to spill over into other disciplines of the humanities, such as history, anthropology, and biblical studies. This work represents an interdisciplinary study in the fields of linguistics and biblical studies.

Statement of the problem. The purpose of this study is to discover discourse-level linguistic features that are used in the Greek text of the New Testament book of 1 Corinthians. To facilitate this process the following questions can be asked. What linguistic features of discourse can be discovered in the Greek text of 1 Corinthians, and how do these impact the theory of textlinguistics and the understanding of the text under study? The answers to these questions can be uncovered by answering the following subsidiary questions:

Is there information in the rhetorical situation and cultural background of the book of 1 Corinthians that would affect our understanding of the grammatical style and conceptual framework of this book?

What is the relationship between themes, theses, and macrostructures in general, and what light does 1 Corinthians shed on this relationship?

What structural and rhetorical patterns of discourse can be discovered in the Greek text of 1 Corinthians? Is one perspective sufficient to view these patterns?

What is the nature of the grammatical shifts known as PEAK in hortatory texts? Does peak function to mark a HORTATORY CLIMAX in hortatory texts in the same way that it marks climax in narrative texts? Does 1 Corinthians show a grammatical peak and/or a hortatory climax?

Are there any motivations for clause-level word order in Koiné Greek as evidenced in 1 Corinthians that can be attributed to linguistic features operating at a discourse level?

Limitations. There are other questions that could be asked which are beyond the scope of this study. Specifically, the following limitations apply to this work.

Although there is justification given below for selecting the third edition of the Greek text found in the United Bible Societies' *Greek New Testament* as the basis for this research, this is not a study in the textual criticism of 1 Corinthians, nor, in general, is the linguistic effect of textual variants discussed in this study.

It should be noted that the study of any ancient document is a study in the performance of a given language, and the exact degree of linguistic competence of the writer cannot be fully determined. Generalizations about grammatical rules at a discourse level will be true only to the extent that the text under study is the product of a competent user of the language. Since 1 Corinthians is usually considered to be a document of enduring literary significance, it will here be assumed that its author exhibited a high degree of linguistic competence in producing this work.

Although discourse studies, especially in conversational analysis, often focus on the area of phonology, including the prosodic features of a language, such features are difficult to determine in an ancient document and will be considered beyond the scope of this study.

Without getting into the question of authorial intent, it is assumed in this study that certain scholarly techniques, such as a study of the historical, cultural, and rhetorical situations plus a grammatical and lexical analysis of the text, allow the modern student to understand the meaning of a given text within reasonable tolerances.

Terms. Discourse analysis is a relatively new field. However, it has been around long enough to establish a technical vocabulary. The following terms need to be defined in order to clarify the discussion in subsequent chapters.

DISCOURSE is used in this work in two ways. First, it is used in a general way to refer to a level of analysis of any linguistic unit larger than a sentence. In this sense, discourse analysis is roughly equivalent to text analysis or the study of textlinguistics. Second, it is used in a specific way to refer to a linguistic unit that constitutes a whole that can, to some extent, meaningfully stand on its own. Such a unit is typically composed of paragraphs or smaller discourses. The complete book of 1 Corinthians is analyzed as a discourse composed of several smaller discourses plus an introduction and conclusion.

PARAGRAPH in this work is used to refer to a linguistic unit which is larger than a sentence but smaller than a discourse. Such a unit is typically composed of sentences or recursively embedded smaller paragraphs. MACROPARAGRAPH is used to refer to a paragraph which is an immediate component part of a discourse. Such a paragraph may express a complete idea or concept, but cannot stand on its own without losing its original significance in the work in which it is found. MICROPARAGRAPH is used to refer to the simplest form of paragraph, one composed only of sentences, that is, having no recursively embedded paragraphs.

TEXTTYPE in this work is used to refer to a category of types of text based upon grammatical differences. The five texttypes identified in this study are narrative, procedural, expository, hortatory, and persuasive.

MACROSTRUCTURE in this work is used to refer to a collection of mental concepts that controls the form and content of a discourse. An overt macrostructure may be seen as an abstract, summary, or thesis statement of a work.

PEAK is used in this work to refer to a region of grammatical turbulence where linguistic features do not occur in their normal usage within the discourse under study.

TAGMEMICS in this work is used to refer to a linguistic theory developed initially by Kenneth L. Pike (1967, 1982) and expanded by various others. In the view of tagmemics, any linguistic data can be viewed in one of three ways: statically, dynamically, or relationally (sometimes called after physics: particle, wave, or field). The theory divides linguistic data into three hierarchical areas: phonological (the sound system), grammatical (the morpho-syntactic system), and referential (the mental meaning system as it relates to perceived reality). Since REFERENTIAL has at least four different technical meanings in the discipline of linguistics, the term CONCEPTUAL will be used in this work to refer to this third area. A linguistic unit in any of these three areas is referred to as a TAGMEME. A tagmeme is described by a slot and class relationship (optionally including role and cohesion in the FOUR-CELLED TAGMEME). This is usually represented by the notations in (1).

(1)   Two-celled tagmeme notation   Four-celled tagmeme notation

       Slot:Class | Slot | Class |
                                            |------|----------|
                                            | Role | Cohesion |

COMPETENT is used in this work to refer to language usage by a speaker or writer which most other speakers and writers of the language would agree is in conformity with the grammatical rules of the language.

STYLE is used in this work to refer to any repeated linguistic feature or collection of features, without regard to whether such features or collections are under the control of competent grammatical rules or are in free variation, subject only to the author's choice.

The word FEATURES is used in this work in a generic way to refer to various linguistic facets, aspects, and factors at work on a discourse level. Specifically, it does not refer to any theoretical construct, such as phonetic features usually assumed to make up a phoneme.

1.2 The study of discourse in the field of Linguistics

As an interdisciplinary study, this work draws upon the scholarship in two fields—linguistics and biblical studies—and brings them together to produce new insights for both. Some cross-disciplinary studies of this nature have already been done.[1] Since the work in discourse linguistics is

---

[1]Longacre has led the way with Old Testament studies on both the flood narrative (1979a) and the Joseph narrative (1989a) in the book of Genesis. He has been followed by Clendenen, who has applied the methodology to a study of the Hebrew hortatory texts of Jeremiah 10:1–16 (1987) and the book of Malachi (1989).

K. Callow (1974) provided an early attempt at combining discourse studies with the New Testament, although her emphasis was on the receptor language in Bible translation. At the 1980 seminar of the Society of Biblical Literature, Boers read a paper which dealt with the discourse structure and macrostructure of John 4. Levinsohn (1987) has done research on cohesion in Acts. In addition, Booth's (1991) dissertation

relatively recent, it seems best to give a brief overview of the theory behind it at this point.

The study of linguistics can be divided into several subdisciplines, including phonology, grammar, semantics, pragmatics, and sociolinguistics. The study of discourse has ties with all of these areas, although it receives special emphasis by the last two of these fields. It is not tied to any special linguistic theory, such as generative transformational grammar, X-bar syntax, government and binding, or generalized phrase structure grammar. It has especially drawn the attention of linguists who have worked in case grammar, such as Grimes (1975), Fillmore (1981), and Longacre (1983b). But others, who hold to nongenerative theories, have also worked in discourse, including Pike and Pike (1983) in tagmemics, Fleming (1988) in stratificational grammar, and Halliday and Hasan (1976) in systemics. In general, the field of discourse analysis is so new that no grammatical theory has fully incorporated it enough to exclude other theories, nor has discourse analysis limited itself to any single grammatical theory. Consequently, the work done by any linguist in the field of discourse can be used by others, since it is not limited to a particular grammatical theory.

Grammatical theories have traditionally held that the largest grammatical unit is the sentence (Bloomfield 1933; Chomsky 1957). For these theories, a discourse is a combination of sentences, the form of which is totally dependent upon the text producer's choice. In this view, the form of any given sentence is due to the author's emphasis or style. Subsequent work by discourse analysts, however, has indicated that the competent speaker or writer is constrained by several factors as to the type of sentence which can be used in any given situation. The following review will concentrate on several of these factors, including texttype, foregrounding and backgrounding, macrostructures, frame structures, cohesion and coherence, constituent structures, participant and prop identification, and peak markers.

---

is a discourse analysis focusing on peak-marking features in the Gospel of John. In the New Testament area, however, most of the textlinguistic work on the source language has been in hortatory texts. Friberg's 1978 master's thesis was on the discourse structure of Galatians. Three master's theses have been done at the University of Texas at Arlington on various chapters of 1 Corinthians: Hoopert's (1981) on chapters 1–4; Matsumura's (1983) on chapters 5–7; and Youngman's (1987) on chapters 8–10. In addition, Miehle (1981) and Longacre (1983a) have worked on the book of 1 John. Radney (1988) has worked on clause ordering, primarily in the book of Hebrews. Both Hymes (1986) and this writer (Terry 1992) have worked on the book of James. Nida et al. (1983) have done work in various parts of the Greek New Testament. Recently Levinsohn (1992) has produced a coursebook to promote the study of discourse features of New Testament Greek. Also, Black (1992) has edited a collection of essays on discourse analysis of New Testament texts.

A major factor in discourse studies has been the identification of texttypes. Beekman, Callow, and Kopesec (1981:36–38) have listed four major texttypes: narrative, procedural, expository, and hortatory. Larson (1984:365–66) has listed six types: narrative, procedural, expository, descriptive, hortatory, and repartee. Nida (1984:29–30) has listed five types: narration, description, argument, dialogue, and lists. Longacre (1983b:3–14) potentially has sixteen etic types based upon the presence or absence of four binary features: agent orientation, contingent temporal succession, projection (i.e., future orientation), and tension. These are usually written with a plus (+) or minus (–) in front of the feature. Depending upon the particular language being studied, these texttypes would be limited to a smaller number of emic types. In practice, Longacre often bases his typology only upon the first two features, thus limiting the major texttypes to four, namely: narrative, procedural, behavioral, and expository. In this system, hortatory is described as behavioral with +projection. Recently he has added persuasive to his list of major texttypes (personal communication). Clendenen (1989:50) rightly suggests identifying the addition of an argument to a text with tension in Longacre's scheme. It seems likely that persuasive text is –agent orientation, –contingent temporal succession, and +tension.

It is important not to confuse genre with texttype. A particular genre is produced by a combination of several factors, among them texttype, text structure, and semantic content. It is possible to have several genres that use the same texttype and thus show grammatical similarities in some ways while being structurally and semantically quite different from one another. For example, a fairy tale, a short story, and a biography have three different genres, but all use narrative texttype.

Closely identified with a study of texttypes has been a study of the foregrounding and backgrounding of information. Discourse theory posits that different texttypes signal information as being either foregrounded or backgrounded in different ways. Often these signals are based on the choice of verb mode and/or tense, but sometimes on other particles in the sentence. Hopper and Thompson (1980:252) have associated the following factors with foregrounding and backgrounding: number of participants, kinesis, aspect, punctuality, volitionality, affirmation, mode, agency, affectedness of the object, and individuation of the object. Grimes (1975) has devoted several chapters to the difference between the two. Longacre (1989b) has suggested that instead of a distinction between the two broad areas, there exists a distinction between several degrees of foregrounding and several degrees of backgrounding. This is illustrated in his work on Joseph (1989a:81) by a chart showing a cline for ranking verbs as to degree of foregrounding or backgrounding for Hebrew narrative.

The information which is foregrounded in a narrative text is variously called the STORYLINE, the MAINLINE, or the BACKBONE of the text. A THEMELINE may occur in both narrative and other types of text. Foregrounded information in texttypes other than narrative may be called the mainline or backbone, but the term storyline is not appropriate.

The marking for foregrounded sentences varies from texttype to texttype. While the main verb tense in a Greek narrative sentence is the aorist (Robertson 1934:840), an expository passage is much more likely to have a present tense verb as primary. Likewise, hortatory text has imperative mode verbs as primary. In the same way, conditional sentences are much more likely to occur in persuasive text than in narrative. While such statements may be considered intuitively correct by many, they illustrate that, for competent users of a language, there is a strong connection between the mainline verb tense used and the type of text being produced or received. This connection is a feature of discourse grammar.

Finally on this subject, it should be noted that many texts do not contain merely one texttype. Often paragraphs of another texttype are embedded in the text (Longacre 1983b:13–14; and Clendenen 1989:47). It is possible to treat the setting of a narrative as either backgrounded information in a narrative texttype or as expository texttype information embedded in the narrative. In the same way, narrative text may be embedded in hortatory text for illustrative purposes.

Another factor to be considered in analyzing discourse is the influence of macrostructures and frame structures. Both of these structures are cognitive information structures that influence the grammatical surface structure.

The primary work on macrostructures has been done by van Dijk (1972, 1977, 1981). A macrostructure is a conceptual (i.e., mental) summary of a text that determines how the text is produced (for the speaker or writer) or understood (for the listener or reader). The term is also used to refer to a written or oral summary of the text that corresponds to the conceptual macrostructure. Originally van Dijk (1972) posited the macrostructure as a starting point for generating a text, but another person's macrostructure can only be accessed by using one produced by a recipient of the text. There is no other way to get inside a person's head. There is an analytical problem with this, for very often different receivers conceptualize different macrostructures for the same text. To alleviate this, van Dijk (1981:8–15) has suggested four operations to reduce a text to its macrostructure: generalization, deletion, integration, and construction. Longacre has suggested a simplification of the method by applying these operations mainly to foregrounded material (1990a), although most macrostructures also contain some background material. It may be that this information can be handled as mainline to embedded texttypes. In this way, a macrostructure would have a primary mapping to foregrounded material.

Frame structures are also conceptual in nature. They differ primarily from macrostructures in that they are not a part of the text. Rather they are part of the knowledge which the text producer (and hopefully the text receiver) possesses. Since frame structures are in the mind of the text producer, and the text producer supposes that the same or similar structures exist in the mind of the text receiver, this information is not overtly added to the text. In biblical studies, such information is often called background information. With frame structure theory, however, this type of information has been moved from supplemental to integral. De Beaugrande and Dressler (1981:194–201) have shown that it is possible to isolate such information. The work of Minsky (1980) on artificial intelligence also has a bearing on the linguistic understanding of cognition. Other research in this area has been done by Miller and Kintsch (1981) and van Dijk (1981). Frame structures are called various things by different researchers. Van Dijk identifies them as FRAMES, although FRAMEWORK might be a more meaningful term. Other terms that are used include SCHEMAS (or SCHEMATA), PLANS, and SCRIPTS (de Beaugrande and Dressler 1981:90–91). The latter term is usually reserved to refer to frames that store a typical sequence of actions, such as the process of eating at a restaurant. Haberlandt and Bingham (1982) note that, as text activates scripts in the human memory, subsequent text is easier to understand. They also point out that the understanding of a given text is more often based on several scripts than based on a single script.

The primary work on cohesion and coherence in English has been done by Halliday and Hasan (1976). This subject has to do especially with the relationships between two units (sentences, paragraphs, etc.) and the particles that serve as formal markers of those relationships. Charolles (1983) has argued that coherence is ultimately a function of the reader's mind and not a matter of what is in the text. Marks of cohesion, such as pronouns, do not make the text coherent. Rather it is the willingness of the reader to make the pronoun sensibly refer to something which has gone before (or will come after) that produces coherence in a text. Haberlandt and Bingham (1982) show that scripts contribute to the coherence of a text.

There are three main traditions of work on constituent structures on a discourse level: Beekman-Callow, Mann-Thompson, and Longacre. All three are similar and have influenced one another. Beekman, Callow, and Kopesec (1981) have developed a system of analyzing a text by producing a relational structure tree diagram. Mann and Thompson (1988) use a technique of determining text relationships in what they call Rhetorical Structure Theory (RST). In addition to relations, they list five kinds of structures, which they term schemas, which represent four different head-branch relationships: single branching, double headed, double branching, and multiple headed (Mann and Thompson 1988:247).

Perhaps the most work on constituent structures has been done by Longacre. His work on the Joseph narrative (1989a) contains a complete constituent display of Genesis 37 and 39–48. Such a constituent display uses a two-celled tagmeme (slot and filler) description of all relationships in the text higher than sentence level. That is, it shows the relationships between sentences, paragraphs, and discourses within the narrative in question.

Grimes (1975) has distinguished between participants and props in a text by using characters and items that are more central and less central. This general distinction has been picked up by Longacre and developed into a complete etic scheme for discovering participant and prop relationships within a text. In the introduction to the 1990 volume of Occasional Papers in Translation and Textlinguistics 9, Longacre (1990c) suggests that participant reference can be identified using an ordered triplet: participant-reference resources, participant rank, and operations of participant reference. In referring to participants and props, the resources of a language can include noun phrases (nouns plus qualifiers), nouns (with or without an article), generic nouns (such as kinship or occupational labels), pronouns, verb affixes, and null or zero anaphora. Participant rank is divided into three major levels: major participants, minor participants, and props. Among major participants, a distinction may be made between central (protagonists) and noncentral (antagonists) participants. Minor participants may be classified as helpers of central participants, helpers of noncentral participants, introducers, and bystanders. Props may be classified as human, nonhuman animate, inanimate, and natural forces. A study in participant identification involves fully classifying all participants and props within a discourse and searching for recurring patterns that a language may use. The seven functions or operations of participant reference which Longacre distinguishes include first mention, integration as central, routine tracking, restaging after absence, confrontation and/or role reversal, local contrast or thematicity, and author evaluation or comment.

The final feature of discourse to be discussed here is the presence of peak markers. Longacre (1981, 1983b, 1985a, 1990b) has done the most work on peak. Peak can be defined as a zone of grammatical or stylistic turbulence within a discourse that corresponds to its climax and/or denouement. In languages around the world, standard grammatical rules and stylistic conventions seem to change around those parts of a text which show the most conceptual tension. Longacre (1983b:24, 34) has noted that embedded discourses can each have their own peak, resulting in a larger discourse with multiple peaks. He has also noted (p. 24) that there can be both action peaks and didactic peaks in a work where the thematic material comes to a climax at a place other than the narrative climax.

Most of the work on peak has centered around the study of narrative discourses. Although work on other discourse types is just beginning, there is some evidence that peak also manifests itself in hortatory text as well. Longacre (1983a:28–34) has identified 1 John chapter 4 as peak of that book. Clendenen (1989:109, 123) has shown that there appear to be peak markers in the Hebrew text of Malachi. Previous work in the Greek text of James has shown that the discourse in James 3:13–4:10 is marked by at least seven types of peak material and seems to function as a hortatory climax of the book (Terry 1992:121–23).

Longacre (1990b) has classified types of peak-marking features under three major headings which he labels as augmented sequence, immediacy, and maximum interlacing of participant reference.

Several types of peak-marking features are classified as augmented sequence. The text may shift to a series of fast moving actions, resulting in a much higher verb to nonverb ratio and/or the elimination of dialogue from this section. Component actions may be mentioned in some detail, resulting in a slowing down of the action. A single action may be mentioned several times using paraphrasing, that is, the same thing may be said in several different ways. This type of peak marker may be signaled by the use of long sentences where short ones are the rule for the discourse or by short sentences in the peak where long ones are the rule.

Immediacy devices take the hearer or reader to the scene of the action. For example, peak may be marked by a shift in tense or aspect. In narrative this shift is often from the use of a point-action (foregrounded) to a continuous (backgrounded) tense in order to increase vividness. Peak may also be marked by a shift up the agency hierarchy, that is, from third person to second to first. A third example of immediacy is a shift to dialogue or drama where such has not been used before. The peak may also include extra background or setting material. It may be marked by devices such as onomatopoeia, ideophones, and/or profanity. Immediacy peak may also be marked by asyndeton, that is, coordinating particles may be omitted from the peak as the narrative proceeds too rapidly for standard connection.

Maximum interlacing of participant reference may be manifested by a crowded stage in which many participants are brought together at once. If they are not physically together in the narrative, there may be rapid shifting back and forth between various characters in this type of peak marking feature. This type of peak marking may be evidenced by an abandonment of usual participant reference devices in favor of increased use of nouns and pronouns. There may be confrontation devices or role reversal in a peak section. Grammatical structures may become more complex in a peak; word-order changes may come into play. Finally, code switching between languages may be noted in a peak. Clendenen (1987) has noted the use of Aramaic in the chiastic key of chapter 10 of the Hebrew text of Jeremiah.

1.3 The textual basis for the study

The Greek text used for this study of 1 Corinthians is the third edition of the United Bible Societies' (UBS) *Greek New Testament* (Aland et al. 1975; corrected ed. 1983). This is the same text as the twenty-sixth edition of *Nestle-Aland Novum Testamentum Graece* (Nestle et al. 1979). This text is also found in the Fribergs' *Analytical Greek New Testament* with grammatical identification of each word form (Friberg and Friberg 1981). This Greek text has become a standard for twentieth century work in the New Testament. Several tools, both printed and in computer files, have been created to help study it. Several translations are based upon it, including the Today's English Version and the New Revised Standard Version. There is a companion volume to the Greek text written by Metzger (1971) that explains the committee's reasoning on readings that are questionable.

The punctuation for this text exists in two different forms. The original punctuation in the 1975 edition (followed by the Fribergs) is based on linguistic principles similar to those used in English. The corrected edition of 1983 changes the punctuation to follow that of the twenty-sixth edition of the Nestle-Aland text. The punctuation in that work is based on conventions of Greek usage (Nestle et al. 1979:44*). For linguistic analysis the punctuation in the 1975 edition is superior (Terry 1992). In only two places has alternative punctuation been used. 1 Cor. 2:8bc is a conditional sentence; the 1983 punctuation makes it a separate colon, while the 1975 punctuation has a comma following 2:8a, thus subordinating the condition to the preceding relative clause. The revised punctuation, producing a better linguistic form, has been followed to reflect the independent status of the conditional sentence. Secondly, all the editions punctuate 2:13 as a separate colon in spite of the fact that it is a relative clause modifying 2:12. It seems linguistically better to depart from the standard punctuation and take it as a part of the previous colon.

This work is not a study in textual criticism nor will it seek to establish the text chosen for the study. That text has been chosen largely because it has become a standard in modern biblical studies. No doubt there are places where future work in textual criticism will result in minor changes to the text, but it seems to be very close to the original text. Table 1 lists the 37 variants in the text of 1 Corinthians which the UBS textual committee has given a C (a considerable degree of doubt) or D (a very high degree of doubt) rating.

Most of these variants make slight differences in the meaning of a verse; few of them, however, make any significant difference in the overall grammar at the discourse level. For example, the difference between 'mystery' and 'testimony' in 2:1 makes a difference in the meaning of the sentence but it does not affect the grammatical structure of either the sentence or the discourse in which it occurs. Those which do affect the grammar do so in only a minor way. Of the significant variants which affect clause length, none makes any clause longer or shorter by more than two words. If the variants listed in Table 1 were accepted into the text, only fourteen words would be omitted from the text at most, and only sixteen words would be added at most. This would have very little impact on the statistics given later on clause and colon length.

In the same way, only four significant variants (7:34; 10:20; 14:39; 15:54) have to do with word order or sentence division. Two of these variants have no impact at all on the analysis of subject-verb-object word order. Five of the variants (1:28; 2:10, 15; 7:13; and 9:15) do affect conjunctions that introduce clauses, but no conjunction is affected more than once. Only two of the variants (3:17; 5:13) affect tense, only two (10:10; 15:49) affect mood, and only two (10:2; 13:3) affect voice. These few changes would have no significant influence on the statistical analysis of these variables. Five other variants show one case each, affecting only person (10:10), number (14:37), the specification of an actor (8:3), the inclusion of an article (15:10), and the use of the vocative (15:31). These likewise would have little impact on a statistical analysis if the variant readings were accepted as genuine.

There are two variants, one with a UBS textual committee rating of A (text is virtually certain) and one with a rating of B (some degree of doubt), which need to be considered also, not because they are very likely to be the original readings, but because they change the discourse structure of the text in minor ways. The A rating variant is found in 9:20. The participial clause "not being myself under law" is missing from some manuscripts. The clause is found in early manuscripts from all three major text families: the Alexandrian, Western, and Byzantine. But aside from the question of its originality, the discourse analyst is interested in the fact that omission of this clause destroys the balance in a grammatical chiasm in 9:19–22. The clause is needed to balance "not being without the law of God but within the law of Christ" in 9:21.

Table 1
Doubtful textual variants in 1 Corinthians

Verse	Rate	UBS text reading	Variant reading
1:8	C	*[Χριστοῦ]* 'of Christ'	omit
1:14	D	*[τῷ θεῷ]* 'to God'	omit
1:28	C	omit	*καὶ* 'even'
2:1	C	*μυστήριον* 'mystery'	*μαρτύριον* 'testimony'
2:4	D	omit	*ανθρωπίνης* 'human'
2:10	C	*δέ* 'but' or 'now'	*γάρ* 'for'
2:14	C	*τοῦ θεοῦ* 'of God'	omit
2:15	D	*τά* 'the'	*μέν* 'on the one hand'
3:3	C	omit	*διχοστασίαι* 'divisions'
3:10	C	*τοῦ θεοῦ* 'of God'	omit
3:17	C	*φθερεῖ* 'will destroy'	*φθείρει* 'destroys'
4:17	C	omit	*αὐτό* 'itself'
5:4	D	*[ἡμῶν]* 'our'	either omit or add *Χριστοῦ* 'Christ'
5:5	C	omit	variously add *Ἰησοῦ* 'Jesus' and *Χριστοῦ* 'Christ' and *ἡμῶν* 'our'
5:13	C	*κρινεῖ* 'will judge'	*κρίνει* 'judges'
6:11	C	*Χριστοῦ* 'Christ'	omit or add *ἡμῶν* 'our'
7:13	D	*εἴ τις* 'if any'	*ἥτις* 'whoever'
7:15	C	*ὑμᾶς* 'you (PL)'	*ἡμᾶς* 'us'
7:34	D	period after 2nd word	no period at beginning
8:3	C	*ὑπ' αὐτοῦ* 'by Him'	omit
9:15	C	*οὐδείς* 'no one'	*ἵνα τις* 'that anyone'
10:2	C	*ἐβαπτίσθησαν* passive 'were baptized'	*ἐβαπτίσαντο* middle 'had themselves baptized'
10:9	C	*Χριστόν* 'Christ'	*κύριον* 'Lord'
10:10	C	*γογγύζετε* 'murmur' 2nd imp.	*γογγύζωμεν* 'let us murmur' 1st subj.
10:11	C	omit	*πάντα* 'all'
10:20	C	word order: OI and –IV	word order: OIV and –I
11:29	C	omit	*ἀναξίως* 'unworthily'
11:29	C	omit	*τοῦ κυρίου* 'the Lord'
13:3	C	*καυχήσωμαι* 'boast'	*καυθήσωμαι* 'be burned'
14:37	C	*ἐστὶν ἐντολή* (SG) 'is a command'	*εἰσὶν ἐντολαί* (PL) 'are commands'
14:39	D	split infinitive	regular infinitive
15:10	C	*[ἡ]* 'the'	omit
15:14	C	*ὑμῶν* 'of you (PL)'	*ἡμῶν* 'of us'
15:31	C	*[ἀδελφοί]* 'brothers'	omit
15:49	C	*φορέσομεν* ind. 'we shall bear'	*φορέσωμεν* subj. 'let us bear'
15:54	C	word order: –V,sV	word order: V,–sV
16:24	C	omit	*ἀμήν* 'amen'

UBS rating for degree of doubt: C considerable; D very high

The second variant of interest occurs in 14:34–35. Some manuscripts of the Western family move these two verses to a place following verse 40. Once again, the problem from a discourse analyst's view is that this shift destroys a chiastic structure. These verses form the BCC'B' elements of a chiasm. The A and A' elements are found in verses 33b and 36, respectively.

Both of the chiasms in 9:19–22 and 14:33b–36 will be discussed in more detail in chapter 4.

1.4 Methodology

General method. This study is limited to eight of the many aspects of discourse analysis which can be pursued. In order to understand the rhetorical situation and the cultural-historical background of the book better, a study covering author, reader, setting, background, and related items was done. An attempt was made to formulate the macrostructure of the book in order to understand the overall thrust of 1 Corinthians. Next, based on the results of gross chunking and macrosegmentation, a constituent analysis was done. Then a search for markers of peak was conducted throughout the book. Studies were also done on participant reference, clause word order, and quotations. These latter involved charting and the creation of a computer database. When these studies were completed, the data were then checked for possible differences in grammatical and stylistic tendencies between (a) the parts of 1 Corinthians which were in response to the letter the Corinthians had sent Paul, and (b) the parts that were in response to information he had received by word of mouth.

Procedures. In order to understand the rhetorical situation and the historical-cultural background to 1 Corinthians, research was done on the letter itself, on the rest of the New Testament, on other ancient documents of and near that time, and on current scholarly writings. An emphasis was placed on discovering the Greek cultural attitudes and practices regarding wisdom and leadership, fornication, lawsuits, marriage and celibacy, consumption of food previously used in idol worship, head coverings, drunkenness in religious services, ecstasy in religious services, views on the resurrection from the dead, and concerns about finances.

Analysis of macrostructures in 1 Corinthians began by concentrating on the macrostructures of each of the several discourses within the letter. Van Dijk's four methods (1977:143–46; 1981:8–15) were used wherever possible, but in order to make the task manageable, two of Longacre's concepts on macrostructure were applied. The first is that macrostructure material is more likely to be foregrounded in the text than backgrounded. Therefore, most background material was omitted from consideration. The second is that the primary material in a hortatory text consists of forms of commands, suggestions, and requests. Since most of the discourses in 1 Corinthians are hortatory, macrostructure work centered around these primary forms.

The constituent analysis was done from two perspectives. For top-down processing, the text was divided using principles of gross chunking. For bottom-up processing, relationships between colons (Greek linguistic sentences) and paragraphs were considered. This is often known as micro-segmentation. A constituent display for selected passages was prepared and from this work a preliminary salience chart for Greek hortatory text was prepared. Ideally, material that is higher up on the salience chart should be given prominence in the constituent analysis.

A clause chart for the text of 1 Corinthians was prepared according to the layout shown in (2). 1 Cor. 2:1 was chosen to demonstrate how the chart was prepared. Information from the chart was entered into a database.

(2)   1 Cor. 2:1

notes	conjunction	preceding dependent	independent	following dependent
sV	Κἀγὼ	ἐλθὼν πρὸς ὑμᾶς,		
V–		ἀδελφοί,	ἦλθον οὐ καθ᾽ ὑπεροχὴν λόγου	
ViO			ἢ σοφίας	καταγγέλλων ὑμῖν τὸ μυστήριον τοῦ θεοῦ.

The database contains information on twenty-six variables and two other items for each clause of 1 Corinthians. Using the database, as well as a Greek concordance, a search was then made for markers of peak and for features (both at the clause and discourse levels) which control word ordering. The chart and database were also used to study participant analysis, quotations, and any influence which the rhetorical situation may have on features of grammatical discourse. Specifically, preliminary research indicated that passive constructions and conditional sentences are distributed throughout the letter in a manner which may indicate that the extent of their use or nonuse was dependent upon whether Paul at any given point was responding (a) to the Corinthians' letter to him or (b) to a report which he had received by word of mouth. Further study was done to determine whether the distribution of these features was statistically significant and whether there are other features that show the same distributional patterns.

2

Rhetorical Situation and Cultural Background

2.1 Setting and background

The city of Corinth. The peninsula of southern Greece, known as the Peloponnesus, is connected to the main part of Greece by a narrow isthmus about 50 miles west of Athens. At its narrowest part the isthmus is only 3½ to 4 miles wide, separating the Corinthian Gulf to the west from the Saronic Gulf to the east. On the southwest end of the isthmus, just to the north of a mesa which rises to a height of 1,886 feet above sea level, lies the ancient city of Corinth. Situated at the crossroads of the major north-south land route and the major east-west sea route, the city early became a commercial center. The mesa, known as the Acrocorinth or Acrocorinthus, served as a citadel for the city. A six-mile wall protected the city on its north side. The city was on a plain 300 feet above sea level, but had access to both gulfs via the harbors, Lechaeum (or Lechaion), about 1½ miles to the west, and Cenchreae, about 8¾ miles to the east (Scranton 1980; Harrop 1980; Morgan-Wynne 1983:4; and Bruce 1971:18–19).

The ancient city was noted not only for its military and commercial importance, but also for its worship of the goddess of love, Aphrodite. On top of the Acrocorinth stood a temple dedicated to her, which Strabo reported had been staffed by "a thousand temple-slaves, courtesans, whom both men and women had dedicated to the goddess" (*Geography* 8.6.20 [Loeb §378]; cf. Craig 1953:4; Conzelmann 1975:12, expresses his disbelief of this figure). Prostitution was so rampant that "to corinthianize" became

17

a verb meaning "to practice fornication," especially in the Old Comedy (Morgan-Wynne 1983:4; Barrett 1968:2).

All of this came to an end in 146 B.C. when the Roman general L. Mummius destroyed the city and carried its inhabitants off into slavery. Then in 44 B.C. the city was refounded by Julius Caesar as a Roman colony under the name of 'Laus Iulia Corinthiensis'. Because of its location, it quickly gained in importance and in 27 B.C. was made the capital of the Roman province of Achaia (Scranton 1980; Bruce 1971:18). The Roman influence is seen in the fact that names such as Crispus, Titius Justus, and Fortunatus, associated with Corinth in the New Testament, are Roman names. Also Corinth was the only city in Greece to have an amphitheater. The city became the wealthiest and most important city in Greece during the first century A.D. Its population has been estimated as high as 600,000, including its two port cities (Craig 1953:3).

The temple of Aphrodite was reestablished on the Acrocorinth, although Strabo calls it a "little temple" (Conzelmann 1975:12). The city center boasted temples for Apollo and Asclepius, the god of healing (Morgan-Wynne 1983:4). Poseidon was an important god in Corinth, but there were also altars to Hermes, Artemis, Zeus, Dionysus, Heracles, and others (Craig 1953:4). The sanctuaries to foreign gods include two to Isis and two to Sarapis, both Egyptian deities (Smith 1977:210–16; Conzelmann 1975:12; Pausanias *Description of Greece,* Corinth 4.6).

The historical background to 1 Corinthians. The apostle Paul came to the city of Corinth on his second missionary journey, probably in the spring of A.D. 50 (Barrett 1968:5; Craig 1953:4). Acts 18:1–18 records how Paul stayed with Aquila and Priscilla, working with them as tentmakers during the week and preaching in the synagogue on the Sabbath. When Silas and Timothy finally arrived from Macedonia, he devoted himself to preaching and teaching full-time. Opposition arose from the Jews, and Paul moved his preaching to the house of Titius Justus, a God-fearer who lived next door to the synagogue. Crispus, the ruler of the synagogue, was converted, along with many of the Corinthians. In all, Paul stayed about a year and a half, probably until the fall of A.D. 51 (Barrett 1968:5; Craig 1953:4). It was during this time that the Jews dragged Paul before the judgment seat of Gallio, the Roman proconsul. The effort of the Jews to stop his preaching by legal means aids us in dating the event. An inscription found at Delphi places Gallio in Corinth between January 25 and August 1 in A.D. 52. It is therefore likely that he became proconsul in the spring of A.D. 51. This date may be a year too early, but the chronology is close if not exact (Conzelmann 1975:12–13).

After Paul, Aquila, and Priscilla left Corinth for Ephesus, Apollos came to Corinth (Acts 18:27–19:1). Perhaps Peter also visited the city, for we find a Cephas party mentioned in 1 Cor. 1:12. When Paul returned to Ephesus on his third missionary journey, he began correspondence with the church at Corinth that probably included four letters from him and at least one letter from them. In 1 Cor. 5:9–11 Paul refers to a previous letter he had written to them (unless, of course, the word "wrote" is taken as an epistolary aorist referring to 1 Corinthians). Some have identified this previous letter with 2 Cor. 6:14–7:1, but it is more likely that this letter has been lost (Guthrie 1970:425–26).

In reply, the church at Corinth sent a letter to Paul asking questions (1 Cor. 7:1), perhaps carried by Stephanas, Fortunatus, and Achaicus (16:17). Several sections begin with the words περὶ δέ 'now concerning' (7:1, 25; 8:1; 12:1; 16:1, 12); these are usually taken as referring to the Corinthians' questions in their letter (cf. Morris 1958:115, 124, 166, 237, 242). If this is correct, the letter read something like the following reconstruction (this was composed using 1 Cor. 1:2, 14; 7:1, 25, 38; 8:1, 4; 10:23; 11:1; 12:1; 16:1, 12, 17; Rom. 16:23; 3 John 2; 1 Clement 1:1; Morgan-Wynne 1983:7, 10–11; Bruce 1971:102; Barrett 1968:4; Doty 1973:2, 4–5, 30–31):

(3)   The church of God which is at Corinth to Paul. Rejoice.
        We pray that you may be in health, even as we are. We thank God for you, remembering you in our prayers.
        There have been some matters of discussion among us, and knowing your wisdom, we are writing for your decision in these matters.
        Is it a good thing for a man not to touch a woman? If so, does a man do well if he should give his virgin in marriage?
        Should we eat things sacrificed to idols? Some say that we all have knowledge that no idol is anything in the world and that there is no God but one. And we know that all things are lawful.
        Now we remember you in everything and maintain the traditions even as you have delivered them to us. But as to spiritual gifts, is it better to speak in tongues or to prophesy in church?
        How should we take up the collection for the saints in Jerusalem?
        Some among us would like Apollos to return. Send him back to us soon.

This letter is sent by the hand of Stephanas and
Fortunatus and Achaicus whom you know to be faithful in
the Lord. They will tell you more than what we have written.
Gaius, and the church in his house, greets you. Crispus
greets you. Greet Apollos. Greet Aquila and Priscilla, and
the church in their house. Rejoice.

Paul's answer to them was the letter we call 1 Corinthians. Subsequently
Paul paid a second visit to Corinth, which he calls a "painful visit" (2 Cor.
2:1), apparently because he was rebuffed there. He followed this with a
severe letter (2 Cor. 2:3–4, 9; 7:8, 12) which was delivered by Titus. Some
have identified this with 1 Corinthians, while others have identified it with
2 Corinthians 10–13, but most likely it, too, is lost (Guthrie 1970:429–38).
Paul traveled to Troas and on to Macedonia hoping to meet Titus. When
he met him, he rejoiced that his mission had been successful in producing
their repentance. In response he wrote 2 Corinthians (or at least chapters
1–9).

2.2 Literary concerns

The authorship, authenticity, and dating of 1 Corinthians. The fact
that 1 Corinthians was written by Paul to the Christians at Corinth is
beyond dispute. Barrett states, "No serious scholar questions it" (1968:11).
Craig notes, "It has been denied only by fanciful scholars who have looked
upon all the Pauline correspondence as falsifications from the second
century. No letter has better external testimony than this one" (1953:13).
It is referred to by 1 Clement 37:5; 47:1–3; 49:5 (just 45 years after it was
written); Ignatius to the Ephesians 16:1; 18:1; to the Romans 5:1; to the
Philadelphians 3:3 (about A.D. 110); Justin Martyr (Dialogue with Trypho
33); Athenagoras (On the Resurrection of the Dead 18); and numerous
times by Irenaeus, Tertullian, and Clement of Alexandria (Craig 1953:13;
Feine, Behm, and Kümmel 1966:202).

It is not possible to date exactly when 1 Corinthians was written, but it
was probably within a couple of years of A.D. 55. Estimates vary between
A.D. 53 and 57, with the most likely time being the spring of A.D. 54 or 55
(Guthrie 1970:441; Feine, Behm, and Kümmel 1966:205; Barrett, 1968:5;
Bruce 1971:25; Craig 1953:13; Martin 1986:175).

In the opening, Paul associates Sosthenes, a Christian brother, with
himself. Some have connected him with the Sosthenes mentioned in Acts
18:17 (Barrett 1968:31). Bruce notes that he was probably "someone well

known to the Corinthian church who was with Paul in Ephesus at the time of writing" (1971:30). But Conzelmann is right in noting that "the fellow-writer is not a fellow-author" (1975:20). Paul uses the singular Greek pronoun for "I" eighty-six times in the letter (Aland, et al. 1978:82).

The unity of 1 Corinthians. Some have suggested that this letter was originally two or three letters that have been combined by an editor. Among them, Johannes Weiss has suggested the letter was originally in three parts, while Jean Héring has suggested two parts (Guthrie 1970:439). Hurd (1983:44–45) lists six scholars (Loisy, Couchoud, Goguel, de Zwaan, Schmithals, and Dinkler) who have, with variations, followed Weiss's division of the letter. But most scholars view the letter as a unity (Guthrie 1970:439; Feine, Behm, and Kümmel 1966:203–5; Barrett 1968:12–17). Barrett notes that no partition theory is more probable than the unity of the letter (1968:15). After surveying the various scholarly theories that divide the letter into two or three letters of Paul, Hurd (1983:46) comments, "Even when simplified these theories appear radical and somewhat arbitrary." Later he concludes about the division theories, "Most scholars and the present writer, while recognizing the above points, do not believe that this evidence is strong enough to support the burden of proof which this kind of theory must always bear" (1983:47).

Therefore, this study will assume that the work is a unity, composed at one time (but not necessarily at one sitting) in its present order, although it may contain differences between sections that have led some to think it was not. Chapter 5 of this study demonstrates that these differences are, in fact, stylistic differences which seem to be due to the differences in rhetorical situation between answering the Corinthians' letter and addressing problems reported to Paul in oral reports.

2.3 The place of a schema in understanding

One of the difficulties of understanding any ancient writing is that we are so far removed in time and culture from the ancient world. De Beaugrande and Dressler (1981:194) have shown that a reader understands a text not just from the information within it but also from what they call "a discourse-world model," that is, "the integrated configuration of concepts and relations underlying all the texts in a discourse." Within the reader's mind, these concepts are generally related by a pattern that text linguists refer to as a frame or a schema. The resultant understanding of a text is a combination of the information in the text and information in the schema.

Where information which the reader or listener needs to supply is lacking from the schema, the result is either a failure to understand the text or a guess at the missing information, often resulting in a misunderstanding when the guess is wrong. In the absence of good evidence, scholars sometimes are apt to make incorrect guesses as well as less studied readers. With regard to the view that short hair or a shaved head was the mark of Corinthian prostitutes, Fee (1987:511) notes, "But there is no contemporary evidence to support this view (it seems to be a case of one scholar's guess becoming a second scholar's footnote and a third scholar's assumption)." Such a guess evolves into a made-up "fact," which becomes part of a scholar's schema but was never part of the original writer's schema.

With this in mind, it is important to establish the cultural setting for several items mentioned in 1 Corinthians. As Pike (1982:132) has stated, "A context has very high power to determine or to change a meaning." Thus the text cannot be understood as it was originally meant apart from an understanding of its cultural context. Much of the information below is drawn from the texts of ancient authors that shed light on the cultural situation in Corinth. The reader should note that, in all the following areas in which Paul admonished the Corinthians, they were following patterns that were well established in Greek society.

2.4 Aspects of culture at Corinth

Wisdom and leadership. In Greek society, there was a line of thought that the wise men should be the leaders. Perhaps the best example of this comes from Plato's *Republic*, where he has Socrates say, "either philosophers become kings in our states or those whom we now call our kings and rulers take to the pursuit of philosophy seriously and adequately, and there is a conjunction of these two things, political power and philosophic intelligence" (5.473d). These wise ones Plato likens to gold: "yet God in fashioning those of you who are fitted to hold rule mingled gold in their generation, for which reason they are the most precious" (*Republic* 3.415a). It was a viewpoint such as this that Paul was combating when he argued that the Corinthians should not label themselves after individual Christian workers, for to do so was to rely on what the world called wisdom, but was not (cf. 1 Cor. 3:18–22).

Fornication and incest. Sexual license was the rule rather than the exception in much of the ancient Mediterranean world. Hauck and Schulz wrote concerning Greek sexual ethics, "The main cause of prostitution is the Greek view of life which regards sexual intercourse as just as natural, necessary and justifiable as eating and drinking" (Kittel 1968 4:582). Athenaeus devoted Book 13 of the *Deipnosophists* to extramarital sex among the Greeks. He indicates that prostitution was an established and respected function in Corinth. Athenaeus relates that whenever the city of Corinth would pray to Aphrodite in matters of grave importance, the people would "invite as many prostitutes as possible to join in their petitions, and these women [would] add their supplications to the goddess and later [be] present at the sacrifices" (*Deipnosophists* 13.573c). Further, it was the custom for the city to celebrate a festival of Aphrodite for the prostitutes (13.574b–c). The lyricist Pindar wrote in their honor:

> Young girls, who welcome many strangers with your hospitality, ministrants of Persuasion in rich Corinth—who on the altar send up in smoke the auburn tears of fresh frankincense the many times that ye fly in thought up to the Mother of the Loves, heavenly Aphrodite, upon you, my children, free from reproach, she hath bestowed the right to cull the soft beauty in your desired embraces. When Necessity requires it, all things are fair. (Athenaeus *Deipnosophists* 13.574a)

This latter indicates that the Greeks saw nothing wrong with cultic prostitution, and although some complained of the influence of ordinary prostitutes, most saw nothing wrong with it either. Athenaeus relates that the Corinthian courtesan Lais replied to a detractor who had criticized her profession, "What is foul, if it seems not so to those who indulge in it?" (*Deipnosophists* 13.582d).

But the problems of sexual license were not limited to prostitution. The Roman sage and cynic Seneca wrote, "Is there any shame at all for adultery now that matters have come to such a pass that no woman has any use for a husband except to inflame her paramour? Chastity is simply a proof of ugliness" (*On Benefits* 3.16.3). However, as Paul says in 1 Cor. 5:1, even the pagans were aghast at incest. Gaius notes in his *Institutes* (1.63): "Again, I may not marry a woman who was previously my mother-in-law or daughter-in-law or step-daughter or step-mother." Cicero writes about a woman who had broken up her daughter's marriage to marry her son-in-law: "Oh! to think of the woman's sin, unbelievable, unheard of in all experience save for this single instance!" (*In Defense of Cluentius* 4 [Loeb §15]). He goes on to speak of this incident as a "scandal among men" and a "disgrace" (§15–16). So when the Corinthians tolerated incest, they had gone even beyond the bounds of pagan propriety. But fornication and prostitution were often accepted in ancient Greek culture, and Paul's denunciation of them in 1 Corinthians 6 went against the grain of Greek mores.

Marriage and divorce. Divorce was as much a problem in the ancient world as it is today. There was a long standing tradition of divorce in the Greek world. Diodorus of Sicily reports that Charondas, a sixth or seventh century B.C. leader of a Greek colony in Italy, had established a law "which gave a wife the right to divorce her husband and marry whomever she chose" (12.18.1). Closer to New Testament times, Seneca states, "Is there any woman that blushes at divorce now that certain illustrious and noble ladies reckon their years, not by the number of consuls, but by the number of their husbands, and leave home in order to marry, and marry in order to be divorced?" (*On Benefits* 3.16.2). Consequently, when Paul quoted from Jesus that the wife should not leave her husband nor the husband divorce his wife (1 Cor. 7:10–11), he was teaching something novel to Greek society.

Eating meat offered to idols. It was common in worshiping certain Greek gods for the devotee to share the sacrifice with the god and invite his or her friends to eat the worshiper's portion at a banquet, often in the temple of the god. The orator Aristides relates a dream that he had in which the god Asclepius commanded, "After this to go to the Temple and make a full sacrifice to Asclepius, and to have sacred bowls set up, and to distribute the sacred portions of the sacrifice to all my fellow pilgrims" (*Sacred Tales* 2.27). There was a temple of Asclepius near the gymnasium in Corinth (Pausanias *Description of Greece,* Corinth 4.5). In addition, on the road to the Acrocorinthus were temples to Isis and Sarapis (Pausanias *Description of Greece,* Corinth 4.6), who also were worshiped with meals in their temples. Fee (1987:361) notes that at least thirteen papyrus invitations to cult meals have survived. Willis (1985:40–42) gives the Greek text and translations of nine of them. I have redone several of the following translations to make them consistent with one another.[2] Six of them invite the recipient to the temple of a god: Sarapis, Thoeris, or Isis.

(4)   Chaeremon asks you to dine at a table of the lord Sarapis in the Sarapian [temple] tomorrow, which is the fifteenth, from the ninth hour (P. Oxy. 110).

---

[2]The original translations in Willis (1985) were done by Grenfell and Hunt (1916) for (4), (5), (6), (7), and (10), Willis (1985) for (8) and (9), Eitrem and Amundsen (1936) for (11), and Oates, Samuel, and Welles (1967) for (12).

(5)   Apollonius asks you to dine at a table of the lord Sarapis on the occasion of the coming of age of his brothers in the Thoerian [temple] (P. Oxy. 1484).

(6)   Apion asks you to dine in the house of Sarapis at a table of the lord Sarapis on the thirteenth from the ninth hour (P. Oxy. 1755).

(7)   Diogenes asks you to dine at the first birthday of his daughter in the Sarapian [temple] tomorrow, which is well-spread [παχῶν, a possible variant of παχέων 'thick'; cf. Liddell-Scott 1968:1351], from the ninth hour (P. Oxy. 2791).

(8)   The god invites you to a table in the Thoerian [temple] tomorrow from the ninth hour (P. Colon 2555).

(9)   Sarapis asks you to dine at the sacred offering for the lady Isis in her [or, his] house tomorrow, which is the twenty-ninth, from the ninth hour (P. Fouad 76).

This last meal may be taken as either at Isis's temple or at Sarapis's house, depending upon how one understands the significance of the definite article preceding the word 'house'. But three of the invitations which Willis lists are definitely to meals at the host's house.

(10)   Antonius, [son] of Ptolemaeus, asks you to dine with him at a table of the lord Sarapis in the [house] of Claudius Sarapion on the sixteenth from the ninth hour (P. Oxy. 523).

(11)   Sarapion, former gymnasiarch, asks you to dine at a table of the lord Sarapis in his own house tomorrow, which is the fifteenth, from the eighth hour (P. Oslo. 157).

(12)   Dionysios asks you to dine on the twenty-first at a table of Helios, great Sarapis from the ninth hour at his father's house (P. Yale 85).

These invitations illustrate two situations reflected in the book of 1 Corinthians: a meal in an idol's temple (8:10) and a meal in honor of a god at a person's home (10:28). Therefore, the situations which Paul was addressing in 1 Corinthians were ones with which the Corinthians were familiar. They may well have wanted to continue a basic part of social life that they had engaged in before their conversion.

Head coverings. One of the more controversial issues in current scholarship is the question of women's headgear in ancient Greece. Morris has written, "For a woman to appear in public bareheaded was to act in what we would call a 'barefaced' manner. It was the mark of a woman of loose morals. It outraged the proprieties" (1958:151). Bruce has written:

> In the cultural milieux with which Paul was most familiar (both Jewish and Tarsian) it was not normally reckoned proper or seemly for a woman to flout these standards and appear in public with her head uncovered, still less to pray to God in public thus; this is something which he invites his readers to judge for themselves. (1971:107)

But Conzelmann writes, "the Greek practice in regard to headgear and hairstyle cannot be unequivocally stated for the simple reason that the fashion varies" (1975:185). Oepke, in the *Theological Dictionary of the New Testament*, surveys the evidence and says:

> To be sure, the veil was not unknown in Greece. It was worn partly as adornment and partly on such special occasions as match-making and marriage..., mourning..., and the worship of chthonic [i.e., underworld] deities (in the form of a garment drawn over the head). But it is quite wrong that Greek women were under some kind of compulsion to wear a veil in public. (Oepke 1965 3:562)

He goes on to say that the idea that women always wore some sort of head covering in public is taken from two passages in Plutarch. At the end of the first century A.D. in *Moralia*, The Roman Questions 14, Plutarch asks:

> Why do sons cover their heads when they escort their parents to the grave, while daughters go with uncovered heads and hair unbound?... Or is it that the unusual is proper in mourning, and it is more usual for women to go forth in public with their heads covered and men with their heads uncovered?

As Oepke (1965) points out, this passage refers to a Roman custom, not to a Greek one. To be sure, there were Romans in the city of Corinth, for it was a Roman colony. But it was basically a Greek city, following Greek customs (cf. Dio Chrysostom *Orationes* 37.26: "he has become thoroughly hellenized, even as your own city has"). Even the Roman custom changed over time, for Plutarch goes on to say, "But formerly women were not allowed to cover the head at all ... The second [man to divorce his wife] was Sulpicius Gallus, because he saw his wife pull her cloak over her head." (*Moralia*, The Roman Questions 14).

It should be noted that, among the Romans, even the men covered their heads at worship. In *Moralia*, The Roman Questions 10, Plutarch asks, "Why is it that when they worship the gods, they cover their heads, but when they meet any of their fellow-men worthy of honour, if they happen to have the toga over the head, they uncover?" The only exceptions to this covering at worship that he lists are in the worship of Saturn and the god called Honor (Plutarch *Moralia*, The Roman Questions 11, 13). Virgil presents Aeneas as saying, "before the altar veiled our heads in Phrygian robe" (Aeneid 3.545).

The second passage which Oepke notes is Plutarch's *Moralia*, Sayings of Spartans, where he records regarding Charillus, an early king of Sparta, "When someone inquired why they took their girls into public places unveiled, but their married women veiled, he said, 'Because the girls have to find husbands, and the married women have to keep to those who have them!' " (Charillus 2). Although Sparta was a region in Greece, Corinth was not in Sparta, and thus it is difficult to know to what extent (if at all) this custom was practiced in Corinth.

Oepke goes on to give some of the evidence that pagan Greek women did not wear a covering on their head while worshiping.

> The mysteries inscription of Andania (Ditt. Syll.[3], 736), which gives an exact description of women taking part in the procession, makes no mention of the veil. Indeed, the cultic order of Lycosura seems to forbid it [but this may apply to men; the verb in question seems to refer to women, but has a masculine ending—RBT]. Empresses and goddesses ... are portrayed without veils. (1965 3:562)

Other evidence can come from Greek pottery and art. The following data are taken from an analysis of photographs and illustrations in Zinserling's *Women in Greece and Rome* (1973). In that book, 96 pictures show 180 Greek women as depicted in artwork produced during the fifteenth through the first centuries B.C. In addition, 41 pictures show 63 Roman women from art objects ranging in date from the eighth century B.C. to the sixth century A.D. Since Zinserling's purpose was to study ancient women and she does not focus on their headdress, this analysis assumes that she did not have a bias in choosing her illustrations and they reflect a cross-section of surviving Greek and Roman art objects depicting

women. Tables 2 and 3 summarize the status of the headdress of the
women shown in Zinserling's book. Where the counts for women who are
bareheaded, wearing headbands, and hooded do not add up to the total,
the difference is accounted for by art objects with missing heads. An
examination of the data in the tables reveals that there was no uniform
practice in either Greek or Roman customs.

Table 2

The headdress of Greek women in illustrations

Date	Total	Bareheaded	Headband	Hooded
8th B.C.	12	2	5	3
7th B.C.	4	4	—	—
6th B.C.	29	—	20	8
5th B.C.	97	21	50	23
4th B.C.	20	8	4	8
3rd B.C.	11	6	3	2
2nd B.C.	5	2	2	—
1st B.C.	2	—	—	2
Totals	180	43	84	46

Further analysis of the data from the illustrations in Zinserling's book
provides some interesting observations. It is sometimes maintained that for
a Greek woman to appear in public bareheaded was a sign that she was a
prostitute (cf. Morris 1958:151). Zinserling's work contains nine illustrations of Greek hetaerae (i.e., 'companions') taken mostly from Greek
pottery; these show thirteen women and date from the sixth to the fourth
centuries B.C. Of these, one is bareheaded, six are wearing headbands and
six are wearing a special type of headdress shaped something like a
horn-of-plenty. The one who is bareheaded is not wearing any clothing. In
fact, of the six hetaerae wearing the horn-shaped headdress, that is all that
four of them have on except for sandals. It would seem that, rather than
the lack of a headdress marking prostitutes, the presence of a special
horn-shaped headdress was what helped identify them.

Table 3
The headdress of Roman women in illustrations

Date	Total	Bareheaded	Headband	Hooded
8th B.C.	7	5	—	2
7th B.C.	—	—	—	—
6th B.C.	—	—	—	—
5th B.C.	1	—	—	1
4th B.C.	—	—	—	—
3rd B.C.	—	—	—	—
2nd B.C.	1	1	—	1
1st B.C.	16	7	3	6
1st A.D.	9	6	2	1
2nd A.D.	15	10	2	3
3rd A.D.	3	2	—	1
4th A.D.	3	3	—	—
5th A.D.	—	—	—	—
6th A.D.	8	3	1	4
Totals	63	37	8	18

Zinserling's book contains eight pictures that show fifteen Greek women in various acts of worship. A seventh century B.C. water jar shows four bareheaded women dancing with young men in a cult dance (1973:19). A fifth century B.C. jar shows a Maenad (i.e., a frenzied female dancer) worshiping Dionysus, wearing an ivy chaplet in her hair (plate 21). Likewise, another fifth century B.C. jar shows four Maenads with garlands in their hair drinking at a cult celebration of Dionysus (plate 51). A fifth century B.C. statue of what appears to be a girl praying with arms out-stretched shows her bareheaded (plate 28). A fifth century B.C. vase shows a bareheaded woman sacrificing a young pig to the goddesses of the underworld (plate 43). Another fifth century B.C. vase shows a young woman and a slave girl at a scene of the cult of the dead; one is bareheaded and the other is wearing a headband (plate 49). A third century B.C. statue of a serving maid sacrificing at a cult ritual shows her bareheaded (plate 66). Finally, another third century B.C. statue shows a priestess apparently wearing a hood; part of her head is missing and the identification of the headwear cannot be exact (plate 71). But of all the worshipers, only this last one wears a headcovering, and she has an official function as a priestess. To be sure, the examples above predate the first century A.D. by three hundred years or more. But if the customs were at all stable, the evidence above indicates that ordinary Greek women did not wear headcoverings during acts of worship.

Fee (1987:509) presents two sources as evidence that women wore head coverings in religious ceremonies. First, he refers to two plates in Volume 11 of Goodenough's *Jewish Symbols* that show three women in the worship of Isis, two uncovered and one covered (1964, figures 99 and 101). But a two-to-one ratio favoring women without their heads covered is hardly evidence that women wore head coverings in worship. Second, he refers to Lucius Apuleius in *The Golden Ass* (11.10) where, with regard to a procession at the Isis festival, we read, "The women had their hair anointed, and their heads covered with light linen; but the men had their crowns shaven and shining bright." These are not, however, ordinary devotees; these are initiates. Apuleius had previously described women in the procession as wearing "garlands and flowers upon their heads" (11.9). Fee (1987:509) also refers to the ambiguous evidence from Pompeii, but it is unlikely that Italian customs have much bearing on the Greek situation.

It is also worthy of note that Greek women seem to have cut off their hair in times of mourning. Plutarch, in the context of discussing mourning at funerals, says, "So in Greece, whenever any misfortune comes, the women cut off their hair and the men let it grow." (*Moralia*, The Roman Questions 14). This would be similar to the Jewish custom of shaving the head as a symbol of grief or mourning (cf. Deut. 21:12–13; Is. 7:20; 15:2; 22:12; Jer. 16:6; Mic. 1:16; and Josephus *Antiquities* 4.8.23 [Loeb §257]).

Again, note that the customs as regards women's headdress were not uniform, but varied from culture to culture. Jewish women, as well as most women in Tarsus and farther east, did wear a head covering in distinction to the Greek custom, a fact worth mentioning since there was a Jewish community in Corinth (cf. Acts 18:4–5). It would seem that most oriental women covered their heads in public, in the east if not in Corinth. Philo (*De Specialibus Legibus* 3.56), a first century Alexandrian Jew, describes the head-covering (ἐπίκρανον) as "the symbol of modesty, regularly worn by women who are wholly innocent"; and it is related that a certain woman named Qimchith, who was the high priest's mother, was always veiled, even in the house (Oepke 1965 3:562, citing Strack and Billerbeck 1922ff., 2:430). Lightfoot quotes several sources to show that Jewish women were veiled in the streets, but then says, "when they resorted unto holy service they took off their veils, and exposed their naked faces; and that not out of lightness, but out of religion" (1979 4:231). "Evidence of the veil in Tarsus is provided by Dio Chrys[ostom] *Or[ationes]*, 33, 46 [sic; the reference should read 33.48–49] and coins bearing the image of Tyche of Tarsus" (Oepke 1965 3:562). Regarding the veiling of women in Tarsus,

Dio Chrysostom (33.49) indicates that Tarsian women followed an older custom of covering their faces when they went out for a walk. In discussing the customs that showed sobriety of the earlier days, he says:

> Among these is the convention regarding feminine attire, a convention which prescribes that women should be so arrayed and should so deport themselves when in the street that nobody could see any part of them, neither of the face nor of the rest of the body, and that they themselves might not see anything off the road. (33.48)

Ramsey (1960:202) notes that this heavy veiling of women was "utterly different" from the Greek custom.

The variety of customs regarding women's headdress in the ancient world shows that there was no uniform practice, especially in Greece where women often appear without a head covering in religious rites. The evidence seems to indicate that, in the first century among the Romans, both men and women covered their heads at worship, while among the Greeks, both men and women uncovered their heads when they worshiped. Thus the tradition which Paul advocated in 1 Corinthians 11 was, contrary to popular opinion today, not grounded in the social customs of Corinth, but opposed to them.

Lord's Supper. Drunkenness in the ancient world was sometimes considered a part of a religious rite, especially in the worship of Dionysus, who was considered the discoverer of wine (cf. Diodorus of Sicily 4.3.4–5). It was the custom at a meal to greet undiluted wine with the words "To the good Deity *[δαίμονος]*" and wine mixed with water with the words "To Zeus Saviour" (Diodorus of Sicily 4.3.4). Diodorus mentions a second Dionysus, also called Sabazius, who was worshiped in secret, shameful night meetings (4.4.1). This worship involved, among other things, the consumption of wine, as shown by a passage at the beginning of Aristophanes's play *Wasps*. The play opens with a dialogue between two household slaves on watch at night. One of them attributes his sleepiness to having drunk wine with the words: "Nay, 'tis a sleep from great Sabazius holds me" (line 9). To be sure, drunkenness at religious ceremonies was not entirely condoned. In a fragment preserved from Menander's play *The Peevish Man [Δύσκολος]*, we find the condemnation: "Look at their mode of offering sacrifices, the burglars that they are. They bring couches and wine-jars, not for the god's sake but their own" (129K.1–3). But with this background connection between drunkenness and religion, one should not be entirely surprised to find the Corinthians getting drunk at the Lord's Supper.

Ecstasy in religion. There was an element in Greek religion, often identified with the worship of Dionysus, that emphasized ecstasy and frenzy. For example, in describing the worship of Osiris, Plutarch describes it as being much like the worship of Dionysus:

> If, however, for the benefit of others it is needful to adduce proofs of this identity [that Osiris is identical with Dionysus], let us leave undisturbed what may not be told, but the public ceremonies which the priests perform in the burial of the Apis, when they convey his body on an improvised bier, do not in any way come short of a Bacchic procession; for they fasten skins of fawns about themselves, and carry Bacchic wands and indulge in shoutings and movements exactly as do those who are under the spell of the Dionysiae ecstasies (*Moralia,* Isis and Osiris 364e [Loeb §35]).

But ecstasy was not limited to Dionysian worship. Even the more restrained worship of Apollos could be marked by ecstasy. Plutarch notes that in the past the oracles at Delphi used "strange words" [γλῶττας, i.e., Attic for 'tongues'] (Plutarch *Moralia,* Oracles at Delphi 406f [Loeb §24]). In commenting on Greek religion in the middle of the second century A.D., Tatian says, "Some woman by drinking water gets into a frenzy, and loses her senses by the fumes of frankincense, and you say that she has the gift of prophecy" (Address of Tatian to the Greeks, 19).

In fact, to Romans, the Greek religion seemed to be marked by a lack of reverence. Dionysius of Halicarnassus writes of religious rites at Rome in contrast with those of Greece:

> And no festival is observed among them as a day of mourning or by the wearing of black garments and the beating of breasts and the lamentations of women because of the disappearance of deities, such as the Greeks perform in commemorating the rape of Persephone and the adventures of Dionysus and all the other things of like nature. And one will see among them, even though their manners are now corrupted, no ecstatic transports, no Corybantic frenzies, no begging under the colour of religion, no bacchanals or secret mysteries, no all-night vigils of men and women together in the temples, nor any other mummery of this kind; but alike in all their words and actions with respect to the

gods a reverence is shown such as is seen among neither Greeks nor barbarians. (*The Roman Antiquities* 2.19.2)

Once again, with this in mind, the modern reader of 1 Corinthians should not be surprised to find the Christians at Corinth placing a high value on those spiritual gifts which seemed to be the most ecstatic.

Women in religion. Women often served as priestesses and prophetesses in Greek religion. The most famous oracle in all Greece was the one at Delphi, the "earth's navel" (Euripides *Ion* line 6). But the prophet there was a woman, a prophetess (cf. lines 42, 91, 321). In describing that oracle, Plutarch (*Moralia,* The Oracles at Delphi 405c–d [Loeb §23]) tells that a maiden became a prophetic priestess. At times there was more than one prophetess there, but Plutarch (*Moralia,* Obsolescence of Oracles 414b [Loeb §8]) states that there was only one priestess at Delphi in his time. With this in mind, the reader can understand why, in a section on prophecy and speaking in tongues, Paul found it necessary to discuss the principle which the churches followed about women keeping silent in the assembly. It would run against a Greek's upbringing to suggest that there was a time and place when a prophetess should not speak.

The resurrection. Greek thought generally denied a resurrection of the body from the dead. Aeschylus has Apollo say, "When the dust hath drained the blood of a man, once he is slain, there is no resurrection *[ἀνάστασις]*" (*Eumenides* 647–48). In Aeschylus's play *Agamemnon,* a member of the chorus says, "I know no way how by mere words to bring the dead back to life" (lines 1360–61). Herodotus reports that Prexaspes told Cambyses, "If the dead can rise, you may look to see Astyages the Mede rise up against you; but if nature's order be not changed, assuredly no harm to you will arise from Smerdis" (3.62). The chorus in Sophocles's *Electra* says, "Yet him, thy sire, from Acheron's dark shore / By prayers or cries thou never can'st restore, / No, never more" (lines 137–39).

It is true that Aristotle mentions the possibility of a resurrection in *On the Soul* 1.3.406b. But this seems to be a possibility that he thinks his readers will reject; thus it is an argument against the idea that a soul which has left a body could enter it again. Rather, in that same paragraph he argues, "the soul has the same movements as the body." Later he argues against the Pythagorean view that any soul can enter into any body, for "every body has its own peculiar shape or form" (*On the Soul* 1.3.407b). To follow this to its logical conclusion, if a body has decayed, the soul would no longer be able to reenter it, for it would now have a different shape and form.

By the second century A.D., opponents of Christianity were arguing that this dissolution of the body makes a resurrection impossible. Athenagoras the Athenian wrote:

> These persons, to wit, say that many bodies of those who have come to an unhappy death in shipwrecks and rivers have become food for fishes, and many of those who perish in war, or who from some other sad cause or state of things are deprived of burial, lie exposed to become the food of any animals which may chance to light upon them. (*On the Resurrection of the Dead,* 3)

To be sure, this comes from a century after the writing of 1 Corinthians, and it can be maintained that this objection arose in response to Christianity. But the Jews had taught the resurrection hundreds of years before this, and it is likely that the argument had emerged much earlier.

With this in mind, it becomes apparent that those at Corinth who were arguing that there was no resurrection of the dead were simply following the line of thinking that they had held for years before their conversion. They were trying to make Christianity more palatable to Greeks, but at a cost that would destroy an essential tenet of Christianity.

Contributions. Corinth is described as a "prosperous and wealthy" city (Dio Chrysostom *Orationes* 37.36). As such, it was a favorite stop for orators who gave speeches and collected fees. In the writings of Dio Chrysostom, one finds an account of a failed attempt to collect such a fee: "Again, Herodotus the historian also paid you a visit, bringing tales of Greece, and in particular tales of Corinth—not yet fallacious tales—in return for which he expected to receive pay from the city." (*Orationes* 37.7). When Paul argued that he had not availed himself of his right to be supported by the Corinthians (1 Cor. 9:15–18) and again when he suggested that they should select some individuals to carry their gift to Jerusalem (1 Cor. 16:3), he was trying to avoid being identified with these traveling orators.

2.5 Christianity and culture at Corinth

In his book *Christ and Culture,* Yale theologian Richard Niebuhr (1951) has postulated five categories to embrace different viewpoints of the relationship between Christianity and culture throughout the centuries. The first two are extremes and these he labels CHRIST AGAINST CULTURE and THE CHRIST OF CULTURE. By Christ against culture he does not mean that Christ is opposed to all aspects of culture, for people cannot exist without culture. Christians partake of culture just as others do; they speak a language, marry one another, wear clothing, and do many other things that they share in common with non-Christians. Niebuhr is speaking, however, of an attitude toward those aspects of culture that come into conflict with Christianity. These practices of a culture that are opposed to the teaching of Christ must not be followed. At the other extreme—the Christ of culture—Christ is viewed as sanctioning every aspect of the society. Such a viewpoint cannot be held until the culture has been greatly affected by Christianity.

The other three categories that Niebuhr names are all various attempts at synthesis between the first two views. He labels these CHRIST ABOVE CULTURE, CHRIST AND CULTURE IN PARADOX, and CHRIST THE TRANS-FORMER OF CULTURE. In his fifth chapter, Niebuhr lists Paul as one of the individuals holding to the second synthesis—Christ and culture in paradox—which he labels the "dualist" view. It is perhaps significant that, in assigning Paul to this category, he fails to refer to 1 Corinthians. It is true that Paul does make a few appeals to Greek culture in this letter: he appeals to the normal hair length in 11:14 (cf. Plutarch *Moralia,* The Roman Questions 14) and to the shame of a woman speaking in public in 14:35 (cf. Plutarch *Moralia,* Advice to Bride and Groom 31–32). But as noted above, in many aspects Paul is quite against the practices of Greek culture. In fact, several of the items that Paul challenges, such as the importance of human wisdom and disbelief in the resurrection, strike at the heart of the Greek world view. It would seem that Paul's approach to culture, at least for the book of 1 Corinthians, best fits in the category Christ against culture.

3
Overall Discourse Structure

3.1 Methodology

The presupposition behind the search for macrostructures is as follows: for any given well-structured discourse there exists an overall idea that the author of the text has in mind as he produces it. To the extent that the text is well-formed, that controlling idea is reproduced in the mind of the receiver as he reads or listens to the text. It is the macrostructure which is identified when a person gives a brief summary of the discourse. Where a text contains several loosely related discourses, each discourse will have its own macrostructure.

Van Dijk (1977:144–46) has suggested four procedures for isolating the macrostructure of a given discourse. The first may be called ATTRIBUTIVE DELETION, in which attributes and other less important parts of the text are irrecoverably deleted. The second may be called PREDICTIVE DELETION, in which information is deleted that is inductively recoverable. The third may be called SIMPLE GENERALIZATION, in which information is grouped and replaced by a more generic term. The fourth may be called INTEGRATION, in which descriptions of processes are combined into a more general term, which entails all of the processes.

Ideally, such a procedure should yield something like the thesis of the discourse, which most readers would intuitively arrive at by reading the discourse. For a lengthy discourse, however, this procedure can be quite tedious. With this in mind, a shortcut proposed by Longacre (1990a) can be taken. Longacre has noted that the most important material for any given discourse is usually encoded in a given mode and/or tense. A chain of these tenses he calls MAINLINE (STORYLINE in narrative; THEMELINE in other texttypes). For example, in Greek narrative text, the storyline is usually given in the aorist tense. For hortatory text, the themeline is marked by the imperative (and other methods of encoding command forms).

In this study, the following methodology has been chosen for determining the macrostructure. First, the text was divided into its major sections using both conceptual (topical) and grammatical (syntactic) concerns. Next, hortatory forms (imperative, hortatory subjunctive, and statements containing words such as *appeal* and *ought*) were identified for each section. Third, using topic sentences, key words, and the hortatory themeline, the key ideas were abstracted from the text. Then, these were reduced to macrostructural statements for each section. Finally, an attempt was made to combine these macrostructures into one overall macrostructure.

3.2 Macrosegmentation

Structure of the letter. The body of the letter of 1 Corinthians is composed of ten discourses, whose main topics are division (chapters 1–4), fornication (5–6), marriage (7), eating food offered to idols (8–10), head coverings (11), the Lord's Supper (11), spiritual gifts (12–14), the resurrection from the dead (15), the contribution for the saints (16), and the coming of Apollos (16). The discourses on marriage, eating meat offered to idols, spiritual gifts, and the contribution seem to be written in answer to the Corinthians' letter. The discourses on division, fornication, head coverings, the Lord's Supper, and the resurrection seem to have arisen from reports brought by some members of Chloe's household (1:11) and by Stephanas, Fortunatus, and Achaicus (16:17). There are indications of oral reports also in 5:1, 11:18, and 15:12, although there is no indication of the source of this information.

The discourse on marriage actually seems to be in answer to two questions (7:1, 25). However, the responses to both are similar, and it seems best to treat this as one discourse.

The motivation for the order in which the subjects are addressed is not entirely evident. Presumably the subjects that are introduced by περὶ δέ 'now concerning' are in the same order as in the Corinthians' letter, although even this is not certain. The sections on fornication and marriage are found together, probably because both have to do with sexual issues. In the same way, the worship concerns of head coverings, the Lord's Supper, and use of spiritual gifts are grouped together, even though the first two interrupt what would have been a continuous reply to the Corinthians' letter. Perhaps the lengthy treatment given the subject of division, the back reference to that subject in 11:18, and the primary place accorded it indicate that it was foremost in Paul's mind. In the same way, the ordering of the discourse on the resurrection as the last major discussion may indicate its importance, although it is possible that the contribution received only four verses of attention due to constraints imposed by the size of the scroll on which the letter was written (note that the subject merits two chapters in 2 Corinthians). But Paul may have seen the end of the scroll coming and decided to address the question of the resurrection before he ran out of room.

This study takes the position that only those sections that are introduced by περὶ δέ 'now concerning' are in fact Paul's answers to the Corinthians' letter. All other sections are in response to oral reports which Paul received from various sources. This position, however, is not universally accepted. In perhaps the most significant study dealing with this question, Hurd (1983) has argued that some of the sections which do not begin with 'now concerning' are also answers to questions in the Corinthians' letter. These sections include 5:9–13a, 6:12–20, 11:2–16, and 15:1–58 (cf. Hurd 1983:93). Let us examine each of these in more detail.

First, Hurd (1983:83) argues that 5:9–13a (on not associating with fornicators) can perhaps be considered as material dealing with the written questions in the letter from the Corinthians. Hurd admits that these verses occur within "the context of Paul's discussion of oral information" (p. 83). But he argues that "this item was not based on an item of information connected with the news concerning the incestuous man and is thus free of its present context" (p. 83); thus, since it contains information about Paul's previous letter, it can be considered to be a part of the material in the epistolary dialogue between Paul and the Corinthians. It is not the purpose of this study to deny that these verses shed light on that dialogue. But there is a great difference between verses shedding light on a previous stage of a dialogue and responding to the latest stage of that dialogue. Even though Paul refers to his previous letter (5:9–11), he does not suggest that the Corinthians had written back disputing his instructions. Rather, he is pointing out that the instructions he has just given regarding the incestuous man are nothing new—in a general statement he said the same thing in his previous letter. The incestuous man belonged to the class of fornicator discussed in 5:9–11 and the class of those inside the church in 5:12, thus he is still under discussion in verses 5:9–12a. These verses are, therefore, properly included with the material written in response to oral reports.

Second, Hurd (1983:86–89) argues that 6:12–20 (the last major paragraph on fornication) is transitional between the responses to oral material and those to the Corinthians' letter. He points out that these verses prefigure several sections which come later in this letter: the Old Testament quotation "the two shall become one flesh" (6:16; from Gen. 2:24) foreshadows the discussion on marriage in chapter 7; the maxim "all things are lawful for me" and the reference to food (6:12–13) foreshadow the discussion of food offered to idols in chapters 8–10; the terminology "members of Christ" (6:15) anticipates that used in chapter 12; and in these verses is the first reference to the resurrection (6:14), a theme given fuller expression in chapter 15 (Hurd 1983:87–88). In addition, Fee (1987:252) notes that the verb form ($\varepsilon\xi o\upsilon\sigma\iota\acute{\alpha}\zeta\omega$) of the word for 'rights' or 'authority' ($\varepsilon\xi o\upsilon\sigma\acute{\iota}\alpha$) is found in this section. The concept of rights is found again in chapter 9 and mentioned as authority in 11:10. That these verses contain transitional elements is not here denied; it may be the case, however, that Paul is using many different persuasive techniques here that he later repeats on other topics. The sexual overtones of the one flesh quote can fit the topic of fornication as well as marriage. The resurrection is a common theme that occurs often in Paul's letters, not just in foreshadowing a major chapter on the subject. The expression "members of Christ" is similar to the concept of members of the body of Christ in chapter 12, but there the emphasis is on the body as being the church, while that concept is absent here. Certainly the semantic domains covered by $\varepsilon\xi o\upsilon\sigma\acute{\iota}\alpha$ 'authority, rights' in chapters 9 and 11 are different from that covered by the verb form here, where it means something like overpowered or mastered (Arndt and Gingrich 1957:278).

In addition, there is little or no evidence that these verses in chapter 6 were written in response to a question about fornication in the Corinthians' letter. To be sure, the two maxims "all things are lawful for me" (6:12) and "food for the stomach and the stomach for food" (6:13) are thought by many scholars to be sayings of the Corinthians that could have been in their letter (Hurd 1983:67–68, 86–87). The first is repeated in 10:23 in a section that is definitely written in response to the Corinthians' question about food offered to idols. Since the second also talks about food, it is possible that both maxims were in the Corinthians' letter, but in the section on eating food offered to idols rather than part of a question about fornication.

Actually, these verses function as a section providing justification for the command that Paul has given in 5:3–5 to deliver the incestuous man to Satan, showing that fornication is wrong for a Christian. Fee (1987) comments: "This is the standard view, found in most of the older commentaries. After an aside over the matter of lawsuits, Paul returns to the issue of sexual immorality from 5:1–13, for which he is now giving a general theological argument" (p. 250). While there seem to be elements that reflect statements in the Corinthians' letter in 6:12–20, the section itself is better viewed as being written in response to an oral report that Paul had received.

Third, Hurd (1983:90–91) argues that 11:2–16 is written in response to a question in the Corinthians' letter about head coverings, and with this Fee agrees (1987:492). Many commentators have seen 11:2 as a reflection of a statement of the Corinthians' letter (cf. Hurd 1983:68), and this same position is adopted in the reconstructed letter found in chapter 2 of this study. Most likely their letter contained a sentence that said something like, "Now we remember you in everything and maintain the traditions even as you have delivered them to us." As Fee (1987) notes, "how does he know that they have 'kept the traditions' (v. 2) unless they have so expressed themselves, most likely in their letter?" (p. 491). In saying that this section is in response to the Corinthians' letter, Hurd (p. 90) appeals to Faw's (1952:221) notion that δέ can introduce a response to a letter just like περὶ δέ can. The problem with Faw's position is that not only do the sections in response to the letter begin with the postpositive conjunction δέ, so do sections like 1:10 and 11:17, which are stated to be a reaction of an oral report received by Paul. In fact, with the possible exception of the second discourse, all the discourses in 1 Corinthians begin with δέ, whether in response to oral reports or to the Corinthians' letter. If, as suggested below, the transitional paragraph in 4:18–21 about Paul's travel plans should be taken with the second discourse rather than the first, all discourses begin with δέ. But whether it is all sections or just all but one, the fact that 11:2 contains a δέ is hardly an argument in favor of the section being in response to the Corinthians' letter.

Certainly it is possible that, after mentioning that they keep the traditions, the Corinthians went on to say something like, "But we want to know why our women cannot keep our Greek custom of uncovering their heads when they pray?" At least three factors make this unlikely, however. First, he seems to pair 11:2–16 and 11:17–34 with "I praise you" (v. 2) and "I do not praise" (v. 17). The second of these two sections is stated as being in response to a report that Paul had heard (11:18). Without any indication of a question by the Corinthians in 11:2–16, it seems better to take this paired section as a response to an oral report. Also, the particle δέ seems to have an adversative sense 'but' in 11:17 (Fee 1987:500–1). Even though Paul can praise them as a group for keeping the traditions, he has some teaching to give on a subject that 'someone' (τις) is being contentious about (v. 16). Unlike the situation with the Lord's Supper, the problem is not extensive, so the indefinite singular τις is used. How could

Paul have known that there was someone advocating the abandonment of the Christian tradition unless he had been told? Finally, to foreshadow the research presented in chapter 5 of this study, the grammatical variables studied as a part of style are more like those in chapters 1–6 than like those in chapters 7–10. Thus it is more likely that the specific issue of head coverings was something that Paul had heard about in an oral report.

The final passage that does not start with περὶ δέ that Hurd (1983:91–92) argues is in response to the Corinthians' letter is 15:1–58. Hurd notes that Paul "explicitly refers to at least one question that the Corinthians were asking: 'How can some of you say there is no resurrection of the dead?' (15:12)" (1983:91). But this is not a question from the Corinthians; rather, it is a statement which 'some' (τινες) among them were making. Just as in the discussion of 11:2–16, how could Paul have known that this was the statement of some of the Corinthians without an oral report to that effect? Rather than 15:12 indicating a question in the Corinthians' letter, it provides evidence that Paul had information about the situation of a kind that does not come in letters but is transmitted in oral reports. As for Hurd's (1983:91) contention that the text is logical and persuasive like his answers to the Corinthians' letter, suffice it to say that this is entirely due to the fact that the chapter is trying to effect a change of belief, not a change of behavior. The material is presented using persuasive texttype rather than hortatory, and this is sufficient to account for the perceived differences.

With these points in mind, it seems fair to say that it is best to treat only those sections which are introduced by περὶ δέ 'now concerning' as replies to questions in the Corinthians' letter and the other sections as responses to oral information which Paul had received. When this is done, the letter divides nicely into a cyclical structure of ABA'B'A''B'', where A is a response to oral reports and B is a response to the Corinthians' letter. This is shown clearly in table 4. First, two subjects are covered in response to oral reports; then there are two subjects in response to their letter. This is followed by a two–one–one–two pattern of two responses to oral reports, one to the letter, one to an oral report, and two to the letter. The motivation for this pattern is not clear, although it may provide groupings of related topics (discourses 2 and 3 on sex; 4, 5, and 6 on pagan worship forms; and 6 and 7 on the Christian assembly). In addition, Paul's travel plans are found both between the first two discourses and the last two discourses. If the division defended below and indicated in table 4 is correct, these travel plans are found at the beginning of the second discourse and the end of the next to last discourse, showing an even greater balance in the overall structure of the book.

Table 4
Discourse structure of 1 Corinthians

Chapter	Response to oral report	Response to letter
1	Introduction (1:1–9)	
	1. Church division (1:10–4:17)	
	A Division (1:10–17)	
2	B Wisdom (1:18–2:16)	
3	A' Division (3:1–4)	
	C Servanthood (3:5–15)	
	D Wisdom and division (3:16–23)	
4	C' Servanthood (4:1–17)	
	2. Fornication (4:18–6:20)	
	Travel plans (4:18–21)	
5	A Fornication (5)	
6	B Lawsuits (6:1–8)	
	A' Fornication (6:9–20)	
7		**3. Marriage** (7)
		A Marriage (7:1–16)
		B Circumcision and slavery (7:17–24)
		A' Marriage (7:25–40)
		4. Idol food (8:1–11:1)
8		A Idol food (8:1–13)
9		B Rights (9:1–27)
10		A' Idol food (10:1–11:1)
11	**5. Head coverings** (11:2–16)	
	6. The Lord's Supper (11:17–34)	
		7. Spiritual gifts* (12–14)
12		A Spiritual gifts (12)
13		B Love (13)
14		A' Spiritual gifts (14)
	8. The resurrection* (15)	
15	A The resurrection (15:1–32)	
	B Quit sinning (15:33–34)	
	A' The resurrection (15:35–58)	
16		**9. Contribution** (16:1–4)
		Travel plans (16:5–11)
		10. Apollos (16:12)
	Conclusion (16:13–24)	

*Discourses 7 and 8 are peak sections foreshadowed by the thanksgiving in 1:4–9.

Paul's use of chiasmus in major sections. Several of the discourses in 1 Corinthians show chiasmus of major sections in the form ABA'. The B section in these discourses has often been mistakenly identified as a digression or excursus (Guthrie 1970:425; Feine, Behm, and Kümmel 1966:198–99; Morgan-Wynne 1983:7). For the moment skipping the discourse in chapters 1 through 4, we find this feature in the discourses in 4:18–6:20 (fornication, lawsuits, fornication), 7:1–40 (marriage, circumcision and slavery, marriage), 8:1–11:1 (eating meat offered to idols, right of the teacher to receive pay, eating meat offered to idols), and 12:1–14:40 (spiritual gifts, love, spiritual gifts) (Turner 1976:97). In the latter three, a transition is made that ties the second subject in with the first in such a way that the second subject actually becomes an argument for the first. Failure to note the unity and chiastic structure of chapters 8 through 10 have led to the misunderstanding that Paul is allowing freedom to eat meat offered to idols. Chapter 8 cannot correctly be seen as independent of chapter 10. The whole thrust of the section is to confirm the ruling of the apostolic decision at Jerusalem in Acts 15, albeit presented in a persuasive way, rather than as an authoritarian dogma. The relationship between fornication and lawsuits is not so obvious, although it may have been to the first readers (Guthrie 1970:444). Perhaps the lawsuits were over problems aggravated by fornication. Richardson (1980:347–48) lists eight possible scenarios for this possibility, but it remains precisely that, only a possibility. More likely, the section on lawsuits is establishing the church's right to judge the offender (cf. 5:12 "those inside the church whom you are to judge"). In addition, chiasmus can also be found in some of the subsections of these discourses: it has been noted in 5:2–6 and 13:1–13 (Conzelmann 1975:5; Osburn 1976:150–52).

In the same way the first discourse shows a form of chiasmus with the topics of division and wisdom, although the form is not the simple ABA'. These topics are combined with the topic of servanthood (introduced in 3:5) to form a double chiasmus. The chiasmus may be charted in the following way:

(13)   first set: division, wisdom, division (1:10–3:4)
        second set: servanthood, wisdom and division, servanthood (3:5–4:17)

When this is done, the structure of the first discourse shows the double chiastic form of ABA' C(A''/B')C'.

In passing, it might be well to note Bailey's (1983:154–56) division of 1 Cor. 1:10–15:58 into five large chiastic sections, which are themselves arranged chiastically as shown in (14).

(14)   X the cross (1:10–4:16)
     Y men and women relating to sex (4:17–7:40)
     Z idols (8:1–11:1)
     Y' men and women relating to worship (11:2–14:40)
    X' the resurrection (15:1–58)

Bailey (1983:154–56) divides each of these sections into the chiastic scheme in (15).

(15)   K a statement of a tradition
     L a practical/ethical problem
     M a general theological statement
      N (an optional level)
     M' a general theological statement
     L' a practical/ethical problem
    K' a concluding appeal

When this scheme is applied to one of the major chiastic elements, we get a second chiasmus given in (16).

(16)   K The tradition (4:17–21)
     L Incest and church judgment (5:1–6:11a)
     M Theology of human sexuality (6:11b–14)
     M' Theology of human sexuality (6:15–20)
     L' Christian patterns of sexuality (7:1–40a)
    K' Concluding appeal (7:40b)

But there are major problems with this view. First, Bailey's scheme ignores the obvious division at 7:1 where Paul notes that he is answering the Corinthians' letter. Second, it subordinates the section on the Lord's Supper (11:17–34) to the question of men and women so much that it does not even find a place on Bailey's outline of the book (1983:156). Third, the second suggested chiasm covering 4:17–7:40 lumps the obvious A and B sections (see table 4, discourse 2) of incestuous fornication and lawsuits together as one L section in Bailey's scheme and splits the A' section on fornication into two general theological statements as M and M' divisions. In the resulting structure, marriage (L') becomes parallel to incest and lawsuits (L). Fourth, in order to make the scheme work, Bailey balances the statement of a tradition with an appeal in a way that is often unrelated. Fifth, this scheme ignores the two short answers to the Corinthians' letter in chapter 16. Sixth, it makes the whole letter use only one rhetorical device, chiasm, and ignores other devices such as cycle and inclusio, for which there is evidence in the letter. Seventh, Bailey's suggested appeal in 7:40b ("I think I have the Spirit of God") can only be considered an appeal in the most mitigated sense. Finally, this scheme begins the second section with 4:17, a division which Fee labels quite arbitrary (1987:188). In Bailey's scheme, this division is needed to make the chiasmus fit. There are enough examples of chiasmus in 1 Corinthians without trying to find more than are actually there.

The unity of the fourth discourse. In the preceding section it was suggested that chapters 8 and 10 cannot be correctly understood as independent of one another. Before going further, it is necessary to examine this suggestion more closely since many scholars have understood them, not only as independent, but even as contradictory. Weiss and his followers have divided the text of 1 Corinthians into two or three letters based primarily on what they see as instances of Paul changing his mind about what he should teach on the subject of food offered to idols (cf. Hurd 1983:44–45, 69–70). The material in 1 Cor. 10:1–22 is obviously opposed to eating meat offered to idols, first comparing it to idolatry in the Old Testament and then comparing it to sharing food with demons. This would seem to be in accord with the apostolic decree of Acts 15 which forbade Christians from eating food offered to idols (cf. Barrett 1965:138–44). On the other hand, the last verses of 1 Corinthians 10 give times when it is not wrong to eat food offered to idols (when it is bought in the meat market and when it is served by a friend at a private meal). In addition, 1 Corinthians 8 is often interpreted as accepting the Corinthians' argument that it is all right in itself to eat food offered to idols, but Paul argues that one must be careful in doing so not to lead a weaker brother into sin. Chapter 9 is then interpreted as a defense of Paul's apostleship because he is flying in the face of the apostolic decree and has to establish his right to do so (p. 150).

All of this is to miss the force of Paul's argument. This section deals with three different situations regarding meat offered to idols in which two principles of Christianity seem to be at odds. These two principles are that Christians are not to take part in the worship of idols and that Jesus declared all foods clean for Christians to eat. The three situations are eating idol-food in an idol's temple, at a private meal given by a non-Christian friend, and at home using food bought in the meat market. Paul argues that the latter principle takes precedence in regards to food purchased in the meat market and found on the table at a friend's house, unless of course the friend wants to make it a matter of accepting the worship of idols.

But in the situation of eating meat in an idol's temple, where the worship of an idol could be seen as being in the fore, Paul gives four arguments to support the claim that the former principle takes precedence: (1) the person eating with knowledge that an idol has no real existence may lead a weaker brother who does not know this into sin (8:1–13); (2) Paul himself has set an example of giving up his own rights for the sake of the Gospel, and the Corinthians should do likewise (9:1–27); (3) the Old Testament forbids idolatry (10:1–13); and (4) one cannot eat both the Lord's Supper at the Lord's table and idol-meat at a demon's table without making God jealous (10:14–22). The latter two arguments in 10:1–22 are obviously opposed to the eating of meat in the temple of an idol. But the first two arguments are not so easily understood. Paul uses a conditional approach: he introduces the Corinthians' position in 8:1–6 and seems to accept it as valid for the moment. That is, Paul begins by taking the Corinthians' arguments and saying in effect, "Let's assume for a minute that you are right, that if you are not personally worshiping the idol, you have a right to eat food offered to that idol, even in its temple." Even so, he goes on to argue, there are two problems with eating food offered to an idol: a weaker brother may be made to sin, and a Christian should be willing to give up rights for the sake of the Gospel. Having noted these problems that come with accepting the Corinthians' position, he goes on in chapter 10 to argue that it is in fact wrong to eat meat in an idol's temple. When the reader sees that Paul is only conditionally accepting the Corinthians' proposition that he later tears down, it becomes clear that all four arguments are points against the Corinthians' position and in accord with the apostolic degree of Acts 15.

Paul does not explicitly state that he is for the moment assuming the Corinthians' argument to be valid, which is the cause for the usual misunderstanding by many scholars. As Westerners, most Bible scholars are looking for explicit markers to lay out an argument in unambiguous terms. The Oriental approach, however, is much more subtle: the listener or reader is given the argument, but is supposed to figure out what the speaker or writer is saying and what the relationship is between the parts of the discourse. As Orientals, the Hebrews often used such an approach in the Old Testament, where the setting is missing from passages and transitions are made from one item to another without explicit conceptual markers showing the relationship. But this is not just a Jewish feature of rhetoric. In speaking of Greek style, Demetrius (*On Style* 4 [Loeb §222]) refers to Theophrastus as his authority "that not all possible points should be punctiliously and tediously elaborated, but some should be left to the comprehension and inference of the hearer." To understand the relationship requires induction on the part of the reader.

The endings of two discourses. In a couple of places it is questionable whether chapter beginnings actually mark the beginnings of the major embedded discourses. It is generally agreed that 11:1 is the last statement of the discussion on meat offered to idols rather than the first on the subject of head coverings (cf. Morris 1958:150). In the same way, there is some difficulty in knowing whether to assign the transitional verses 4:18–21 to the first or second discourse.

It is traditional among commentators to carry the discussion of the first discourse through 4:21 and begin the new discourse on fornication with 5:1. This view is not without its problems. Some commentators who take this view note that 5:1 begins abruptly (Findlay 1979:807; Morris 1958:86), or *medias in res* (Lenski 1946:205), or as a "sudden bursting of the storm" (Edwards 1885:118; cf. also Robertson and Plummer 1914:95). A few note either that the discourse should begin with 4:21 (Calvin 1948:177), or that 4:21 ties the two discourses together (Alford 1983:1000). Fee (1987:194) notes that there are verbal ties between 4:18–20 and 5:2–6, and Hurd (1983:89) lists 4:18–21 as a transitional passage. Several ancient manuscripts marked 4:21 as beginning kephalaion 2 (an ancient system of chapters) while manuscript Vaticanus marked the new section as beginning with 4:16. Various manuscripts also began paragraphs either at 4:16, 17, or 18 as well as at 4:14 and 5:1 (Nestle et al. 1957:432; Nestle et al. 1979:447).

If indeed the new discourse begins at 5:1 (or even at 4:21), this would be unique among the discourses of 1 Corinthians, for all the other discourses (1:10; 7:1; 8:1; 11:2; 11:17; 12:1; 15:1; 16:1; and 16:12) begin with a verse containing the conjunctive particle δέ 'now'. In addition, they all end with verses that contain a transitional particle, either δέ 'but' (7:40; 11:16; 11:34; 14:40; 16:12), ὥστε 'so' (11:33; 14:39), οὖν 'therefore' (10:31), or γάρ ... δέ 'for ... but' (6:20; 16:11). But neither 5:1 nor 4:21 contain inter-colon transitional conjunctions (4:21 does contain ἤ 'or' and 5:1 contains καί 'and', but both connect clauses within a colon).

For the purposes of this analysis, it is suggested that the first discourse actually ends with 4:17 and the new discourse begins with 4:18. In favor of this are the following facts: First, the verses 4:18–21 are all on a single subject—Paul's proposed visit to Corinth. This subject is picked up again in 16:5–9. It hardly seems right to begin the new discourse in the middle of this subject. This small section can fit with either the preceding discourse or the following as far as content is concerned. But when put with the following discourse it provides a meaningful introduction to the stern words of chapter 5. Second, it also contains ideas elaborated on in chapter 5: those of being puffed up (vv. 18–19) and having power (vv. 19–20). These words are picked up in 5:2 and 5:4, respectively. Third, it contains the phrase "kingdom of God," a term which is picked up again in 6:9–10.

Fourth, beginning the discourse on fornication with 4:18 would make this discourse begin with a verse containing δέ 'now' and have the discourse on division end with verses containing οὖν 'therefore' (v. 16) and διὰ τοῦτο 'because of this' (v. 17). Fifth, commentators have noted the difference in tone between 4:14, where Paul is admonishing the Corinthians as children, and 4:21, where Paul is threatening to come against the arrogant with a whip (cf. Bailey 1983:162; Barrett 1968:117). Finally, verses 16 and 17 contain similar ideas to those found in other verses that end discourses. The idea of imitating Paul in verse 16 also brings to a close the discourse on eating meat offered to idols in 11:1 and the idea of the practice of all the churches in 4:17 closes the discourse on head coverings in 11:16. Therefore it seems best to take the first discourse as ending at 4:17 and 4:18 beginning a transition into a new section. But however one divides the text at this point, the macrostructure is not affected because the material in the paragraph in question is merely transitional and not central to either section.

3.3 Macrostructure

The hortatory distribution in the letter. The letter as a whole may be treated as being a hortatory text, but the hortatory sections are not distributed uniformly throughout the letter. Shorter discourses, such as those on head coverings and the contribution, show hortatory sections throughout. In the same way, the chiastic discourse on marriage has commands in all three chiastic sections. The chiastic discourse on fornication and lawsuits has overt command forms only in the first and last sections on fornication. The hortatory force in the inner section on lawsuits is mitigated to rhetorical questions. With the exception of the appeals at the beginning (1:10) and end (4:16) of the first discourse, most of the hortatory forms there are found in the inner section of the second chiastic set about wisdom and division. Three discourses (the longer chiastic ones about meat offered to idols and spiritual gifts, and the shorter one about the Lord's Supper) have the hortatory section reserved until the last part of the discourse. The only hortatory material in the discourse about the resurrection are admonitions not to sin (15:33–34) and to remain steadfast (15:58). Both of these are in result sections that follow from the main point: that of believing in the resurrection of the dead. This discourse is primarily persuasive in nature rather than hortatory, and even then its call to belief is mitigated to a rhetorical question (15:12).

The argument summaries and key ideas of the discourses. In the first discourse, after beginning with an appeal for the Corinthians to be united, Paul makes two main arguments. The first is that it is human wisdom, not divine, which leads people to be puffed up and boast in men. The second is that the men they are boasting in are merely servants of God and are not to be followed themselves. Rather than saying "I belong to" some man, the Corinthians should realize that they all belong to Christ (3:22).

The key ideas of the first discourse can be summarized as follows: I appeal to you by the name of Christ that all of you agree and that there be no divisions among you (1:10); in God's wisdom, the foolishness of preaching Christ crucified is wiser than the wisdom of men, so that no person might boast (1:21, 23, 25, 29); we impart a secret hidden wisdom of God revealed through the Spirit (2:7, 10); while there is jealousy and strife among you, you are fleshly, not spiritual (3:1, 3); Apollos and Paul are servants: farmers and builders for God (3:5, 6, 9, 10); the wisdom of this world is foolishness with God, so let no one boast of men, for you all belong to Christ (3:19, 21, 23); we are servants of Christ and stewards of God's mysteries (4:1); do not be puffed up in favor of one against another or boast as if you have things you did not receive (4:6, 7).

The second discourse begins with a rebuke because one of the Corinthian Christians is living with his father's wife (probably the man's stepmother). Paul commands that the offender should be delivered to Satan. The discourse then turns to the problem created when the Corinthian Christians sued one another in public lawsuit. Paul suggests that the church should decide such disputes; otherwise, it would be better to suffer loss. Paul ends the discourse with an admonition against fornication.

The key ideas of the second discourse can be summarized as follows: Deliver the man who is living with his father's wife to Satan (5:1, 5); when one of you has a grievance against another, he should not go to law before unbelievers but rather before the saints (6:1); the unrighteous will not inherit the kingdom of God (6:9); flee fornication, for our body is meant for the Lord, not for a prostitute, and we are united to the Lord by the Holy Spirit in our body (6:13, 18, 19).

The third discourse, on marriage, seems to be in answer to a couple of questions which the Corinthians had written in their letter. Paul argues that it is best for each one to stay either married or unmarried, as they were when they became Christians. He states that celibacy can lead to a more productive Christian life than marriage, but celibacy is not for everyone. Therefore, it is no sin to get married.

The key ideas of the third discourse can be summarized as follows: A husband and wife should have sex with each other to avoid fornication (7:2, 3, 5); it is best for the unmarried to remain so if they can practice self-control (7:8); the Lord says a husband and wife should not separate (7:10); everyone should remain in the state in which he was called (7:20); the unmarried should not seek marriage, but if passions are strong, let them marry; it is not a sin (7:25–26, 36).

The fourth discourse is on eating meat offered to idols. This also seems to be in answer to one of the Corinthians' questions. He argues first of all that one must not use his Christian liberty in such a way as to lead a weaker brother into sin. Next he discusses the right he has as an apostle to be supported by the church and how he has given up this right for the sake of the Gospel, implying that the Corinthians should not insist on their rights either. In chapter 10 he argues from Old Testament examples that idolatry must not be practiced. Then he argues that a Christian cannot share in the Lord's Supper and in an idol's sacrifice also, for to do so is in fact to share in the worship of demons. He summarizes by giving specific examples which show that it is not wrong to eat meat if one does not realize that it has been sacrificed to idols.

The key ideas of the fourth discourse can be summarized as follows: Take care lest the liberty which you have because of your knowledge that an idol is nothing does not cause a weak brother to fall into sin (8:4, 9); I have not made use of my right to make a living by preaching the Gospel, so that I might win people for Christ (9:14, 15, 19); do not be idolaters, but be warned by the example of what happened to the Israelites (10:6, 7); flee from idolatry, for when you eat food offered to idols you share with demons rather than with the table of the Lord (10:14, 20, 21); eat meat sold in the meat market or at a friend's dinner without raising questions, unless someone says, "This has been offered in sacrifice" (10:25, 27, 28).

The fifth discourse contains five arguments as to why women should cover their heads when they pray or prophesy and men should not. First Paul argues that Christ is the head of man and man is the head of woman. Then he argues from the creation that woman was created from and for man. His third argument (because of the angels) is obscure, but perhaps refers to the belief that angels are present in worship. The next argument is from the lesson of nature. His final argument is that the churches of God have no such custom as women praying bareheaded. From his use of *anyone* in 11:16, it would seem that the problem was not extensive.

The key ideas of the fifth discourse can be summarized as follows: A man ought not cover his head when he prays or prophesies, because to do so would dishonor Christ, while a woman ought to cover her head, lest she dishonor her husband (11:4, 5, 7, 10).

The discourse on the Lord's Supper, on the other hand, deals with a more extensive problem. Here, in contrast to verse 2, Paul writes "I do not commend you." He begins with an admonition not to use the Lord's

Supper as a time for satisfying hunger and thirst. He then gives an account of Jesus instituting the Lord's Supper. Next, he admonishes them to examine themselves before they eat, and closes with instructions to wait for one another and satisfy their hunger at home.

The key ideas of the sixth discourse can be summarized as follows: When you meet to eat the Lord's Supper, wait for one another, and remember the body and blood of the Lord Jesus, as He said (11:20, 24, 25, 33).

The seventh discourse is on the proper place of spiritual gifts. Paul begins with the argument that all the gifts come from the same Spirit of God. The gifts are different but, by analogy with the human body, he shows that all are needed. He next argues that love is more important than any of the spiritual gifts. Then he contrasts prophecy and speaking in tongues, and concludes with instructions regulating the use of spiritual gifts in the assembly.

The key ideas of the seventh discourse can be summarized as follows: Just as the body is one and has many members, so you are one body in Christ, with each person having gifts given by the Spirit for the common good (12:4, 7, 12, 27); love, which remains, is greater than the spiritual gifts, which will pass away (13:8, 13); seek spiritual gifts, especially prophecy, which is greater than speaking in tongues, because it builds up the church (14:1, 5, 12); all things should be done decently and in order, which means that those who speak in tongues without an interpreter and women should keep silent in the assembly (14:28, 34, 40).

The eighth discourse is on the resurrection from the dead. Some of the Corinthians were following Greek philosophy by saying that there will be no resurrection from the dead (15:12). Paul begins by arguing the reality of Christ's resurrection. He repeats the Christian tradition that the death, burial, resurrection, and appearances of Christ are of first importance. Then he demonstrates that the resurrection of Christ is tied to the resurrection of Christians at Christ's coming. He next discusses the nature of the resurrection body. He writes of the events of the second coming and concludes with praise to God.

The key ideas of the eighth discourse can be summarized as follows: Just as Christ was raised from the dead, so at His coming all who belong to Him will be made alive (15:20, 22, 23); unlike our physical body, the body which is raised will be imperishable, glorious, powerful, spiritual, and immortal (15:42–44, 53).

The ninth discourse concerns the contribution for the saints. In four verses he encourages the Corinthians to put some money aside every Sunday for this purpose. If the gift they collect is worthwhile, he will accompany their representatives when they take it to Jerusalem. The letter continues with travel plans for Paul and Timothy.

The key ideas of the ninth discourse can be summarized as follows: Each of you should put something aside and store it up for the contribution for the saints at Jerusalem (16:1, 2); I will come visit you after Pentecost and spend some time with you (16:5, 7, 8); welcome Timothy and send him back to me (16:10, 11).

The final discourse is merely a statement that Apollos will not come at this time. After concluding exhortations, he commends Stephanas and Fortunatus and Achaicus. The letter closes with greetings and a postscript in Paul's own handwriting.

The key ideas of the tenth discourse and conclusion can be summarized as follows: Apollos will come when he has an opportunity, but not now (16:12); be subject to and acknowledge those workers who have devoted themselves to the service of the saints (16:15, 16, 18).

The macrostructures of the discourses. With the above argument summaries and listings of key ideas, we can now abstract a macrostructure for each of the ten discourses and the conclusion in 1 Corinthians given in (17)–(27).

(17)   Discourse 1 (1:10–4:17)
        I appeal to you to avoid division and strife due to following men (Paul, Apollos, and Cephas), for such boasting is due to the wisdom of men, but in God's wisdom they are servants of Christ.

(18)   Discourse 2 (4:18–6:20)
        Flee fornication and lawsuits with one another, and deliver an incestuous fornicator to Satan.

(19)   Discourse 3 (7:1–40)
        Let everyone remain in the marital status in which he was when called, but it is not a sin to get married if an unmarried person cannot control his passions.

(20)   Discourse 4 (8:1–11:1)
        Do not eat meat offered to idols in an idol's temple, for this is not a right but idolatry and can lead a weak brother into sin; but eat meat bought at the meat market or at a friend's dinner without asking any questions.

(21)   Discourse 5 (11:2–16)
        A man ought not cover his head when he prays or prophesies, but a woman should.

(22)   Discourse 6 (11:17–34)
       When you meet to eat the Lord's Supper, wait for one another and
       remember the body and blood of the Lord.

(23)   Discourse 7 (12:1–14:40)
       Seek spiritual gifts, especially prophecy, which builds up the church,
       but above all, show love.

(24)   Discourse 8 (15:1–58)
       Just as Christ was raised from the dead, so you should believe that
       Christians will be raised at His coming with a spiritual body.

(25)   Discourse 9 (16:1–11)
       Every Sunday let each of you put something aside and store it up
       for the contribution for the saints at Jerusalem. I will come after
       Pentecost, and Timothy will come now.

(26)   Discourse 10 (16:12)
       Apollos will not come now.

(27)   Conclusion (16:13–18)
       Be subject to and acknowledge those workers who have devoted
       themselves to the service of the saints.

The macrostructure of the fourth discourse. Before proceeding further, it is necessary to stop and examine the macrostructure of the fourth
discourse, because alternative macrostructures have been formulated by
other researchers. These alternative macrostructures focus on rights and
see the question of eating food offered to idols as incidental. Youngman
(1987:121–23) suggested the following theme for 1 Cor. 8:1–11:1: "Using
the general topic of 'food' as an example, I exhort you to exercise self-
control in the use of your highly-valued rights, lest you sin or cause others
to sin." Then a few pages later he modified it to "do everything out of love
for God and people; restrict the exercise of your rights for the sake of the
Gospel" (p. 128). This latter macrostructure does not mention either food
or idols at all. In this he was preceded by Hoopert (1981:50) who wrote
about the same section: "This expresses a theme statement for the Epistle
to this point, namely, 'I exhort you, brothers, that you say "no" to your
own selfish interests, and even to your own individual rights, for the sake
of Christ'. "
Do these generalized statements of principles correspond to a macrostructure of this section? The answer is no. For one thing, a

macrostructure is a mental structure that determines the form and content of a discourse. Van Dijk (1972) originally postulated the macrostructure as a generative device for a text in an attempt to extend generative grammar from the sentence level to the discourse level. These statements proposed by Hoopert and Youngman are so general that they could generate many different texts, not just this one. Second, such generalized statements omit information which is central to the fourth discourse and which cannot be retrieved from mental frames. The discourse is primarily about eating food offered to idols, and this fact cannot be recovered from the suggested macrostructures of Hoopert and Youngman. Third, the suggested macro-structures embody a principle expounded in chapter 9 of the fourth discourse, but that principle is not the central one to the discourse. Actually, as previously noted, the discourse is working out the balance between two principles: (a) a Christian should not worship idols in any way; and (b) a Christian is allowed to eat any food if it is done with thanksgiving. But even the statement of these two principles which Paul tries to balance in the fourth discourse does not constitute the macro-structure for this discourse. The macrostructure must lay out the way in which the two principles are applied within this given text. Mere statement of the logically underlying principles does not give the macrostructure.

3.4 Theme

A unifying theme for 1 Corinthians. Niebuhr (1951:10) has rightly noted, "Not only pagans who have rejected Christ but believers who have accepted him find it difficult to combine his claims upon them with those of their societies." This is especially seen in this letter which Paul wrote to the Corinthians. They, like many others after them, found it difficult to be completely Christian in those areas in which their former lifestyle con-flicted with Christianity.

Since 1 Corinthians deals with several areas in which the Corinthian Christians had problems, students of the New Testament have had diffi-culty in finding a single theme that unites the whole letter. Unifying themes that have been suggested by scholars have included the following: op-ponents of Paul who were Judaizers, Palestinian Christians claiming superiority over Paul, and Jewish Christian Gnostics (Guthrie 1970:422–23; Conzelmann 1975:14–15). Schmithals ([1956] 1971) has advocated the lat-ter idea forcefully enough that those who have written on the subject have had to agree or disagree with him (Ziesler 1986:264). Most have disagreed, although some have accepted some of his argument with a degree of modification. After demonstrating that a hypothesis of Gnostic opponents is not necessary to an understanding of the book, Conzelmann (1975:15) says that there are traces of the beginnings of what later was called gnosticism. He thus describes the Corinthians as proto-Gnostics. In the same way, Bruce (1971:21) says that the doctrine of some of the Christians at Corinth might legitimately be called incipient Gnosticism. In a somewhat extended passage, Nock (1964:xiv) writes:

> Would you have found a church or conventicle of some type or other of Gnostics in Corinth at the time of Paul's correspondence with his converts there? ... Evidence for something of the sort might conceivably appear. In the meantime, since originality is not necessarily confined to movements or authors that have disappeared, I must continue to hold that in the environment of early Christianity there were materials which could be built into Gnostic systems—but no Gnostic system; that there was an appropriate mythopoeic faculty—but no specific myth; that there was a 'Gnostic' state of mind—but no crystallized formulation of that state of mind and no community or communities clinging to the formulation.

In searching for a unifying theme, several scholars have sought to identify the different false doctrines that Paul opposes with one or more of the parties referred to in the first chapter: the Paul-party, the Apollos-party, the Cephas-party, and the Christ-party (Barrett 1964:283–85; Craig 1953:7–8). But as Conzelmann (1975:14) has stated, "Since Paul does not enter into any special opinions on the part of the groups, it is impossible for specific positions which Paul combats to be assigned to any specific group." This is best illustrated by the fact that different scholars have assigned various doctrines to the different groups.

Rather than seeing all the false doctrines as being the product of one particular group or dividing the false teachings among the groups, it seems better to attribute the problems that Paul discusses to various individuals.

It is the conflict with culture and customs that gives the book of 1 Corinthians its lasting appeal. Although the customs in different societies may vary, the conflict of Christ with culture is ever present. 1 Corinthians has been one of the most practical books of the New Testament scriptures, not because it provides arguments against a particular heresy, but because it addresses principles and problems that are common to all ages.

Culture as a unifying theme. The question may be asked as to whether the discourse macrostructures given above can be further combined into one overall macrostructure. Some of them seem to have little in common with others. Yet there are two themes which run throughout the whole book. First, every problem which Paul discusses has its roots in Greek culture, and second, almost every argument appeals to Christ in some way.

If a unifying theme is sought, it is found first in the conflict of Christianity with the cultural background of Corinth. As Conzelmann (1975:15) has noted, "We have here to do with people who have only recently become Christians; what were the ideas they brought with them into the community?" Most, if not all, of the problems which Paul discusses in 1 Corinthians can be attributed to the influence of the Corinthian cultural setting on the Christians there. It is generally accepted that the glorification of wisdom, the eating of meat offered to idols, and the denial of a bodily resurrection were aspects of Greek culture. In addition, ecstatic utterances may have been found in some Pythian and Dionysiac religions (Bruce 1971:21), although the speaking in tongues in 1 Corinthians should not be viewed as a part of pagan religion. But Greek religion may have been an influence on the Corinthians' high estimate of this gift. Some of the problems that Paul deals with are moral problems, such as fornication, drunkenness, and the desires of greed and for revenge that accompany lawsuits. But even these problems are culturally based, for Greek society did not place a strong condemnation on them.

Perhaps the most misunderstood cultural influence in modern days is the Greek attitude toward women wearing head coverings. Regarding this, Guthrie (1970:445) writes, "Paul urges Christian women to respect the social customs of their time, in spite of their new-found freedom." But in fact, as shown in chapter 2 of this study, Greek women were under no obligation to wear a covering on their head in Greek society, especially when they were at worship. Rather than Paul pleading for respect of social customs, in 1 Corinthians 11 he is arguing for the maintenance of the Christian tradition (11:2). Some women were being influenced more by what society allowed than by what Christianity taught.

The centrality of Christ. Although the cultural influences behind the problems at Corinth stand out, the word *culture* is not found in the text. Rather the key concept in 1 Corinthians is the Lord Jesus Christ. A list of the nouns and verbs that show theological significance and are used more than ten times (found in table 5) clearly shows that the book of 1 Corinthians is primarily theocentric and Christo-centric. The term *Christ* is found 64 times in 1 Corinthians. This is second in frequency of usage only to the Epistle to the Romans (which has the word 66 times) among the New Testament books. The term *Lord* is found 66 times, and Jesus 26 times (Aland, Bachmann, and Slaby 1978:2–304).

Table 5
Key words in 1 Corinthians

English	Greek	No. uses	English	Greek	No. uses
God	θεός	106	member	μέλος	16
Lord	κύριος	66	spiritual	πνευματικός	15
Christ	Χριστός	64	to give	δίδωμι	15
to have	ἔχω	49	power	δύναμις	15
body	σῶμα	46	to be able	δύναμαι	15
woman/wife	γυνή	41	love	ἀγάπη	14
spirit	πνεῦμα	40	to do	ποιέω	14
rother	ἀδελφός	39	to drink	πίνω	14
to speak	λαλέω	34	dead	νεκρός	13
man/husband	ἀνήρ	32	glory	δόξα	12
man/human	ἄνθροπος	31	holy	ἅγιος	12
to say	λέγω	30	to call	καλέω	12
to eat	ἐσθίω	27	wise	σοφός	11
Jesus	Ἰεσοῦς	26	flesh	σάρξ	11
to know	οἶδα	25	to prophesy	προφητεύω	11
church	ἐκκλησία	22	weak	ἀσθενής	11
world	κόσμος	21	faithless	ἄπιστος	11
tongue	γλῶσσα	21	to receive	λαμβάνω	11
to raise	ἐγείρω	20	knowledge	γνῶσις	10
to write	γράφω	18	grace	χάρις	10
to come	ἔρχομαι	18	to baptize	βαπτίζω	10
wisdom	σοφία	17	apostle	ἀπόστολος	10
word	λόγος	17	to judge	ἀνακρίνω	10
to wish	θέλω	17	head	κεφαλή	10
to judge	κρίνω	17	authority	ἐξουσία	10
to know	γινώσκω	16			

Note: Compiled from Aland, Bachmann, and Slaby 1978:2–304 passim.

The arguments that Paul advances in trying to solve the various problems are rooted in Christ. Paul's argument about divisions in chapter 1 begins with an appeal in the name of our Lord Jesus Christ (1:10). He implies that they were baptized in the name of Christ (1:13–15). For Paul, Christ is the crucified One, the power of God, and the wisdom of God (2:23–24); He is the foundation of the church (3:11). In discussing fornication, Paul notes that Christ is our Passover lamb (5:7); therefore, we should cleanse out the old leaven of sin from our lives. He argues that for a Christian to commit fornication is to join Christ to a prostitute (6:15). He refers to the command of the Lord in the instructions about marriage (7:10–11). In discussing food offered to idols, Paul states that Christians have one Lord, Jesus Christ. When we eat the Lord's Supper, we share in the body and blood of Christ (10:16). Paul exhorts the Christians to imitate him, as he imitates Christ (11:1). In discussing head coverings, he argues that Christ is the head of every man (11:3). In the discussion on the Lord's Supper, he recounts the words of Jesus on the night that He was betrayed (11:23–25). In the discourse on spiritual gifts, he calls Christians the body of Christ (12:27). He grounds his discussion of the resurrection in the resurrection of Christ (15:3–23).

A unified macrostructure. With these two concepts in mind, the following tentative macrostructure is suggested. Whether this was in fact the motivating idea which was in Paul's mind when he produced 1 Corinthians is highly questionable, but it can be said to fairly represent a summary of the text which he produced. It reads as follows:

(28)   Obey Christ rather than following social customs, such as boasting about allegiances to certain leaders, committing fornication and suing one another, getting a divorce, eating meat offered to an idol, having women pray bareheaded, getting drunk, valuing ecstatic utterances, doubting the resurrection, and spending all your money on yourself.

Themes as metastructures. The question remains: is this in fact a mental concept which Paul had in mind before beginning 1 Corinthians or not? While it does represent a good generalization that fairly summarizes the whole book, it is open to some of the same criticisms that were previously made of Hoopert and Youngman's work in macrostructures. For one thing, this suggested macrostructure is so general that it could generate any number of given texts. For another, it introduces the terms *Christ* and *social customs* from the theme, but such terms do not appear in most of the sectional macrostructures. The term Christ does appear in the discourses as they are worked out by Paul, and various social customs are dealt with in 1 Corinthians, but these seem to be a part of a recurrent theme rather than a part of a macrostructure. Finally, this suggested macrostructure would make the macrostructures of the component discourses of less importance than the theme, although an over-all macrostructure ought to be discoverable out of the macrostructures of the constituent discourses.

A recurrent theme in a discourse is not necessarily a part of its macrostructure. This is not to say that it is not a controlling mental concept, but rather that it is not necessarily a part of the central idea. Such a theme does play a part in structuring the discourse. But it is woven into the fabric of the text, appearing, disappearing, and reappearing. As such, the mental structure that embodies the theme may be referred to as a METASTRUCTURE because it occurs throughout the text.

Actually the proposed metastructure for 1 Corinthians may be more than a simple theme or recurrent motif. The appeal to Christ in the various arguments which Paul presents throughout 1 Corinthians may very well be labeled a recurrent motif. But Christ's relation to culture is more likely to be a part of his underlying world view than merely a theme that he decided to emphasize. In this world view, Christ was Lord of the universe, and pagan religion, Greek or otherwise, was wicked. Thus in Paul's mind, each aspect of pagan religion that made its way into the Christian community must give way before the authority of Christ. The metastructure which manifests itself in 1 Corinthians is deeply rooted in its author's world view.

By postulating that a mental structure, which can be labelled a metastructure, exists in the conceptual realm, the suggestion is being made that some discourses are more complex than one simple macrostructure can encompass. A discourse may actually contain more than one macrostructure in addition to several themes or metastructures. It is the integration of the macrostructures, metastructures, and rhetorical organization principles that determines the final overall structure of a given discourse.

First Corinthians is one of these complex discourses that requires more than a simple statement of a single macrostructure to account for its final form. Ten macrostructures of component discourses have been isolated together with a metastructure that may be stated: obey Christ rather than following social customs. These conceptual structures are mapped onto a mixture of rhetorical patterns that include a cyclical (ABA'B'A''B'') treatment of response to oral information and response to the Corinthians letter. Several of the component discourses take the form of a simple chiastic structure (ABA'). The discourse is laid out with balance in mind as regards the number of discourses per cyclical unit, forming a pattern (2–2–2–1–1–2). Balance is seen in the location of the transitional paragraphs about Paul's travel plans, between the first two discourses and also between the last two. All of these elements are needed to explain the high level organization of the complex book of 1 Corinthians.

4
Constituent Analysis

Unlike the visual and plastic arts which work with two and three dimensions, a text is linear in its nature, especially if it is a spoken text. The concepts that a text producer endeavors to duplicate in the mind of the receptor, however, are multidimensional. In order to place a multidimensional text into a linear stream of speech or writing, the mind calls upon techniques such as embedded concepts and relationships, skewed ordering, and patterned presentation. This means that a student of a text, especially an ancient text such as 1 Corinthians where it is no longer possible to ask the author what he meant by something, must utilize various methods of understanding in an effort to reconstruct the underlying concepts that prompted the text.

Tagmemic theory asserts that any given text can be analyzed from three different perspectives. These are often called (after physics) particle, wave, and field. Pike (1982:12–13) declares that a person has the choice of using any or all of these three perspectives:

> On the one hand, he often acts as if he were cutting up sequences into chunks—into segments or *particles*. At such times he sees life as made up of one "thing" after another. On the other hand, he often senses things as somehow flowing together as ripples on the tide, merging into one another in the form of a hierarchy of little *waves* of experience on still bigger waves. These two perspectives, in turn, are supplemented by a third—the concept of *field* in which intersecting properties of

experience cluster into bundles of simultaneous characteristics which make up the patterns of his experience.

The triple perspective which tagmemic theory provides allows the modern interpreter to approach a text from more than one viewpoint. The particle perspective, especially as it is refined by constituent structure analysis, allows the reader to examine embedded concepts and relationships and determine what is a normal method of presentation and what may be altered for emphasis or other purposes. The wave perspective allows the reader to examine areas of the text where the conceptual realm may have different boundaries than the grammatical. The reader is thus freed from constructing topic boundaries based only on grammatical units. Finally, the field perspective allows the reader to perceive ways in which the concepts in the text may be patterned and presented in nonlinear fashion. Thus as one begins to look at the constituent elements of a text, it becomes apparent that a single perspective will not do for a proper analysis. The use of multiple perspectives allows the analyst to see relationships and structures that might well be overlooked in any analysis using only a single perspective.

This chapter analyzes smaller structures of 1 Corinthians using all three types of perspective that Pike has identified. First, the particle view is obtained by analyzing the hierarchical nature of the text using a search for structural paragraphs, an examination of orthographic paragraphs, and Longacre's approach to constituent paragraph structure and verb ranking (cf. Longacre 1989a:64–118). Next, some transitions are looked at using the wave perspective. Finally, grammatical, lexical, and conceptual patterns are studied using the field perspective. The chapter concludes with a discussion of the value of such a multiple perspective approach as it relates to interpretation of the biblical text.

4.1 Particle

The linear structure of a text. The most obvious way to divide a text is into a linear hierarchy of units, with each unit being embedded within larger units and being composed of one or more smaller units. The traditional method of outlining biblical books depends upon this technique of analyzing a text. Longacre (1983b:285) has posited that any text can be analyzed hierarchically by distinguishing eight levels of units: discourse, paragraph, sentence, clause, phrase, word, stem, and morpheme. Generally speaking, units on a lower level combine to form units on a higher level; however, levels can be skipped so that, for example, a sentence can be analyzed as being a combination of words. This is due to the fact that it is possible to have one unit constructions. There can be one paragraph discourses, one sentence paragraphs, one clause sentences (usually called simple sentences), one word phrases, and one morpheme words. It is even possible to collapse all the levels so as to have a one morpheme discourse, as when someone shouts "Fire!"

In addition, Longacre (1989a:279–80) has noted that it is possible for units to be formed recursively. A paragraph may be composed of two or more paragraphs. A word may be composed of two or more words; for example, *football* is made by combining the words *foot* and *ball*. Recursion can also work in combining elements that are not on the same level. A paragraph can be composed of a topic sentence plus an amplification paragraph. A prepositional phrase can be composed of recursively embedded prepositional phrases (e.g., the power of the Spirit of the God of heaven). This kind of recursion can also happen on the word level (e.g., right, righteous, and righteousness).

Longacre (1989a:280–81) has also noted a third kind of combination of units that he calls backlooping. This is where higher level units are embedded within lower level units. A typical example of such a construction is a relative clause modifying a noun phrase (e.g., the God who brought Israel out of Egypt). Another common type of backlooping occurs when a quoted paragraph is embedded in the object slot of a quotative sentence. But backlooping can even happen in some not so common ways. For example, a noun phrase can be embedded in a slot that usually expects a noun, such as *the King of England's crown* where the phrase *King of England* is marked with a possessive morpheme just like a noun would be. Both Pike (1967:107) and Longacre (1983b:280) have noted Martin Luther King, Jr.'s "see-how-far-you've-come-ism," where a whole clause is embedded in a slot that usually takes a noun stem.

The colon as linguistic sentence. What then defines the linguistic declarative sentence in Greek? Two endmarks of punctuation are used in declarative text by modern editors of Greek texts: the period and the colon. The period defines the end of the Greek sentence in current usage, and the raised dot (also called a colon) defines the end of the colon. The colon is in every respect a linguistic sentence: the nucleus is an independent clause and it is modified by various types of subordinate clauses. In his work on New Testament Greek semantics, Louw (1982:95) notes, "In this analysis the colon is defined, not in terms of its semantic unity, but in terms of certain specific grammatical structures which in many ways parallel what would be regarded as sentences in English." It may well be that what modern editors mark as a multi-colon Greek sentence corresponds to a simple type of paragraph. This same kind of confusion as to what a linguistic sentence is exists in English. Fries (1952:10–11) once asked a number of English teachers to decide how many sentences existed within a text that could be punctuated with both periods and semi-colons. They could not agree on the actual number of sentences in the text. Despite the ambiguity as to what constitutes a sentence, in both Greek and English, it seems best to choose the colon as the linguistic sentence, since it is the minimal possible sentence.

This colon marked in current editions of the Koiné Greek New Testament should not be confused with what the ancient Greek grammarians referred to as a κῶλον 'colon', for this unit corresponds more to the modern clause (Demetrius, *On Style* 1 [1–8]). The colon as marked by modern editors was called a περίοδος 'period' by ancient grammarians such as Demetrius (*On Style* 1 [10–11]).

Louw (1982:100) has also chosen to make the colon the unit of choice for discourse analysis in the Greek New Testament. Besides the basic fact that the Greek colon as currently marked seems to correspond to the linguistic sentence, Louw gives an additional reason for using the terminology colon to describe the linguistic unit analyzed: "In certain linguistic analyses the term *sentence* (with the abbreviation S) has been employed in speaking of any syntactic string which may be less or even more than a colon."

This study differs from Louw's use of the term in only one respect: Louw (1982:102) rejects the possibility of having a compound colon. He writes, "All of this means that so-called simple sentences and complex sentences (those with dependent clauses) are regarded as colons, while so-called coordinate sentences (those in which potentially independent clauses are combined by coordinate conjunctions) are regarded as consisting of two or more colons." There are four reasons for not following Louw in his rejection of compound colons. First, the standard Greek punctuation of colons in current editions of the New Testament sometimes includes coordinated independent clauses within a single colon. To redefine the colon as Louw does would have each researcher working with different units. Second, Louw (1982:101, 97) wants "the man went to Boston and the boy played in his room" to be two colons, while he understands "the horse and the bull are grazing" to be a single colon with a compound subject (although it is typically analyzed as two kernel sentences in the deep structure) and "my good friend came and gave me a book" to be a single colon with a compound predicate. Against this is the fact that a Greek verb can be a colon on its own, since subject agreement is marked on the verb and can function as an indicator of the subject of the clause. Thus a compound predicate can usually also be analyzed as compound clauses in Greek. Third, the fact that one can have compound subjects in a subject slot and compound predicates in a predicate slot would argue that by analogy one could also have compound clauses in a clause slot of a colon. Finally, evidence indicates that *καί* 'and' often occurs between clauses in a compound colon but rarely between colons. Of 105 instances of *καί* where the word occurs as the only conjunction in uncontracted form in 1 Corinthians, 95 occur within the colon and only 10 occur at the beginning of a colon. This is similar to the findings of Levinsohn (1987:96–120) in the book of Acts, where he discovered that *καί* was used mainly to join elements within what he called DEVELOPMENT UNITS.

With this brief introduction to the concept of four kinds of embedding (normal, skipped, recursive, and backlooped) and the selection of the Greek colon as the linguistic sentence, it is possible to analyze the text of 1 Corinthians as a combination of units or particles. This study focuses on the relationships of the higher level units, especially paragraphs.

Structural paragraphs. All sentences in a paragraph share some kind of relationship with one another. Using Pike's four-celled tagmeme as a descriptor, that relationship can always be described in terms of role. More will be said about the role relationship further in this chapter. For the present, the question must be posed: Are there relationships between sentences which bind them together in paragraphs and can these relationships be described in a purely structural way (i.e., in tagmemic terms, merely using slot and class)? The answer is yes. There are several kinds of paragraphs in 1 Corinthians that are marked by grammatical features in the surface structure.

First, there is a question-answer paragraph that, in its simplest form, consists of two colons: the first a question and the second an answer. Examples of this in 1 Corinthians include 11:22, as shown in (29), and 14:15.

(29) Q *ἐπαινέσω   ὑμᾶς;*   (11:22)
         shall^I^praise you?
      A *ἐν τούτῳ   οὐκ   ἐπαινῶ.*
         in   this   not   I^praise

Second, there is a question-command paragraph that consists of a question followed by a command. This form often functions as a type of conditional command. If the question can be answered affirmatively, the command should be obeyed. Examples of this include 7:18 (bis), 21, and 27 (bis), as shown in (30).

(30)   A   Q   δέδεσαι   γυναικί;   (7:27)
              have^you^been^bound to^a^wife?
           C   μὴ ζήτει λύσιν·
              not seek a^loosing.
       A' Q   λέλυσαι   ἀπὸ γυναικός;
              have^you^been^loosed from a^wife?
           C   μὴ ζήτει γυναῖκα.
              not seek a^wife.

For a field perspective of the various patterns in this structure, see (39).

The example in 7:21 is of a double command, the second one introduced by ἀλλ' εἰ 'but if', with the conditional clause introducing an additional condition, as shown in (31).

(31)   Q   δοῦλος ἐκλήθης;   (7:21)
              [were you] a^slave being^called?
       C   μή σοι   μελέτω·
           not to^you let^it^matter
       C   ἀλλ' εἰ καὶ   δύνασαι ἐλεύθερος γενέσθαι,
           but   if indeed you^can free   become,
           μᾶλλον χρῆσαι.
           rather use^[it]

Third, there are paragraphs that show a grammatical chiastic structure. Examples of these include 9:19–22, 10:7–10, and 13:8–13, as shown in (50), (51), and (61). Such paragraphs can be viewed either as structures from a particle perspective or as patterns from a field perspective. Since nonlinear paragraphs are handled better from the field perspective, these will be discussed below in more detail in the section on chiasmus under the heading of Field.

Finally, there are paragraphs which are composed of parallel units, either smaller embedded paragraphs or linguistic sentences (colons). These can be categorized by whether they are composed of two (binary) or more than two (multiple) units. They can also be categorized by whether they are composed of statements, questions, or commands. Where these parallel structures are composed of two or three colons, they are sometimes referred to as couplets or triplets, respectively.

There are three examples in 1 Corinthians of paragraphs composed of parallel microparagraphs, that is, low level paragraphs whose only constituent units are linguistic sentences (colons). All examples are binary, limited to two parallel units. 1 Cor. 15:39–41 is an example of two parallel microparagraphs involving statements. Today's English Version (TEV) starts a new orthographic paragraph in the middle of this structure, but such would not seem to fit the Greek text. 1 Cor. 7:18 and 7:27 are examples of two parallel microparagraphs involving questions, as shown in (30). Most of the examples of parallelism involve colons rather than microparagraphs. By far the greatest number of parallel structures involve binary colon statements. There are varying degrees of parallelism in 1 Corinthians, but the following are clear examples of this type of microparagraph: 3:5, 14–15; 6:12; 7:22; 9:17; 10:21, 23; 11:4–5, 8–9; 12:15–16, 26; 14:4, 15; and 16:23–24. 1 Cor. 12:26 is shown in (32) as an example.

(32)　A　καὶ εἴτε πάσχει ἓν　μέλος,　　　　　　　　(12:26)
　　　　　and if　suffers one　member,
　　　　　συμπάσχει　　πάντα τὰ μέλη·
　　　　　suffer^together all　　the members;
　　　A'　εἴτε δοξάζεται　[ἓν]　μέλος,
　　　　　if　is^glorified one　member,
　　　　　συγχαίρει　　πάντα τὰ μέλη.
　　　　　rejoice^together all　　the members.

There are also several examples of parallel structures that involve binary colon questions. Among the clearest examples are 7:16; 9:1, 5–6; 10:16; 11:22 (bis); and 15:55, with the latter shown in (33) as an example.

(33)　A　ποῦ　　　σου,　θάνατε, τὸ νῖκος;　　　　　　(15:55)
　　　　　where^[is] your, [O] death,　the victory?
　　　A'　ποῦ　　　σου,　θάνατε, τὸ κέντρον;
　　　　　where^[is] your, [O] death,　the sting?

First Corinthians also contains some examples of parallel binary colon commands. Among these are 7:12–13; 10:25, 27; and 14:28, 30. 1 Cor. 7:12–13 is shown in (34).

(34)　A　εἴ τις ἀδελφὸς γυναῖκα ἔχει ἄπιστον,　καὶ αὕτη　(7:12)
　　　　　if any brother a^wife　has unbelieving and she
　　　　　συνευδοκεῖ οἰκεῖν μετ' αὐτοῦ, μὴ ἀφιέτω　　αὐτήν·
　　　　　consents　to^live with him,　not let^him^divorce her.
　　　A'　καὶ γυνὴ　εἴ τις ἔχει ἄνδρα　　ἄπιστον,　(7:13)
　　　　　and woman if any has a^husband unbelieving
　　　　　καὶ οὗτος συνευδοκεῖ οἰκεῖν μετ' αὐτῆς,
　　　　　and he　consents　to^live with her,
　　　　　μὴ ἀφιέτω　　τὸν ἄνδρα.
　　　　　not let^her^divorce the husband.

Turning from binary to multiple colon parallelism, there are several examples of triple colon statements in 1 Corinthians. Among the clearest are 4:8, 10; 7:32–34; 12:4–6; 13:1–3; and 15:42–44. 1 Cor. 12:4–6 is given in (35) as an example.

(35)   A   *Διαιρέσεις   δὲ   χαρισμάτων   εἰσίν,*   (12:4)
       varieties   now   of^gifts   there^are
       τὸ   δὲ   αὐτὸ   πνεῦμα·
       the   but   same   Spirit;
    A'   *καὶ   διαιρέσεις   διακονιῶν   εἰσιν,*   (12:5)
       and   varieties   of^service   there^are,
       καὶ   ὁ   αὐτὸς   κύριος·
       yet   the   same   Lord;
    A'' *καὶ   διαιρέσεις   ἐνεργημάτων   εἰσίν,*   (12:6)
       and   varieties   of^working   there^are,
       ὁ   δὲ   αὐτὸς   θεός, ὁ   ἐνεργῶν τὰ   πάντα   ἐν
       the but   same   God who   works   them   all   in
       πᾶσιν.
       everyone.

There are also five examples of parallelism in multiple colon questions: 1:20; 9:7; 12:17, 19; 12:29; and 12:30. The second one is given as an example in (36).

(36)   A   *τίς   στρατεύεται   ἰδίοις   ὀψωνίοις   ποτέ;*   (9:7)
       who   soldiers   [at his]   own   expense   ever?
    A'   *τίς   φυτεύει   ἀμπελῶνα   καὶ   τὸν   καρπὸν   αὐτοῦ   οὐκ   ἐσθίει;*
       who   plants   a^vineyard and   the   fruit   of^it   not   eats?
    A'' *ἢ   τίς   ποιμαίνει   ποίμνην   καὶ   ἐκ   τοῦ   γάλακτος*
       or   who   tends   a^flock   and   from the   milk
       τῆς   ποίμνης   οὐκ   ἐσθίει;
       of^the   flock   not   eats?

All of these examples are triplets, except for 12:29, which contains four grammatically parallel questions.

Thus the book of 1 Corinthians contains four basic types of grammatically structured paragraphs: question-answer, question-command, chiastic, and parallel. These units form the smallest types of paragraphs in 1 Corinthians. Ideally, any analysis of paragraph structure in this book would not start a new paragraph in the middle of one of these units. Unfortunately, in English translations, this has not always been the case.

Orthographic paragraphs. Using analytical techniques, discourse analysis does not always turn up the same paragraph junctures that are marked by translators and editors in a text. Even translators and editors differ among themselves as to exactly where a new paragraph should begin. Some do not begin paragraphs very often, while others begin paragraphs rather frequently. A comparison of paragraph beginnings between the New American Standard Version and the Today's English Version, as shown in table 6, will bear this out. The translators of the New American Standard Version begin new paragraphs less frequently than the editors of the Greek texts, while the Today's English Version begins new paragraphs with such a frequency that they cut across structural Greek paragraphs and even colon boundaries. This technique may be legitimate paragraphing for a simple English translation (for English paragraphing rules may well vary from Greek rules), but it is of little use to the discourse analyst who is trying to draw on the understanding of others to help determine paragraph boundaries in the Greek text.

Orthographic paragraphing is of limited use in discourse analysis because it generally ignores the recursive nature of paragraphs. Most translations have only one level of paragraph indication. An exception is the twenty-sixth edition of the Nestle-Aland *Novum Testamentum Graece,* which indicates three levels of paragraphing by orthographic technique: major section breaks are indicated by spacing before a paragraph, major paragraph breaks are indicated by indention from the left margin, and minor paragraph breaks are indicated by additional spacing within a line. Where translations indicate only one level of paragraphing, there is little indication as to whether indention is taking place to signify major paragraphs, intermediate paragraphs, or minor paragraphs.

Table 6
Orthographic paragraphs for 1 Corinthians

	Vocative	1p	2p	NA26	UBS	NASV	RSV	NIV	NEB	TEV	JerB	TT
1:1		F		XX	XX	XX	XX	XX	XX	XX	XX	XX
1:2							X	X		X		
1:3							X	X	X	X		
1:4		F		X	X	X	X	X	X	X	X	X
1:10	brothers	F	B	XX	XX	X	X	X	X	X	X	X
1:13		P						X				
1:14		F	B							X		
1:17		B									X	
1:18		B		X	XX	X	X	X	X	X		X
1:20		P						X				
1:21										X		
1:25		P							X			
1:26	brothers		F	X	X	X	X	X		X	X	X
2:1	brothers	F	P	X	XX	X	X	X	X	X	X	X
2:6		B		X	XX	X	X	X	X	X	X	X
2:10											X	
2:10b								X	X			
2:13		B								X*		
2:14		P					X					
3:1	brothers	B		X	XX	X	X	X	X	X	X	X
3:5		P	P				X	X	X	X	X	
3:10		F	P	x	X	X	X	X	X	X	X	X
3:16			F	x			X	X	X	X	X	X
3:18			P	X	X	X	X	X	X	X	X	X
4:1				X	XX	X	X	X	X	X	X	X
4:6	brothers	F	F	X	X	X	X	X	X	X	X	X
4:8			B				X	X	X	X		
4:14		B		X	X	X	X	X	X	X	X	X
4:16		B	B	x								
4:18		B		x				X		X	X	
5:1		P		XX	XX	X	X	X	X	X	X	X
5:3		B	B				X					
5:6		P	P	x			X	X	X	X	X	X
5:9		B	F	x	X	X	X	X	X	X	X	X
5:12		P	P					X		X		
5:13			F								X	
6:1			B	X	XX	X	X	X	X	X	X	X
6:7				x			X	X		X		
6:9			B	x			X	X		X		
6:12			B	X	XX	X	X	X	X	X	X	X
6:15			F							X	X	
6:18			F					X		X	X	
7:1			B	XX	XX	X	X	X	X	X	X	X
7:1b			P							X*		
7:6		F	P						X	X		
7:8		B		X	X	X	X	X	X	X	X	X
7:10		F		x			X	X	X	X	X	
7:12		B					X	X	X	X	X	X
7:15								X				
7:17			P	X	XX	X	X	X	X	X	X	X
7:25		F		X	XX	X	X	X	X	X	X	X
7:26		B								X		
7:29	brothers	B		x				X	X	X	X	X
7:32		F	F	x			X	X	X	X	X	X
7:35		F							X	X		
7:36		P		x	X	X	X	X	X	X	X	X

	Vocative	1p	2p	NA26	UBS	NASV	RSV	NIV	NEB	TEV	JerB	TT
7:39				x	X	X	X	X	X	X	X	X
8:1		B		XX	XX	X	X	X	X	X	X	X
8:1b		B								X*		X*
8:4		F		x								
8:7				X	X	X	X	X	X	X	X	X
8:9		P	F					X		X		
9:1		B		X	XX	X	X	X	X	X	X	X
9:3			P	x	X	X	X	X	X	X		
9:7		P						X				
9:8		F					X			X	X	
9:12b		B		x	X		X	X	X	X		
9:13		P	F	x								
9:15		F					X	X		X	X	X
9:19		B		X	X	X	X	X		X	X	X
9:23		B								X†		
9:24		P	F	X	X	X	X	X	X		X	X
10:1	brothers	B	F	X	XX	X	X	X	X	X	X	X
10:6				x			X	X	X	X	X	X
10:11			P					X	X	X	X	
10:12										X		X
10:14	my beloved		B	X	X	X	X	X	X	X	X	X
10:18		P	F					X	X	X		
10:19		F		x								
10:23		P		X	XX	X	X	X	X	X	X	X
10:25			F					X	X	X		
10:27			B					X†		X†		
10:29b		P	P						X	X		X
10:31		P	F	x			X	X		X		X
11:1		B	B			X†	X†	X†			X†	
11:2		B	B	XX	XX	X	X	X†	X	X	X	X
11:3		B	B					X				
11:7				x							X	
11:11								X				
11:13			F	x					X	X	X	
11:16		F							X		X	
11:17		B		X	XX	X	X	X	X	X	X	X
11:23		B		X	XX		X	X	X	X	X	X
11:26			B							X		
11:27			P	X	XX		X	X	X			X
11:28											X	
11:33	my brothers	P	F	x			X	X	X	X	X	X
11:34		F	P					X				
12:1	brothers	B	F	XX	XX	X	X	X	X	X	X	X
12:1b		B	F							X*		
12:4		P		X	X	X	X	X	X	X	X	X
12:7								X				
12:12				X	XX	X	X	X	X	X	X	X
12:14		P		x			X	X	X	X	X	
12:18											X†	
12:21		F						X		X		
12:22		B									X	
12:27			F	x			X	X	X	X	X	X
12:31			F								X	
12:31b		F	P	X	XX	X	X	X	X	X		X
13:1		B		X	X	X	X	X	X	X	X	
13:4		P		X	X		X	X	X	X	X	X
13:8				X	X		X	X	X	X	X	X
13:10		F								X		
13:13		P		x				X		X	X	
14:1			F	X	XX	X	X	X	X	X	X	X
14:5b		P	P							X		

	Vocative	1p	2p	NA26	UBS	NASV	RSV	NIV	NEB	TEV	JerB	TT
14:6	brothers	F		X	X		X	X			X	X
14:7		P						X		X		
14:13			P	X			X	X	X	X	X	
14:18		F	P	x					X	X		
14:20	brothers	P	F	X	X	X	X	X	X	X	X	X
14:22		P						X				
14:23			F							X		
14:26	brothers			X	XX	X	X	X	X	X	X	X
14:29								X†				
14:33b				X	X		X	X	X	X	X	X
14:34						X†						
14:36									X	X	X	
14:37		F		X	X	X	X	X				X
14:39	my brothers		F	x			X	X	X	X	X	
15:1	brothers	F	F	XX	XX	X	X	X	X	X	X	X
15:3		B	P				X	X	X	X	X	
15:8									X†	X†		
15:9		F		x				X		X		
15:12		P	P	X	XX	X	X	X	X	X	X	X
15:20		P		X	X	X	X	X	X	X	X	X
15:23				x								
15:29				X	X	X	X	X	X	X	X	X
15:30		F						X				
15:33		P	F					X		X		X
15:35		P		X	XX	X	X	X	X	X	X	X
15:39				x						X	X	
15:40										X		
15:42				x	X		X	X		X		X
15:44				x				X	X	X		
15:50	brothers	B		X	X	X		X	X	X	X	X
15:51	behold	B					X†			X†		
15:54											X	
15:58	my beloved brothers		F	x		X	X	X	X	X	X	X
16:1		F	B	XX	XX	X	X	X	X	X	X	X
16:5		B		X	XX		X	X	X	X	X	X
16:8		B								X		
16:10			F	X	X	X	X	X	X	X	X	X
16:12		B	P	x	X		X	X		X		X
16:13				X	XX	X	X	X	X	X	X	
16:15	brothers	F		X	X	X	X	X	X	X	X	X
16:17		F	P							X†		
16:19			P	X	X	X	X	X	X	X	X	X
16:20b										X†		
16:21			P	X	X	X	X	X	X	X	X	X
16:22								X	X	X	X	
16:22b	Marana		F						X			
16:23			P					X	X	X	X	
16:24								X	X	X	X	

Key: 1p first person; 2p second person

JerB Jerusalem Bible; NA26 Nestle-Aland Greek text 26th ed.; NASV New American Standard Version; NEB New English Bible; NIV New International Version; RSV Revised Standard Version; TEV Today's English Version (Good News Bible); TT Translators' Translation; UBS United Bible Societies' Greek New Testament

P preceding; F following; B both

X major paragraph; x minor paragraph; XX section

* in middle of colon; † in middle of structured paragraph

Because different translations and editions indicate different levels of paragraphing, however, they can be compared to form a general idea of the relative level of the paragraph breaks in a text. In table 6, two editions of the Greek text of 1 Corinthians and seven English translations are compared as to paragraph breaks. Those breaks in which seven to nine versions agree can be considered major paragraph breaks. In the same way, breaks on which there is agreement between four to six versions can be considered intermediate and breaks with agreement on only one to three can be considered minor paragraph breaks. The assignment of the classifications major, intermediate, and minor to groups of three is an arbitrary one based on a linear progression; it is reasonable, however, that a change in topic which more editors and translators notice is likely to be more significant than one which fewer editors and translators notice.

Table 6 also lists three other grammatical indications of paragraphing: the presence of vocatives and the word ἰδού 'behold', the use of first person verbs in the colons preceding and following the break, and the use of second person verbs in the colons preceding and following the break. By way of clarification, the term COLON FOLLOWING THE BREAK is used to refer to the first colon in the new paragraph and the term COLON PRECEDING THE BREAK is used to refer to the last colon in the previous paragraph.

Vocatives are commonly used to signify the beginning of a paragraph in Greek (cf. Miehle 1981:98 and Longacre 1983a:3, 13, 22, 25, 30 for 1 John as well as Hymes 1986:80 and Terry 1992:113, 118 for James; see also Levinsohn 1992:198). Eighteen of the twenty-five vocatives in 1 Corinthians occur in the colons that begin paragraphs. In addition, three vocatives (two in 7:16 and one in 7:24) occur in the final colon of a paragraph. The first discourse not only contains a vocative (ἀδελφοί 'brothers') in its first colon in 1:10, but also a vocative (ἀδελφοί μου 'my brothers') in its second colon in 1:11. The remaining three vocatives (one in 15:31 and two in 15:55) are found in the eighth discourse in what is probably peak material (see chapter 5 of this study for further discussion of peak). The vocative in 15:31 is omitted by many manuscripts, probably because it is not used in this place in the normal Greek way of beginning a paragraph. It is also possible to treat μαράνα (Aramaic for 'Lord') in 16:22 as a vocative, although it is not likely that the transliterated Aramaic μαράνα θά 'O Lord, come' is a paragraph by itself, as the New English Bible prints it.

The Greek word ἰδού 'behold' is a particle used as an exclamation, not a vocative; however, it often functions in the same way as a vocative in marking the beginning of paragraphs in Greek. For this reason, the Revised Standard Version and the Today's English Version mark 15:51 as the beginning of a new paragraph; there are structural parallels between

15:50 and 15:51, however, that indicate that they belong together. Any paragraph that 15:51 begins must be a minor paragraph indeed.

In epistolary text, it is common for the writer to refer to himself and to the readers. This is especially true around paragraph boundaries where the writer is more likely to relate the discussion of general principles to the parties involved. Table 6 indicates whether first and second person verbs are found in the colon following or preceding the paragraph boundary or both. Their presence or absence is summarized in table 7.

Table 7

First and second person in orthographic paragraph
boundaries in 1 Corinthians

Paragraph Level	1st person		2nd person		Either 1st or 2nd	
	Present	Absent	Present	Absent	Present	Absent
Major 66 total	62.1% (n=41)	37.9% (n=25)	48.5% (n=32)	51.5% (n=34)	84.8% (n=56)	15.2% (n=10)
Intermediate 29 total	55.2% (n=16)	44.8% (n=13)	41.4% (n=12)	58.6% (n=17)	79.3% (n=23)	20.7% (n=6)
Minor 56 total	58.9% (n=33)	41.1% (n=23)	39.3% (n=22)	60.7% (n=34)	73.2% (n=41)	26.8% (n=15)
Substructural 10 total	40.0% (n=4)	60.0% (n=6)	30.0% (n=3)	70.0% (n=7)	50.0% (n=5)	50.0% (n=5)

Table 7 shows that there is a direct relationship between any interpersonal endings and paragraph level. Among major paragraph breaks, 56 (84.8%) have either first- or second-person verbs in the surrounding colons. Intermediate paragraph breaks show 23 (79.3%) with interpersonal verbs in the colons on either side of the break. Minor paragraph breaks show 41 (73.2%) with interpersonal verbs in the surrounding colons. Substructural paragraph breaks show only 5 (50%) with interpersonal verbs. Thus the higher the paragraphing level, the more likely interpersonal verb endings (either first or second person) occur in the surrounding colons. In addition, on a discourse level all 10 (100%) of the discourses in the letter show either first- or second-person verbs in the colons surrounding the beginning of the discourses.

This tendency for paragraph breaks is especially true for discourse breaks. Table 8 shows the boundary markers for the beginnings of the ten proposed discourses in 1 Corinthians and the introduction and conclusion.

All ten discourses show either the first or second person in the first colon in the discourse, half of them showing both. Only the boundary at 7:1 shows that the first colon does not contain a first-person verb. In addition, all the boundaries except for 15:1 show either first or second person in the preceding colon. All of the discourses begin with the Greek conjunction δέ 'now'. It is worth noting that, if the beginning of the second discourse is chosen to be 5:1 instead of 4:18, then all but one of these generalizations are not valid. This tends to confirm that the second discourse begins at 4:18 rather than 5:1 as concluded in chapter 3.

Table 8
Markers for discourse boundaries in 1 Corinthians

Boundary		Introductory words		Vocative	1st person	2nd person
1:1	Int				following	
1:10	1	δέ	now	brothers	following	both
4:18	2	δέ	now		both	
7:1	3	περὶ δέ	now about			both
8:1	4	περὶ δέ	now about		both	
11:2	5	δέ	now		both	both
11:17	6	δέ	now		both	
12:1	7	περὶ δέ	now about	brothers	both	following
15:1	8	δέ	now	brothers	following	following
16:1	9	περὶ δέ	now about		following	both
16:12	10	περὶ δέ	now about		both	preceding
16:13	Con					

Table 9 shows a summary of beginning words for paragraph breaks on the major and intermediate levels. It is worth noting that δέ is the overwhelming conjunction of choice for beginning major paragraphs. This is similar to the result that Levinsohn found in analyzing conjunctions in the book of Acts, where he found that δέ was used to connect major segments that he labeled development units (1987:83–96). The word γάρ 'for' signaling an explanation to follow is second with six usages. It is also significant that 27 (41%) major paragraphs begin without any conjunction, while only 2 (7%) intermediate paragraphs show no conjunction at the beginning.

Table 9
Introductory words for orthographic paragraphs in 1 Corinthians

Introductory word		Major paragraphs	Intermediate paragraphs
none		27	2
ἀλλά/ἀλλ'	but	2	1
γάρ	for	6	2
δέ/περὶ δέ	now	22	9
διό	therefore	—	1
διόπερ	therefore	1	—
ἐάν	if	2	1
εἰ	if	3	3
εἴτε	if	—	1
ἤ	or	—	1
ἤδη	already	1	1
καθάπερ	just as	1	—
καί/κἀγώ	and (I)	3	2
νῦν/νυνί	now	1	2
οὖν	therefore	—	3
οὕτως	thus	1	1
τί	what/why	1	1
ὡς	as	2	1
ὥστε	therefore	2	2

Note: Paragraphs that begin with more than one conjunction are counted more
than once in the above table.

Not too much should be made of the fact that two words are used to
begin major paragraphs but not intermediate paragraphs. This may only
mean that they are not used often enough in this text to occur in this role.
The four words that begin intermediate paragraphs but not major paragraphs are more significant. It is also possible that this lack is due to
infrequent usage. The concepts of consequence (διό and οὖν 'therefore')
and alternative (ἤ 'or'), however, which three of the words embody,
suggest that subordinate ideas follow and are thus perhaps to be expected
on an intermediate level. At any rate, it is noteworthy that οὖν begins
three intermediate paragraphs but no major paragraphs.

Advantages of constituent structure analysis. The study of orthographic paragraphs, while useful, can only take the discourse analyst so far
into the discourse. Generally such paragraphs are the result of intuitive
guesses by editors and translators rather than being based on any kind of
structural analysis. To examine the paragraph structure in depth, one must
turn to a study of the relationships between recursively embedded paragraphs. Louw (1982:98) has noted, "In general any total discourse that is
longer than one paragraph must obviously be analyzed primarily in terms
of the relationships between the constituent paragraphs."

There are many ways to analyze these relationships in a text from a
particle perspective. But constituent structure analysis has certain advantages over other methods of analysis. First, it focuses the analysis on
role, the basic relationship between higher level units. The analyst is forced
to identify the role that each unit plays in the discourse and the primary
unit to which it is related. Second, it shows clearly the level of embedding
of each unit in the discourse. An outline also shows level of embedding,
but the embedding is based on topics and subtopics rather than on the
relationships between units. Constituent structure analysis, on the other
hand, focuses on the grammatical hierarchy as well as the conceptual.
Third, it takes into account the texttype and structural characteristics of
the units (such as parallelism, question forms, and cyclical and chiastic
presentations) under investigation. Fourth, it charts enough variables so as
to allow the analyst to categorize types of paragraphs by kind of branching,
level of embedding, and texttype. Finally, it allows the analyst to relate the
results to a salience level chart and formulate a theory of verb ranking for
a given text. When enough texts have been analyzed, this permits the
analyst to formulate theories of salience levels and verb ranking for
different texttypes and even genres.

Constituent paragraph structure. Relationships between paragraphs
are not always overtly marked. Rather they are often inherent only in the
meaning of the paragraphs. For this reason Young, Becker, and Pike
(1970:319) speak of a generalized plot as "a sequence of semantic slots."
On a lower level, paragraphs also may be said to exhibit plots. These plots
are often marked on the surface structure of a text by what may be called
PLOT CUES. Plot cues are words and phrases which "indicate the relationship of one linguistic unit to another within a specific, or surface, plot" (p.
322). Since the term plot is usually reserved for narrative texttype, it is
perhaps better to refer to these overt markers as RELATIONAL CUES. If
paragraph B is an instance of paragraph A, it may well begin with a
relational cue such as *for example* or *for instance*. If paragraph B contains

a cause for paragraph A or a reason for it, the relational cues *because, since, therefore,* or *consequently* may be found in the text.

But even where such overt markers do not exist, the semantic relationships between paragraphs which they signify do exist. In commenting on a Beekman-Callow relational structure tree diagram of 1 John, Miehle (1981:105) has noted, "Even on the lower levels of structure, I have been prompted more by the semantic rather than the grammatical structure." This is where Pike's four-celled tagmeme defined in the first chapter of this study becomes a useful tool. The third cell is that of role, an acknowledgement that grammar is more than syntax; it contains an element of semantics even within its structure.

For example, in Greek the category VOICE is used to distinguish active, middle, and passive. These categories do not just refer to structural forms, but to semantic relationships within the sentences in which they are used. Even when the structures of the middle and passive voice are the same, the relationships signified by the middle and the passive are quite different. Further, these relationships are grammatical, not merely conceptual. There is a significant semantic difference, but not an ultimate conceptual difference, between *the key turned in the lock* and *the key was turned in the lock*. In both, the speaker and listener may conceptualize a person turning the key, even though neither sentence specifies such. The semantic difference is entirely due to the grammar, not to the conceptual picture drawn by word choice. Pike (1982:111–13) includes role in the grammatical tagmeme, allowing this semantic element to be presented as an integral part of grammar, thereby emphasizing his idea that units should be treated as form-meaning composites.

Longacre has taken this concept a step further by analyzing two-celled paragraph tagmemes with what can be taken as role:class instead of the traditional slot:class. This is consistent with the two-celled tagmeme since originally both were combined (e.g., slot could be filled by subject-as-actor, where actor is a role; Pike 1982:77). Role seems to be more significant in determining relationship than slot does. Longacre (1970; 1980) has given a fairly detailed treatment of this method of analysis. It is well illustrated for a biblical text in his analysis of 1 John (1983a) and in the fourth chapter of his book *Joseph* (1989a:83–118), an analysis of the Hebrew text of Genesis 37 and 39–48.

Several of the different types of paragraphs which have been identified to date based on role are listed in table 10. The terminology in the table is generally from Longacre (1989a:83–118), who labels the head or nucleus of the paragraph the THESIS, although at one time he used the term TEXT for some units. Also following Longacre (1989b:450–58), his earlier terminology for constituent elements of the sequence paragraph has been changed here from BUILD-UP to SEQUENTIAL THESIS. The term build-up applies best to narrative material before the climax, but even in this material an item in the sequence may not build up the storyline. In the same way, the coordinate paragraph is sometimes analyzed as two items rather than two theses (Longacre 1989a:116). Amplification and clarification paragraphs are similar, but the former merely gives additional information, while the latter does so in order to make the thesis clear. Clendenen (1989:131) has labeled the evidence paragraph the attestation paragraph. But the terminology followed here is current and understandable.

Most of the entries in table 10 are listed as right branching paragraphs, that is, paragraphs in which the thesis comes first. The exceptions are the condition paragraph and the quote paragraph, both of which are left branching, that is, paragraphs in which the thesis comes last. These are the normal (unmarked) ordering for these paragraphs, but it is possible for paragraph types which are normally right branching to be left branching and vice versa. There are three other possibilities listed in table 10. Although it may have an introduction as a left branch, the simple paragraph is often without such a branch, having only a head or nucleus. Next, the coordinate paragraph, the dialogue paragraph, and the simultaneous paragraph are usually double headed, although they may be multiple headed. Finally, the sequence paragraph is usually multiple headed.

In addition, paragraphs can be categorized according to structural features such as the ones illustrated in (29) through (36). Following Longacre's terminology, the question-answer paragraph can be called rhetorical question-answer or simply RHETORICAL, the question-command paragraph called RHETORICAL COMMAND, the chiastic paragraph called CHIASTIC, and the parallel paragraph called PARALLEL (1979b:131). When paragraphs have rhetorical and rhetorical command structure, they often become left branching. Longacre also has identified running quote and cyclic paragraphs as further examples of what he calls stylistic types (p. 131). A paragraph can thus be identified by a combination of its stylistic structural type, its branching direction, its texttype, and its basic role relationship as listed in table 10.

Table 10

Types of paragraphs based on role

Paragraph type	Constituents
Alternative	(Intro.) + Thesis + Alternative
Amplification	(Intro.) + Thesis + Amplification
Antithetical	(Intro.) + Thesis + Antithesis
Clarification	(Intro.) + Thesis + Clarification
Comment	(Intro.) + Thesis + Comment
Condition	(Intro.) + Condition + Thesis
Coordinate	(Intro.) + Thesis$_1$ + Thesis$_2$
Dialogue	Initiation + (Continuation) + Response
Evidence	(Intro.) + Thesis + Evidence
Generalization	(Intro.) + Thesis + Generalization
Illustration	(Intro.) + Thesis + Illustration
Motivation	(Intro.) + Thesis + Motivation
Paraphrase	(Intro.) + Thesis + Paraphrase
Quote	(Intro.) + Quote formula + Quote
Reason	(Intro.) + Thesis + Reason
Result	(Intro.) + Thesis + Result
Sequence	(Setting) + SeqT$_1$ + SeqT$_2$ + SeqT$_n$
Simple	(Intro.) + Thesis
Simultaneous	(Intro.) + Thesis + Simul. Thesis

Note: This table was derived in part from Longacre (1989a:83–118) and Clendenen (1989:131). Optional constituents are listed in parentheses. SeqT is an abbreviation for Sequential Thesis.

Illustrations of this method of analysis are given in tables 11 (for 1 Cor. 1:10–17), 12 (for 1 Cor. 2:6–16), 13 (for 1 Cor. 3:10–15), 14 (for 1 Cor. 6:12–20), and 15 (for 1 Cor. 10:23–11:1). All of these are major paragraphs according to the study of orthographic paragraphs done above.

This method of analysis provides a much clearer picture about the relationships, the level of embedding, and even the boundaries between paragraphs than a study of orthographic paragraphs does. For example, table 6 shows minor paragraphs beginning at 2:10 and 2:14; table 12, however, shows that 2:10 is actually a place where a series of right branching paragraphs ends and the relationship returns to a higher level paragraph. In the same way, 2:14 is the second half of an antithetical paragraph, and the contrast has proven a good place to mark an ortho-graphical paragraph. The analysis also shows that 2:10b is not an ideal place to mark an orthographic paragraph (as the NIV and NEB have done) because to do so obscures the relationships.

The sample sections analyzed in tables 11–15 have been chosen to give a cross-section of material from different texttypes. Table 11 shows a combination of texttypes, table 12 shows a text of primarily persuasive texttype, table 13 has a text of mostly expository texttype, and tables 14 and 15 are mainly hortatory texttype.[3] The assignment of texttype here is arbitrary, based upon an intuitive assessment of purpose. A charting of texttype is shown in appendix A. The sections analyzed have been chosen from material which is nonpeak in nature, so that any shift in grammatical markers due to peak will not be a factor. Peak is discussed further in chapter 5.

The displays in tables 11–15 are given in a literal English translation by this writer for convenience in reading, but the analysis is based upon the Greek text, as shown in appendix B. In one case (2:7–8 in table 12) the punctuation of the corrected third edition of the United Bible Societies' Greek New Testament has been followed for the relative clause rather than that of the original third edition.

There are no examples of procedural texttype in the book of 1 Corinthians and very few stretches of narrative texttype. For this reason, no section of these texttypes has been analyzed. The book in general is hortatory, but it contains extensive sections of persuasive and expository texttype. Youngman has rightly noted, "Expository material is an integral part of all but perhaps the most simple hortatory text; it may even form the major part of what is overall a hortatory text" (1987:115). Persuasive and hortatory text differ from expository in the larger amounts of motivational material which they include. They differ from one another primarily in that hortatory text is trying to effect action in the reader, while persuasive text is trying to effect a change in belief and value systems. It is quite possible that in some languages there is no structural difference between these two; however, in Koiné Greek hortatory text differs primarily from persuasive by having imperative verbs (and other mitigated command forms) as its mainline.

Of special interest is the hortatory aside of 3:10b–11 shown in table 13. This is a parenthetical comment exhorting the reader to be careful in building up the church. Usually a hortatory passage in a hortatory discourse will be on mainline. This microparagraph, however, could be removed without doing harm to Paul's argument that he and Apollos are merely servants and not to be followed themselves.

---

[3]The following abbreviations are used in these tables: E expository; H hortatory; N narrative; P persuasive. The Greek text for tables 11–15 is found in appendix B.

Table 11
Constituent display of 1 Cor. 1:10–17
Mixed texttypes

Point 1: (H) Motivation paragraph
  Thesis: (H) Reason paragraph
    Thesis: **10** Now I appeal to you, brothers, through the name
                       of our Lord Jesus Christ, that you all speak the
                       same thing and that there be no divisions among
                       you, but that you be united in the same mind and
                       the same viewpoint.
    Reason: (E) Amplification paragraph
      Thesis: **11** For it has been indicated to me about
                              you, my brothers, by the household of
                              Chloe that there is strife among you.
      Amplification: **12** This is what I am saying, that each of you
                              says, "I am of Paul," and "I of Apollos,"
                              and "I of Cephas," and "I of Christ."
  Motivation: (P) Comment paragraph
    Thesis: (P) Coordinate paragraph
      $Thesis_1$:   **13** Has Christ been divided?
      $Thesis_2$:   Paul was not crucified for you, was he?
      $Thesis_n$:   Or were you baptized into the name of
                             Paul?
    Comment: (P) Reason paragraph
      Thesis: (P) Clarification paragraph
        Thesis: **14** I thank God that I baptized
                          none of you except Crispus and
                          Gaius; **15** lest anyone should say
                          that you were baptized into my
                          name.
        Clarification: (N) Antithetical paragraph
          Thesis: **16** Now I did baptize also the
                            household of Stephanas.
          Antithesis: For the rest, I do not know
                           whether I baptized any
                           other one.
      Reason: **17** For Christ did not send me to baptize
                          but to preach the Gospel, and not in
                          wisdom of word, lest the cross of Christ
                          be emptied of its power.

Table 12
Constituent display of 1 Cor. 2:6–16
Persuasive texttype

Point X: (P) Amplification paragraph
   Thesis: **6**   But we do speak wisdom among the mature, but not
              a wisdom of this age nor of the rulers of this age,
              who are being done away with.
  Amplification: (P) Amplification paragraph
    Thesis: (P) Reason paragraph
      Thesis: **7**   But we speak the hidden wisdom of God in
                a mystery, which God predestined before the
                ages for our glory, **8** which none of the
                rulers of this age understood;
    Reason: (P) Evidence paragraph
      Thesis: for if they had understood, they would not
              have crucified the Lord of glory.
      Evidence: **9**   But, just as it is written,
                 "What eye has not seen,
                   and ear has not heard,
                and has not entered in the
                   heart of man,
                which God has prepared for
                   those who love him."
  Amplification: (P) Amplification paragraph
    Thesis: (P) Clarification paragraph
      Thesis: **10** But to us God has revealed [them]
              through the Spirit.
      Clarification: (P) Amplification paragraph
        Thesis: For the Spirit searches all things,
               even the depths of God.
        Amplification: Rhetorical (P) Evidence paragraph
          Evidence: **11** For what man knows the
                  [thoughts] of a man except
                  the spirit of the man
                  which is in him?
          Thesis: So also no one understands the
               [thoughts] of God except the
               Spirit of God.

Amplification: Chiastic (P) Antithetical paragraph

Thesis A₁: **12** Now we have received not the spirit of the world, but the Spirit which is from God, that we might know the things freely given us by God **13** which also we speak not in words taught by human wisdom but taught by the Spirit, interpreting spiritual truths in spiritual words.

Antithesis B: **14** The soulical man does not accept the [teachings] of the Spirit of God, for they are foolishness to him, and he is not able to understand them because because they are spiritually discerned.

Thesis A₂: (P) Evidence paragraph

Thesis: **15** The spiritual [person] discerns all things but he himself is discerned by no one.

Evidence: (P) Comment paragraph

Thesis: **16** "For who has known the mind of the Lord so that he may instruct him?"

Comment: But we have the mind of Christ.

Note: The punctuation of 2:7–8 follows the corrected third edition of the UBS *Greek New Testament*.

Table 13
Constituent display of 1 Cor. 3:10–15
Primarily expository texttype

Point X: (P) Illustration paragraph
   Thesis: verse 5
   Illustration: (P) Coordinate paragraph
      Thesis$_1$: verses 6–9
      Thesis$_2$: verses 10–15 analyzed below
Thesis$_2$: (E) Amplification paragraph
   Thesis: (E) Comment paragraph
      Thesis: **10** According to the grace of God given to me, as a
                wise master builder I laid a foundation, but
                another man is building on [it].
     Comment: (H) Reason paragraph*
       Thesis: But let each one watch out how he builds on [it].
       Reason: **11** For another foundation no one can lay than
                that which is laid, which is Jesus Christ.
   Amplification: (E) Reason paragraph
     Thesis: **12** Now if any one builds on the foundation with
              gold, silver, precious stones, wood, hay, straw,
              13 each one's work will become apparent, for the
              Day will make [it] evident;
     Reason: (E) Amplification paragraph
       Thesis: because it will be revealed with fire, and the fire
              itself will test each one's work [to see] of what
              sort it is.
      Amplification: (E) Antithetical paragraph
        Thesis: **14** If anyone's work which he has built
                remains, he will receive a reward.
        Antithesis: **15** If anyone's work is burned up, he
                will suffer loss, but he himself will be
                saved, but [only] thus, as through fire.

*This paragraph functions as a hortatory aside.

Table 14
Constituent display of 1 Cor. 6:12–20
Hortatory texttype

Point N: (H) Reason paragraph
  Reason: (H) Antithetical paragraph
    Introduction: (H) Coordinate paragraph
        Thesis$_1$:   **12** All things are permissible for me, but not all things are expedient.
        Thesis$_2$:   All things are permissible for me, but I will not be brought under authority by anything.
    Antithesis: (H) Antithetical paragraph
        Thesis: **13** Food for the stomach and the stomach for food—
        Antithesis: but God will do away with both this and that.
    Thesis: (H) Comment paragraph
        Thesis: But the body is not for fornication but for the Lord, and the Lord for the body.
        Comment:**14** And God both raised the Lord and will raise us up through his power.
  Thesis: (H) Motivation paragraph
    Motivation: (H) Result paragraph
        Thesis: **15** Do you not know that your bodies are members of Christ?
      Result: Rhetorical (H) Clarification paragraph
        Thesis: Shall I take therefore the members of Christ and make them members of a prostitute?
      Clarification: (H) Reason paragraph
        Thesis: Definitely not!
        Reason: (H) Antithetical paragraph
          Thesis: (H) Evidence paragraph
            Thesis: **16** Or do you not know that the one joined to a prostitute is one body with her?
            Evidence: For it says, "The two shall be one flesh."

                        Antithesis: 17   But the one joined to
                                                 the Lord is one spirit
                                                 [with him].
        Thesis: (H) Motivation paragraph
            Thesis: (H) Reason paragraph
                Thesis: 18   Flee fornication.
                Reason: Every sin which a man does is outside
                                     the body; but the fornicator sins
                                     against his own body.
            Motivation: (H) Result paragraph
                Thesis: Rhetorical (H) Amplification paragraph
                    Amplification: 19   Or do you not know
                                                that your body is a
                                                temple of the Holy Spirit
                                                within you, which you
                                                have from God, and you
                                                are not your own?
                Thesis: 20   For you were bought with a price.
                Result: So glorify God in your body.

                                Table 15
                   Constituent display of 1 Cor. 10:23–11:1
                             Hortatory texttype

Point N: (H) Generalization paragraph
    Introduction: (H) Coordinate paragraph
        Thesis$_1$:   23   All things are permissible, but not all things
                                 are expedient.
        Thesis$_2$:   All things are permissible, but not all things
                                 build up.
    Generalization: Chiastic (H) Coordinate paragraph
        Thesis A$_1$: 24   Let no one seek his own [good], but the
                            [good] of another.
    Thesis: (H) Coordinate paragraph
        Thesis B$_1$: 25   Eat everything sold in the meat market, raising
                            no questions because of conscience. 26 For
                            "the earth [is] the Lord's, and its fulness."
        Thesis B$_2$: (H) Antithetical paragraph

Thesis: **27** If any of the unbelievers invites you [to
                    dinner] and you wish to go, eat everything
                    set before you, raising no questions
                    because of conscience.
Antithesis: (H) Reason paragraph
    Thesis: **28** But if someone says to you, "This is
                        a sacred sacrifice," do not eat
                        because of that one who informed
                        [you], and conscience—**29** but I mean
                        not your conscience but that one's.
    Reason:(H) Coordinate paragraph
        $Thesis_1$:   For why is my liberty
                         determined by another's
                         conscience?
        $Thesis_2$: **30** If I partake with thankfulness,
                         why am I slandered because of
                         that for which I give thanks?
Thesis A_2: (H) Comment paragraph
    Thesis: (H) Amplification paragraph
        Thesis: **31** Therefore, whether you eat or drink,
                            or whatever you do, do all things to
                            the glory of God.
        Amplification: **32** Do not be a stumbling-
                                   block either to Jews or to
                                   Greeks or to the church of
                                   God, **33** just as I also try to
                                   please everyone in
                                   everything, not seeking my
                                   [own] benefit, but that of
                                   many, that they may be
                                   saved.
    Comment: **11:1** Be imitators of me, just as I also am of
                      Christ.

Note: Thesis A_2 is chiastically coordinate with Thesis A_1.

The major paragraph analyzed in table 15 comes at the end of the fourth
discourse. It is interesting because it is composed of hortatory texttype in
a hortatory discourse, but it discusses issues that are related, but not
central, to the question at hand. Having argued using four major points
that Christians should not go up to an idol's temple to eat, Paul here turns

to the related questions of whether Christians were free to eat food sold in the meat market or served at a friend's house. These issues Paul solves, not by extended argument, but by summary commands. A similar hortatory summary of related issues is found at the end of chapter 14 in the seventh discourse. Having contrasted the spiritual gifts of speaking in tongues and prophecy, he there gives commands designed to regulate speakers with these two gifts, as well as women, in the public assembly. Again, these are related issues, but they are off the central point. The major paragraph analyzed in table 15 is also of interest because it shows a chiastic structure in referring to a generalization (argued in detail in 1 Corinthians 9) used to provide backing for the commands given. The theses labelled A_1 and A_2 are the two parts of a chiastically coordinate paragraph filling a generalization slot even though they are not consecutive. A fourth level antithetical paragraph also shows chiastic structure in table 12. The standard display developed by Longacre has been modified to include the labels A and B to show the chiasm in these cases.

This modification to the method made necessary by the chiasmus here points up a major limitation in analyzing a text in this way. The method is primarily geared toward analyzing texts which are linearly organized, although it is capable of being modified in this way to bring out the relationships of nonlinear text. For a text that is heavily nonlinear (that is, where related paragraphs on the same level are not situated next to one another), another method of analysis which shows field structures rather than particle structures would be preferable.

A second limitation of constituent structure analysis is the lack of focus on topic and change of topic. These are variables which must be considered in any analysis of a discourse. To be sure, topic is not ignored using this method; it is handled in the macrosegmentation or gross chunking segment of the analysis. But these techniques focus on major topics and tend to ignore subtopics that may occur at lower paragraph levels.

There are other limitations of this method of analysis which must be noted. Sometimes two different paragraphs have different relationships to a third paragraph (or colon) because they are related to different clauses within that paragraph. For example, in table 11 the parenthetical statement in 1:16 serves as a clarification of the statement in 1:14 (apart from 1:15); the colon in 1:17 also relates to 1:14 (and to 1:15 as well) by giving a reason for Paul's thankfulness, but it would be a mistake to separate verses 14 and 15 in this relationship. The display as currently constructed does not allow this information to be shown. It depicts paragraphs as being related to other paragraphs and sentences (colons in the case of Greek), not to clauses, but the actual relationship can be on the clause level (cf.

Longacre 1968:53–191 passim for an earlier type of display that allows some clause relationships to be shown).

In the same way, sometimes there are additional relationships on a clause level which this method does not illuminate. A paragraph may be primarily related to another paragraph while also secondarily related in a different way to a clause within that paragraph. For example, in table 12 the first part of verse 10 is primarily the thesis of an amplification on verse 7 about the secret and hidden wisdom of God. But there also exists a contrast between verse 10 (those to whom this wisdom has been revealed) and the relative clause in verse 8 (the rulers of this age who did not understand). Many texts are more complicated than can be shown by any linear method of analysis.

A final limitation of this methodology is the potential danger of misusing it by trying to analyze the paragraph relationships based solely on the words and phrases which Young, Becker, and Pike have labeled plot cues. Usually such relational cues serve to tie a colon or paragraph with the previous colon or paragraph. But the role relationship may be with a colon or paragraph that is some distance away.

Because the relational cues can point to more than one kind of relationship and because the relationship may not be with the immediately preceding colon, it is possible to misanalyze a text using constituent structure analysis. For example, 1:18 begins with the word γάρ 'for' which usually signals either reason or elaboration (i.e., amplification). But it would be a mistake to see 1:18 as simply an elaboration on the cross of Christ mentioned in verse 17; rather, it is the beginning of a new major paragraph on the wisdom of God. The word γάρ here is transitional; it is a relational cue, but one that relates major sections of the first discourse, not merely sentences or minor paragraphs within those sections.

Further, it would also be a mistake to focus on the initial main clauses of 1:17–18 and take γάρ as indicating a reason relationship, thus resulting in the analysis illustrated in (37).

(37)   Thesis: Christ did not send me to baptize...   (1:17)
       Reason: For the word of the cross is foolishness to those
                   who are perishing...   (1:18)

The resulting enthemyme by the great evangelist Paul about the futility of trying to baptize people because the lost will not listen is not only theologically unsound, it also misses the major transitional idea that there should be no church division because such behavior is based on man's wisdom instead of God's. The discourse analyst must look at the actual relationships between whole paragraphs, not just at the transitional words and not just at main clauses. This method allows the actual relationships to be disclosed, but the analyst must be careful to avoid taking a shortcut.

In spite of these limitations, the analysis of constituent structures into displays such as those in tables 11 through 15 is one of the best tools which the discourse analyst has for identifying the relationships between paragraphs in the text. It is superior to the mere marking and ranking of orthographic paragraphs, although that is also useful. But the analyzing of constituent structures, when used with due regard for its limitations, can be used to proceed to two other steps of analysis: the classification and ranking of types of paragraphs, and the ranking of verbs as predictors of paragraph levels.

The first of these additional steps is illustrated in table 16. The level of embedding for each type of paragraph has been listed for each different texttype. This table only gives information for forty-six verses of 1 Corinthians and thus cannot be considered conclusive. But the analysis of even this limited amount of data illustrates the methodology used to investigate the primary levels of each type of paragraph and the types of paragraphs found in each type of discourse.

Further, the table allows the analyst to draw tentative conclusions about the embedded levels and branching characteristics of various types of paragraphs. Table 16 shows that there are certain types of paragraphs, such as reason, amplification, coordinate, and antithetical, which occur across a wide range of embedding levels. Other types, such as generalization and illustration, occur only at high levels in the verses under study. Still other types, such as evidence and clarification, occur only at the fourth level and below. The verses in question show a maximum of seven levels of recursively embedded paragraphs.

These verses also show a strong predominance of right branching paragraphs. Among the persuasive, expository, and narrative paragraphs, the only left branching paragraph is the rhetorical structured paragraph, which is often characterized by left branching. But the hortatory paragraphs show evidence of left branching at higher levels for reason, motivation, and antithetical paragraph types. This seems to indicate the presence of an inductive argument style in which the reasons, motivational material, and contrastive elements are presented before the actual point of the paragraph is revealed. Further study is needed before these generalizations can be considered valid for a wider range of text.

Table 16
Paragraph type, embedding level, and texttype

	Hortatory	Persuasive	Expository	Narrative
Reason	1st L 2nd R 4th R (bis) 5th R (bis)	3rd R (bis)	4th R	
Amplification	3rd R 5th L	1st R 2nd R 3rd R 5th R	3rd R (bis) 5th R	
Motivation	1st R 2nd L 3rd R			
Generalization	1st X			
Illustration			1st R	
Comment	2nd R 3rd R	2nd R 6th R	4th R	
Coordinate	2nd D (tris) 3rd D 5th D	3rd D	2nd D	
Antithetical	2nd L 3rd R (bis) 6th R	4th R	6th R	5th R
Result	3rd R 4th R			
Evidence	7th R	4th R 5th R 6th L		
Clarification	4th R	4th R (bis)		

Key: D double headed; L left branching; R right branching; X chiastic
Note: The highest level of embedding for each type paragraph is in bold print.

Verb ranking and salience levels in Greek hortatory text. The second kind of analysis that can be abstracted from a study of constituent structures is that of verb ranking for a particular kind of texttype. Longacre (1989a:64–82; 1989b:413–60) has done extensive work in relating different verb types to levels of importance in narrative texttype. Two hypotheses underlie this work. First, "It is assumed here that for any language each type of text has a main line of development and contains other materials which can be conceived of as encoding progressive degrees of departure from the main line" (1989b:414). Second, "Within local spans of text an intersentential analysis can be carried out so that the sentences whose main verb(s)/clause(s) are of highest rank are structurally dominant in the local span and those of lower rank are structurally ancillary" (p. 415).

For hortatory texttype, this would mean that verbs which encode commands, prohibitions, appeals, and other primarily hortatory material would signal the main line or command line of the hortatory text. There are also commands which have been mitigated, that is, put in a form that would make them more socially acceptable. When mitigation is taken into account, several different forms of verbs become a part of the command line (cf. Longacre 1983a:3–43 passim, especially 9). In her analysis of 1 John, Miehle (1981:156) lists several different degrees of command mitigation as shown in (38).

(38)   overt imperative (both second and third person)
        ἐντολή 'command' + ἵνα 'that' clause
        ἵνα 'so that' clause
        ὀφείλω 'ought'
        generic + participle [with ὡς 'as' or πᾶς 'all' and the subjunctive]
        participle
        ἐάν/ὅταν 'if/whenever' + clause

The form παρακαλῶ 'I appeal' plus a ἵνα 'that' clause can be added to this list in a fairly high position since the first discourse begins in 1:10 with this form. These hortatory forms are the primary source of macrostructure material for a hortatory text.

It is not just verb forms, however, that mark different levels of salience for different types of material. The rhetorical question is a marker of motivational paragraphs in the hortatory samples analyzed here. Most of the questions in 1 Corinthians are rhetorical questions (Burquest and Christian 1982:5–39). Three of the four questions in the analyzed sample begin with the clause "Do you not know . . ." This occurs nine times in 1 Corinthians (p. 9), but it is by no means the standard way to introduce a rhetorical question. An analyst might be tempted to take the perfect indicative as a marker for motivational text since the perfect is found in the three questions with this clause. But it is the question form, not the verb form, which is the significant indicator here. Grammarians agree that the perfect verb οἶδα 'know' used in this form does not have a typical perfect meaning; rather, it is said to be durative (Robertson 1934:895) with present force (Moulton 1908:147) or meaning (Turner 1963:82). Many rhetorical questions exist without this perfect verb form.

A similar claim can be made for the evidence paragraph which is often marked by a direct quotation. The verb form within the quotation is of little consequence in the analysis, since that form is determined by its function within its original context rather than its present function.

Table 17 gives the results of ordering the verb form and other salience information for the sample passages analyzed in tables 11 through 15. The bands in table 17 are arranged to roughly correspond with the paragraph levels within which information is found. Some of the information types, such as explanation and condition, are more typically embedded within subordinate clauses of high level paragraphs than within lower level paragraphs. This accounts for their rather high level within the table.

Not all grammatical forms are mutually exclusive when assigned to paragraph types. Present indicative verbs are found in both band 2 and band 3. In addition, present indicative verbs may also be found in motivational and evidence paragraphs, where salience is indicated by something other than verb form. The analysis shows that thesis, antithesis, comment, and generalization paragraphs have no effect on determining salience levels; therefore, they are omitted from table 17.

Where a paragraph is recursively embedded within two types of form that are in different bands, its form will be a combination of the two forms if possible, or if not, will take the form of the lowest paragraph level. For example, table 14 shows that 6:15b is embedded within motivation and result paragraphs; it shows both rhetorical question and aorist verb tense. But the next verse further embeds a reason paragraph and thus returns to the present indicative form as signifying reason.

The results obtained in table 17 are valid for the passages analyzed in tables 11 through 15. No claim is made here that a salience level chart for additional data would remain exactly the same. In fact, additional analysis would most likely further complicate the chart, adding new levels and exceptions to the rules. Besides providing a tentative salience level chart for hortatory texttype, the analysis given here demonstrates both the method of determining salience levels and its general validity. It further demonstrates that the techniques that Longacre (1989b) and others have shown to be productive in discovering salience levels for narrative texttype can be used in the same way on non-narrative texts.

Table 17

Salience levels for hortatory texttype in 1 Corinthians

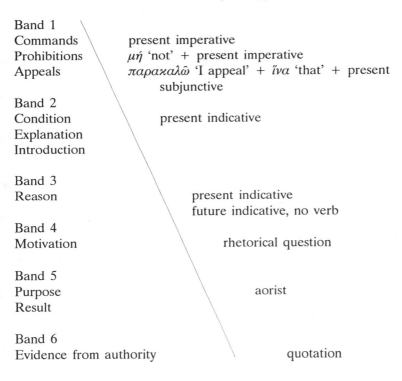

Band 1
Commands   present imperative
Prohibitions   μή 'not' + present imperative
Appeals   παρακαλῶ 'I appeal' + ἵνα 'that' + present
                         subjunctive

Band 2
Condition   present indicative
Explanation
Introduction

Band 3
Reason   present indicative
                                future indicative, no verb

Band 4
Motivation   rhetorical question

Band 5
Purpose   aorist
Result

Band 6
Evidence from authority   quotation

4.2 Wave

Transitions between paragraphs. To this point in the analysis, the focus has been on units or particles. But Pike (1982:24) has noted that this treatment of language is not sufficient. He writes, "The analysis of speech into separate chunks is in *some* manner false—a model useful for some purposes, awkward for others." Thus he suggests that it is also necessary to analyze language as if it were a wave. Applying this to the sounds indicated by letters, he states, "Instruments show that the sounds do slur into one another. One sound is not finished before the begun" (p. 24).

What is true on a small scale is also true on a larg writers block off their material in a very definite where one section ends and another begins. F from one section to another with a paragraph or a sentence designed to make a smooth transition. The analyst who is trying to decide to which section this bit of text belongs is faced with a difficult choice, for in some real sense it belongs to both sections. In such a case, the same sentence can terminate one paragraph while initiating another (cf. Longacre 1985b:167–73).

Paul shows several examples of this in 1 Corinthians. A notable illustration is in 3:9. In 3:5–15, Paul gives two analogies to explain the nature of Christian servants. First he likens them to farm hands working in a field; then he likens them to construction workers erecting a building. The transition between the thoughts happens in the middle of the clause in 3:9 which reads: "You are God's field, God's building." Because the appositive phrase introduces a new topic, such a clause cannot be said to belong to either one idea or the other; it rightfully belongs to both.

The very next paragraph shows a transition across a more significant boundary. Beginning with 3:16, Paul is no longer discussing Christian servants, but has returned to his main topic of congregational unity. In 3:16–17 he likens the Corinthians to a temple of God and says that anyone who destroys that temple will be destroyed by God. Here the way to destroy the temple is to destroy the unity of the congregation. But the figure used is that of a temple, a type of building. This ties in well with the previous paragraph on Christian servants as builders. The figure of building remains, but the topic has changed.

The paragraph in 4:18–21 where Paul discusses his plans to come to Corinth has already been di_ _ssed in chapter 3. There it was suggested that, in a division of _ _ _nto discourses, the paragraph in question functions be++ _ _ _ion to the second discourse than as a concl_ _ _ that it contains some of both elements, first section ends in a discussion of '. This transitional paragraph discusses Corinth. Then in 5:3 Paul specifically in body. In the same way, the word in the first discourse in 4:6, in the _nd in the second discourse in 5:2. _ found twice in 4:8 in the first _α is found in the transitional _ναμις 'power' is found both in the _:20 and in the second discourse in 5:4. _en 4:18–20 are closer to 5:2–4 than 4:6–8; _on th_ the transitional passage 4:18–21 was placed in chapter 3 of this study. But lexical chains _ond discourses together; this is in sharp

_usion _ter as _ the text i_ making the choice difficult. The fact is _ _ _ _ to the first. The fact is _ _ _ _ ica_ _ The _ contrast to the book of James where breaks in lexical chains serve to define the boundaries of different discourses (Terry 1992:111–12).

The transition in 6:9 is of a different kind. Here the grammatical markers signal the paragraph in 6:9–11 as belonging with the material in 6:1–8, but the conceptual markers indicate that it belongs with the material in 6:12–20. The passage in 6:9 is introduced by the word ἤ 'or', which is used most often to show alternative continuity with what has just preceded. In the same way, there is a lexical tie between the word ἀδικεῖτε 'you wrong' in 6:8 and the word ἄδικοι 'unrighteous ones' in 6:9. Further, the phrase "inherit the kingdom of God" is found in both verses 9 and 10. But even though these markers are here to show continuity with 6:1–8, the subject matter has returned to a discussion, not of lawsuits and defrauding one another, as in those verses, but of fornication and other sins, as in chapter 5 and 6:12–20. Verses 9 and 10 present a list of sinners who will not inherit the kingdom of God. The list is strongly reminiscent of the list in 5:10–11. Both 5:10–11 and 6:9–10 share the following words: πόρνος 'fornicator', εἰδωλολάτρης 'idolater', πλεονέκτης 'greedy', μέθυσος 'drunkard', λοίδορος 'reviler', and ἅρπαξ 'robber'. Also, the phrase "kingdom of God" in 6:9–10 is also found in the transition paragraph which leads into the second discourse in 4:20. In addition, "in the name of the Lord Jesus Christ" in 6:11 is very similar to "in the name of our Lord Jesus" in 5:4. Chapter 5 and the end of chapter 6 discuss fornication; 6:9 lists four classes of sexual offenders: πόρνοι 'fornicators', μοιχοί 'adulterers', μαλμκοί 'catamites', and αρσενοκοῖται 'homosexuals'. Conceptually the transition back to the subject of fornication has already been made by 6:9. Fee (1987:250) has argued that 6:12–20 is not concerned with the subject of fornication in general, tying this passage back to the problem of incest in chapter 5; rather, he sees it as dealing with a new problem of Christian men visiting πόρνη 'prostitutes'. In context, if πορνεία can mean 'fornication' and not just 'prostitution' and πόρνος can mean 'fornicator' and not just 'whoremonger', then πόρνη can also mean 'fornicator' (as it does in Ezekiel 16:33–35 LXX) and not just 'prostitute'.

Another transitional passage is found in 10:14. This is usually taken to be the beginning of the paragraph 10:14–22. But it could just as well serve as a summary statement for 10:1–14. Both 10:1–13 and 10:15–22 are discussing the eating of meat offered to idols. The admonition in 10:14 to flee from idolatry fits well with both sections. This sentence contains a vocative, a frequent marker of paragraph beginnings in Greek (cf. Miehle 1981:98 and Longacre 1983a:3, 13, 22, 25, 30 for 1 John, as well as Hymes 1986:80 and Terry 1992:113, 118 for James). The vocative is the adjective ἀγαπητός 'beloved', however, not a noun, and the only other place where this adjective occurs as a vocative in 1 Corinthians is in 15:58, a summary verse at the end of a discourse. In the same way, the introductory conjunction for 10:14 is διόπερ 'therefore, wherefore', a word which is used elsewhere in the New Testament only in 8:13, in the conclusion to the first point of the discourse. It also occurs as an unlikely variant to διό 'therefore, wherefore' in 14:13, a passage often marked as the beginning of a paragraph. All of this indicates that 10:14 is truly transitional in nature. From a unit or particle perspective, it is difficult to tell to which paragraph this sentence belongs; however, from a wave perspective, it belongs to both.

Similarly, it is difficult to tell how to analyze the verses 12:31 and 14:1. They serve as transitional elements into and out of the section on love in 1 Corinthians 13. This section is best analyzed as a discourse rather than a major paragraph. 1 Cor. 13:1–13 can stand alone and, in modern use of these verses, often does. But 12:31 and 14:1 clearly have ties to this section. The passage 12:31 speaks both of charismatic gifts (tying it to chapter 12) and a more excellent way (tying it to chapter 13). The passage 14:1 speaks both of love (tying it to chapter 13) and of spiritual gifts (tying it to chapter 14). The transitional character of these two verses is quite evident.

Finally, it is difficult to tell just how to analyze 16:5–11 in a particle or unit fashion. These verses once again discuss Paul and Timothy's travel plans. They are tied both to 16:2, where Paul relates his intention to go to Corinth, and to 16:12, where he describes Apollos's lack of travel plans. The decision in chapter 3 to keep 16:5–11 with 16:1–4 is based on the fact that 16:2–4 also discusses, in a limited way, Paul's travel plans and 16:12 starts with the discourse-beginning marker περὶ δέ 'now concerning'. But when analyzed in wave fashion, these verses are clearly transitional between 16:1–4 and 16:12.

4.3 Field

Particle and wave perspectives provide two different viewpoints which compliment one another in analyzing the constituent structures of a text. A third perspective, which provides additional insight, is the field perspective, the viewpoint which sees a text from the standpoint of patterns and their relationships.

While linear discourse also shows a pattern, that pattern is often quite easy to discern and can be adequately described in a particle approach. But nonlinear discourse can be better described from a field perspective. Even though some of these patterns, such as inclusio and chiasmus, can be viewed as structures and treated under a particle perspective, they are more clearly seen as patterns in a field perspective. Just as transitions are better suited to description from a wave perspective, patterned text, such as that found in chiasmus, is better suited to be described from a field perspective. When there are multiple patterns overlaid on one another in a given unit of text, the field perspective is no longer only desirable, but necessary.

This section begins with an overview of the different types of patterns utilized in 1 Corinthians which a field perspective can reveal. Then a technique of field perspective is illustrated by examining one of those patterns, chiasmus, in greater detail.

Types of grammatical and conceptual patterns. Where a paragraph structure is made up of two elements, there are two possible patterns: AA' and AB. The AA' pattern is a parallelism structure. The two elements, whether sentences or paragraphs, are either conceptually or grammatically parallel to one another or parallel in both ways. First Corinthians contains numerous examples of this pattern on a microparagraph level, including pairings in 6:7, 12; 7:12–13, 16, 22, 28; 9:1ab, 1d–2b, 5–6, 7; 10:16, 21, 23; 11:4–5, 22; 12:15–16, 17, 26, 28–29; 13:11, 12; 14:4, 15, 23–24; 15:21–22, 55; and 16:23–24. On a slightly higher paragraph level, the microparagraph in 15:13–14 is parallel to the microparagraph in 15:16–17.

The AB pattern contains two paired elements which are connected to one another in some fashion but also are quite different in form. A good example of this pattern is a question-answer paragraph, such as is found in 11:22 and 14:15. A similar structure is a question-command paragraph. Examples of this are found in 7:18, 21, 27. This structure is the functional equivalent of a conditional command; if the question is answered positively, the command applies. The example in 7:27 is a case of two question-command microparagraphs with a parallel pattern, as shown in (39).

(39)   X   A   δέδεσαι   γυναικί;   (7:27)
                   have^you^been^bound to^a^wife?

           B   μὴ ζήτει λύσιν·
                   not seek   a^loosing.

       X' A' λέλυσαι   ἀπὸ γυναικός;
                   have^you^been^loosed from a^wife?

           B' μὴ ζήτει γυναῖκα.
                   not seek   a^wife.

The resulting structure from combining two AB patterns inside an AA' pattern is a cyclical ABA'B' pattern. It also contains a conceptual ABB'A' chiasm: bound to a *wife*, *loosed* from a wife, *loosed* from a wife, bound to a *wife*. While this passage can be viewed as a combination of embedded units as shown in (39), only a field perspective allows these multiple patterns to come into focus.

There are also several possible patterns for paragraphs when they are made up of more than two elements. First of all, there is a parallel structure AA'A'', such as those found in 4:8, 12:4–6, 22–24, 29, 30, 13:1–3, 15:42–44, and 16:19–20. Second, there is a linear structure ABC, where different items follow in some sort of logical order. This structure follows a common Western way of thinking and writing and is not difficult to analyze; it is easily seen even in a particle perspective, as discussed above. Third, there is a cyclical pattern ABA'B' with four elements, as shown in (39) for 7:27, or ABCA'B'C' with six. Other four element cycles are found in 7:32–34 and 14:6–11. In the latter passage, the A elements ask questions about tongues versus clear speech while the B elements give illustrations from various kinds of voices. This also functions as the inner two elements of a chiasmus; see (58) for the layout. Fourth, there is a chiastic pattern ABB'A' with four elements or ABCC'B'A' with six. It is possible to combine the central elements into one in order to have an odd number of elements. Chiasmus is so common in 1 Corinthians that the next section is devoted to a discussion of it. Finally, there is inclusio, an ABCA pattern that repeats the first element.

The simple pattern ABA' can be either a reduced form of chiasmus, a defective cycle, or a simple case of inclusio. The exact rhetorical scheme is impossible to tell since all three of these cases show the same pattern. In this study, however, such a pattern is analyzed as chiasmus since it is so pervasive throughout 1 Corinthians.

Chiasmus on the paragraph level. As noted in chapter 3 of this study, several of the discourses show a form of ABA' chiasmus. But chiasmus is present, not only on the macroparagraph level, but also on the microparagraph and intermediate levels. The major studies of chiasmus in 1 Corinthians have been by Lund (1992) and Bailey (1983). If there is a fault in their work, it is that they tend to find chiasmus throughout the book, even in locations where other rhetorical strategies seem to be used. Lund more readily identifies alternate rhetorical schemes, but even he takes the use of chiasmus to an extreme. But there are many clear cases of chiasmus in this letter, and several of these are discussed below.

It is important to note that three kinds of chiasmus exist in 1 Corinthians: lexical, in which words are repeated in a chiastic pattern; grammatical, in which grammatical structures are repeated in a chiastic manner; and conceptual, in which concepts are repeated chiastically. Some patterns have only a single one of these types, but others show a combination of them.

Bailey (1983:177) identifies 3:1–23 as showing an ABB'A' scheme found in (40).

(40)   A Paul and Apollos (3:1–4)
            B   The illustration of the field (3:5–9b)
            B' The illustration of the building (3:9c–15)
        A' Paul, Apollos, and Cephas (3:21–23)

Certainly this pattern exists, but the problem with it is that it omits the passages about the Corinthians being God's temple (3:16–17) and about the wisdom of men (3:18–20). A pattern without such breaks can be found in 3:21–4:7 as shown in (41).

(41)   A Boasting (3:21)
            B   Paul and Apollos (3:22–23)
                C   Servants of Christ (4:1–5)
            B' Paul and Apollos (4:6)
        A' Boasting (4:7)

But this pattern as well as Bailey's suggested pattern has a difficulty. They both cut across the chiastic macroparagraph structure of the first discourse as given in (42) and shown also in table 4.

(42)   A Division (1:10–17)
            B   Wisdom (1:18–2:16)
        A' Division (3:1–4)
        C Servanthood (3:5–15)
            D   Wisdom and Division (3:16–23)
        C' Servanthood (4:1–17)

This major structure also exists. Bailey's pattern shown in (40) has taken the elements of A'CD in this analysis and made them ABA'. The problem is that his analysis here is too small. But the analysis in (41) also is legitimate, and it too cuts across the boundary lines of the analysis given in (42). This tells us that the rhetorical structure of the first discourse is quite complex and is probably composed of several interwoven patterns (cf. Longacre 1979a on both an episodic and a chiastic structure in the Genesis flood narrative and Pike 1987 on the multidimensional patterns of the Sermon on the Mount). Certainly the C section of (42) in 3:5–15 on servanthood is composed of two major paragraphs, as Bailey notes, which form an AA' parallelism. This multiple relationship patterning cannot be seen from a purely particle perspective; while a single pattern can be viewed as a type of particle structure, it takes a field perspective to view multiple patterns.

Within the first discourse, another chiasm can be noted in the paragraph (3:16–17) about the Corinthians being the temple of God as shown in (43).

(43) A οὐκ οἴδατε   ὅτι   ναὸς   θεοῦ   ἐστε   (3:16)
         not   do^you^know   that temple of^God you^are
      B καὶ   τὸ πνεῦμα τοῦ θεοῦ οἰκεῖ   ἐν ὑμῖν;
         and   the Spirit of God dwells in   you?
         C εἴ τις   τὸν ναὸν   τοῦ θεοῦ φθείρει,   (3:17)
            If   anyone the temple of   God   destroys
            C' φθερεῖ   τοῦτον   ὁ θεός·
                will^destroy this^one [O]   God [S]
      B' ὁ γὰρ ναὸς   τοῦ θεοῦ ἅγιός ἐστιν,
          the for temple of God holy is
   A' οἵτινές ἐστε ὑμεῖς.
       which   are you

The A, B, and C elements are all conceptually and lexically connected.
The second discourse also shows evidence of chiasmus on a smaller scale.
The passage in 6:13–14 (noted by Fee 1987:253–54) shows a complex
pattern of two lexical chiasms embedded within a cyclical XYX'Y' pattern
as shown in (44).

(44) X A τὰ βρώματα   (6:13)
            the foods
         B τῇ   κοιλίᾳ,
            for^the stomach
         B' καὶ ἡ κοιλία
             and   the stomach
         A' τοῖς   βρώμασιν·
             for^the foods
      Y ὁ δὲ θεὸς καὶ ταύτην καὶ ταῦτα καταργήσει.
         and God both this   and these will^destroy
      X' A τὸ δὲ σῶμα οὐ τῇ   πορνείᾳ
             the but body not for^the fornication
          B ἀλλὰ τῷ   κυρίῳ,
             but   for^the Lord,
          B' καὶ ὁ κύριος
              and the Lord
          A' τῷ   σώματι·
              for^the body.
      Y' ὁ δὲ θεὸς καὶ τὸν κύριον ἤγειρεν   (6:14)
          the but God both the Lord   raised
          καὶ ἡμᾶς ἐξεγερεῖ   διὰ   τῆς δυνάμεως αὐτοῦ.
          and   us   will^raise^up through the power   of^him

This multiple patterning is best seen from the perspective of a field. Fee (1987:257) also notes that the next verses contain a lexical and conceptual chiasmus as shown in (45).

(45)   A members of Christ   (6:15)
       B members of a prostitute
       B' the one joined to a prostitute   (6:16)
    A' the one joined to the Lord   (6:17)

The third discourse begins with several examples of lexical chiasmus as noted by Lund (1992:151–52), who has noted that 7:2–5 form a chiasmus as shown in (46).

(46) A *διὰ*   *δὲ τὰς πορνείας*   (7:2)
     because^of but the **fornication**
    B *ἕκαστος τὴν ἑαυτοῦ γυναῖκα ἐχέτω,*
      each^[man] his own   wife   **let^him^have**
      καὶ ἑκάστη τὸν ἴδιον ἄνδρα ἐχέτω.
      and each^[woman] her own husband **let^her^have.**
    C *τῇ γυναικὶ ὁ ἀνὴρ τὴν ὀφειλὴν ἀποδιδότω* (7:3)
      to the^wife the husband **the due   should^give**
      ὁμοίως δὲ καὶ ἡ γυνὴ τῷ ἀνδρί.
      likewise and also the wife to^the husband.
      C' *ἡ γυνὴ τοῦ ἰδίου σώματος*   (7:4)
        the wife **her own body**
          οὐκ ἐξουσιάζει ἀλλὰ ὁ ἀνήρ·
          not rule^over but   the husband^[does];
          ὁμοίως δὲ καὶ ὁ ἀνὴρ τοῦ ἰδίου σώματος
          likewise and also the husband **his own body**
          οὐκ ἐξουσιάζει ἀλλὰ ἡ γυνή.
          not rule^over but   the wife^[does].
    B' *μὴ ἀποστερεῖτε ἀλλήλους, εἰ μήτι ἂν*   (7:5)
      not defraud   **one^another**, except maybe
      ἐκ συμφώνου πρὸς καιρόν, ἵνα σχολάσητε
      by agreement for^a season that you^may^say
      τῇ προσευχῇ καὶ πάλιν ἐπὶ τὸ αὐτὸ ἦτε,
      prayers   and again **together**   be
  A' *ἵνα μὴ πειράζῃ ὑμᾶς ὁ σατανᾶς*
     that not tempt   you   the Satan
     διὰ τὴν ἀκρασίαν ὑμῶν.
     because^of the **lack^of^self-control** of^yours.

The chiasmus is conceptual, with *fornication* equaling *a lack of self-control,* *having* a person being the same as *not defrauding* and *being together,* and *giving due* equaling *not having authority over one's own body.* There is also a lexical chiasmus in verse 4 using the words ἀνήρ 'husband' and γυνή 'wife'. At the same time, the grammatical structure of verses 2–4 is a series of parallel units: AA' BB' CC' DD', where the last three primed elements omit the predicate. Again, a field perspective allows this overlay of patterns to be seen clearly.

A little farther on in the third discourse, Fee (1987:299) has noted that 7:12–14 form what he calls a perfect triple chiasm as shown in (47).

(47) A any **brother** has
         B   an **unbelieving wife**
            C   any **woman** has
               D   an **unbelieving husband**
               D'   the **unbelieving husband** is sanctified
            C'   through his **wife**
         B'   the **unbelieving wife** is sanctified
      A' through her **husband**

Once again note that the lexical chiasmus is embedded within a different grammatical pattern—this time a couple of parallelisms: AB is parallel to CD and D'C' is parallel to B'A'. A field perspective is required to show the overlay of patterns.

The fourth discourse also contains several examples of chiasmus. Youngman (1987:189) has noted that there is a chiastic pattern in 9:4–12 as shown in (48).

(48) A Church workers   (9:4–6)
         B   Secular workers   (9:7)
            C   God's ordinance   (9:8–10)
         B'   Secular work   (9:11)
      A' Church workers   (9:12)

Further, 9:16 contains a lexical and structural chiasmus as shown in (49). It is apparent only in the Greek, for much of the structure is lost in translation.

(49) A *ἐὰν γὰρ εὐαγγελίζωμαι,*
          if for **I^preach^the^gospel**
      B *οὐκ ἔστιν μοι καύχημα·*
          not **is** **to^me** boast
      C *ἀνάγκη γάρ μοι ἐπίκειται·*
          necessity for on^me is^laid
      B' *οὐαὶ γάρ μοί ἐστιν*
           woe for **to^me** **is**
      A' *ἐὰν μὴ εὐαγγελίσωμαι.*
           if not **I^preach^the^gospel**

But the most obvious example of chiasmus in the fourth discourse is found in 9:19–22 as shown in (50). It has been noted by Lund (1992:147), Bailey (1983:167), Youngman (1987:195), and Fee, although the latter states that it is chiastic "in form only, not in content" (1987:423).

Each of the six elements ends with a purpose clause beginning with *ἵνα* 'in order to'. The chiasmus is conceptually defective in the B' element, although Bailey (1983:167) and Youngman (1987:195) argue that the weak are the same as the Gentiles. It is true that the weak person in 8:7 is someone accustomed to idols, that is, a Gentile, but there are weak Christians who are not Gentiles, and Gentiles who are not weak. It hardly seems worth limiting Paul's meaning to preserve the chiasm.

(50) A Ἐλεύθερος γὰρ ὢν ἐκ πάντων   (9:19)
         free   for being from all
         πᾶσιν ἐμαυτὸν ἐδούλωσα,
         to^all myself I^have^enslaved
         ἵνα τοὺς πλείονας κερδήσω·
         that the many   I^might^gain
      B καὶ ἐγενόμην τοῖς   Ἰουδαίοις ὡς Ἰουδαῖος,   (9:20)
         and I^became to^the Jews   as a^Jew
         ἵνα Ἰουδαίους κερδήσω·
         that Jews   I^might^gain
         C τοῖς   ὑπὸ νόμον   ὡς ὑπὸ νόμον,
            to^those under [the]^law as under [the]^law
            μὴ ὢν   αὐτὸς ὑπὸ νόμον,
            not being myself under [the]^law
            ἵνα τοὺς ὑπὸ νόμον   κερδήσω·
            that those under [the]^law I^might^gain
         C' τοῖς   ἀνόμοις   ὡς ἄνομος,   (9:21)
            to^those without^[the]^law as without^[the]^law
            μὴ ὢν   ἄνομος   θεοῦ ἀλλ’
            not being without^[the]^law of^God but
            ἔννομος   Χριστοῦ,
            within^[the]^law of^Christ
            ἵνα κερδάνω   τοὺς ἀνόμους·
            that I^might^gain those without^[the]^law
      B' ἐγενόμην τοῖς   ἀσθενέσιν ἀσθενής,   (9:22)
         I^became to^the weak   weak
         ἵνα τοὺς ἀσθενεῖς κερδήσω·
         that the weak   I^might^gain
   A' τοῖς πᾶσιν γέγονα   πάντα,
      to   all   I^have^become all^things
      ἵνα πάντως   τινὰς σώσω.
      that by^all^means some I^might^save

These are not the only examples of chiasmus in the fourth discourse. Youngman (1987:202) notes another in 10:7–10 as shown in (51). This chiasm is grammatical rather than conceptual. The B and B' colons contain first person subjunctive verbs in their independent clauses, sandwiched between second person imperative verbs in the main clauses of the A and A' colons. There is an apparent imbalance to this nice scheme, however, for the A colon is followed by a quotation from Ex. 32:6 (LXX) to illustrate it and the other colons are not.

(51) A μηδὲ   εἰδωλολάτραι γίνεσθε, καθώς τινες αὐτῶν·
         neither idolators   become **just^as some of^them** [did]
         ὥσπερ γέγραπται, ἐκάθισεν ὁ λαὸς φαγεῖν καὶ
         as   it^is^written, sat^down the people to^eat and
         πεῖν   καὶ ἀνέστησαν παίζειν.
         to^drink and rose^up   to^play
      B μηδὲ   δε   πορνεύωμεν   καθώς τινες αὐτῶν
         neither and **let^us^fornicate, just^as some of^them**
         ἐπόρνευσα, καὶ ἔπεσαν μιᾷ ἡμέρᾳ εἴκοσι τρεῖς χιλιάδες.
         fornicated **and** fell   one day   twenty three thousand
      B' μηδὲ   ἐκπειράζωμεν τὸν Χριστόν, καθώς τινες
         neither let^us^test the Christ, **just^as some**
         αὐτῶν   ἐπείρασαν, καὶ ὑπὸ τῶν ὄφεων
         of^them tested,   **and** by the snakes
         ἀπώλλυντο.
         they^were^destroyed
      A' μηδὲ   γογγύζετε, καθάπερ τινὲς αὐτῶν ἐγόγγυσαν,
         neither grumble, **just^like some of^them** grumbled
         και ἀπώλοντο   ὑπὸ τοῦ ὀλοθρευτοῦ.
         and they^were^destroyed by   the destroyer

A fifth example of chiasmus in the fourth discourse is found in 10:16–21
as shown in (52). Both Bailey (1983:169) and Youngman (1987:208) have
previously noted this example.

(52) A The **cup** of blessing . . . is it not a sharing   (10:16)
         The **bread** . . . is it not a sharing
      B   Are not those who eat the sacrifices **sharers**   (10:18)
        C   That food **offered** to idols is anything   (10:19)
        C' They **sacrifice** to demons and not to God   (10:20)
      B' I do not want you to be **sharers** with demons
   A' You cannot drink of the **cup** of the Lord   (10:21)
      You cannot partake of the **table** of the Lord

Here the correspondences are conceptual rather than grammatical. The
A and A' elements deal with the cup and the bread (or table) of the
Lord's Supper. The B and B' elements relate that eating a sacrifice makes
one a sharer or partner with an altar or a demon, respectively. The C and
C' elements discuss sacrifices offered to idols.

The fifth discourse has an example of embedded chiasmus in 11:8–12 as
shown in (53). Lund (1992:148) has shown that these verses form a

ABCB'A' chiasm with the A, B, B', and A' elements containing lexical
chiasms using the words *ἀνήρ* 'man' and *γυνή* 'woman'.

(53)   A   *οὐ   γάρ   ἐστιν   ἀνὴρ   ἐκ   γυναικὸς,*   (11:8)
           not for   is   **man** from   **woman**
           ἀλλὰ   γυνὴ   ἐξ   ἀνδρός·
           but   **woman** from **man**
       B   *καὶ   γὰρ   οὐκ   ἐκτίσθη   ἀνὴρ   διὰ*   (11:9)
           indeed   for   not   was^created   **man**   because^of
           τὴν   γυναῖκα,
           the   **woman**
           ἀλλὰ   γυνὴ   διὰ   τὸν   ἄνδρα.
           but   **woman** because^of the   **man**
       C   *διὰ   τοῦτο   ὀφείλει   ἡ   γυνὴ   ἐξουσίαν* (11:10)
           because^of this   ought   the woman   authority
           ἔχειν   ἐπὶ   τῆς   κεφαλῆς   διὰ   τοὺς   ἀγγέλους.
           to^have on   the   head   because^of the   angels.
       B' *πλὴν   οὔτε   γυνὴ   χωρὶς   ἀνδρὸς*   (11:11)
           however   neither **woman** without **man**
           οὔτε   ἀνὴρ   χωρὶς   γυναικὸς   ἐν   κυρίῳ·
           nor   **man**   without **woman**   in   the^Lord
       A' *ὥσπερ   γὰρ   ἡ   γυνὴ   ἐκ   τοῦ   ἀνδρός,*   (11:12)
           as   for   the **woman** from the   **man**
           οὕτως   καὶ   ὁ   ἀνὴρ   διὰ   τῆς   γυναικός·
           so   also the **man**   through the **woman**
           τὰ   δὲ   πάντα   ἐκ   τοῦ   θεοῦ.
           the but all^things from the   God

The first two elements have the chiastic order man–woman–woman–man,
while the last two have the order woman–man–man–woman. Once again,
the multiple patterns are most clearly seen from a field perspective.

The whole sixth discourse can be divided into an ABA' chiastic pattern
as shown in (54).

(54)   A   The Lord's Supper at Corinth (11:17–22)
       B   How Jesus instituted the Lord's Supper (11:23–25)
       A' The Lord's Supper at Corinth (11:26–34)

The B element at the center is marked by narrative texttype.

The seventh discourse is the most chiastic of all the discourses, showing
several levels of embedded chiasmus. In this regard, it seems significant
that chapter 5 will show that this discourse is within the peak of the letter.

First, the whole discourse can be seen as one large chiastic pattern (here labeled XYX' to avoid confusion) as shown in (55).

(55)   X Spiritual gifts (12)
         Y   Love (13)
       X' Spiritual gifts (14)

Bailey (1983:178) has pointed out that what is here called the X element (12:1–31) can be itself interpreted as a chiastic pattern. Strictly speaking, the chiasm runs from 12:4–30 rather than over the whole twelfth chapter. The secondary level of chiasmus is here labeled RSR' as shown in (56).

(56)   R Various types of gifts (12:4–11)
         S   The body and its members (12:12–27)
       R' Various types of gifts (12:28–30)

In the same way the Y element (13:1–13) also contains a chiastic pattern, as shown in (57).

(57)   R   Transition (12:31)
         S   Love and spiritual gifts (13:1–3)
           T   Characteristics of love (13:4–7)
         S' Love and spiritual gifts (13:8–13)
       R' Transition (14:1)

This has been noted by Lund (1992:175–76) and Osburn (1976:150–52) among others.

Both Lund (1992:184) and Bailey (1983:178) have noted that the first part of the X' element (chapter 14) is chiastic in structure, although they have differed over how much text it covers. Lund sees the structure as covering 14:5b–13, while Bailey extends it to 14:1b–25. There are two problems with Bailey's analysis: there is not enough depth (forming merely an RSR' chiasm) and his S element could be labeled as saying the same thing as the R and R' elements. Bailey labels the R (14:1b–5) and R' (14:13–25) elements as "prophecy is better than tongues"; he includes in the S element the three parables of the flute (14:7), bugle (14:8–9), and the foreign language (14:11–12). The problem is that the point of the central S element is also "prophecy is better than tongues"; the difference is only that Paul is arguing by analogy. The chiasm should be more specific than what Bailey proposes. Lund's (1992:184) analysis is superior in this respect. The pattern given in (58) basically follows Lund with minor variations to improve the correspondences.

(58) R μείζων δὲ ὁ   προφητεύων ἢ   ὁ   (14:5b)
         greater but theˆ[one] prophesying than theˆ[one]
         λαλῶν   γλώσσαις, ἐκτὸς εἰ μὴ διερμηνεύῃ,
         speaking inˆtongues unless   heˆ**interprets**
      S ἵνα   ἡ ἐκκλησία οἰκοδομὴν λάβῃ.   (14:5c)
         soˆthat the **church**   **edification** mayˆreceive
         T A ἐὰν ἔλθω   πρὸς ὑμᾶς γλώσσαις λαλῶν,   (14:6)
               if   Iˆcome to   you   inˆ**tongues** speaking
               τί   ὑμᾶς ὠφελήσω,
               what you   willˆIˆprofit?
            B ὅμως   τὰ ἄψυχα φωνὴν διδόντα,   (14:7)
               likewise the lifeless **sounds** giving
         T' A' οὕτως καὶ ὑμεῖς διὰ   τῆς γλώσσης   (14:9)
               so   also you   through the **tongue**
               ἐὰν μὴ εὔσημον λόγον δῶτε,   πῶς
               unless intelligible word youˆgive how
               γνωσθήσεται   τὸ λαλούμενον;
               willˆoneˆknow the thingˆspoken?
            B' τοσαῦτα εἰ τύχοι γένη   (14:10)
               soˆmany perhaps kinds
               φωνῶν   εἰσιν   ἐν κόσμῳ,
               ofˆ**languages** thereˆare in theˆworld
         S' πρὸς τὴν οἰκοδομὴν τῆς   ἐκκλησίας ζητεῖτε (14:12)
               for   the **edification** ofˆthe church   seek
               ἵνα   περισσεύητε.
               that youˆmayˆabound
      R' διὸ   ὁ   λαλῶν   γλώσσῃ   (14:13)
         therefore theˆ[one] **speaking inˆaˆtongue**
         προσευχέσθω ἵνα διερμηνεύῃ.
         shouldˆpray that heˆmayˆ**interpret**

The T and T' elements of this chiasm contain an ABA'B' cyclical structure of question-illustration. These multiple overlaid patterns are most clearly seen from a field perspective.

Besides these intermediate levels of chiasmus in the seventh discourse, there are several examples of low level chiasmus in chapters twelve through fourteen. For example, there is a lexical chiasm in 12:3 as shown in (59).

(59) A *οὐδεὶς ἐν πνεύματι   θεοῦ   λαλῶν*   (12:3)
         no^one **by [the]^Spirit** of^God speaking
      B *λέγει, Ἀνάθεμα Ἰησοῦς,*
         says "cursed **Jesus**"
      B' *καὶ οὐδεὶς δύναται εἰπεῖν, Κύριος Ἰησοῦς,*
         and no^one can **say** "Lord **Jesus**"
      A' *εἰ μὴ ἐν πνεύματι   ἁγίῳ.*
         except **by [the]^Spirit** Holy

This has previously been noted by Lund (1992:164).
In the same way, Lund (1992:165) has noted a lexical and conceptual chiasm in 12:12, as shown in (60).

(60) A *Καθάπερ γὰρ τὸ   σῶμα   ἕν   ἐστιν*   (12:12)
         just^as for the **body one is**
      B *καὶ μέλη   πολλὰ ἔχει,*
         and **members   many** has
      B' *πάντα δὲ τὰ μέλη   τοῦ σώματος πολλὰ ὄντα*
         all and the **members** of^the body **many** being
      A' *ἕν ἐστιν σῶμα, οὕτως καὶ ὁ Χριστός·*
         one is   body so   also the Christ.

But perhaps the best example of embedded chiasm is found in 13:8–13, as shown in (61). It has been noted by Lund (1992:176) and Osburn (1976:151–52).

(61) A *Ἡ ἀγάπη οὐδέποτε πίπτει.*   (13:8)
         the **love** never   fails
      B *ἐκ μέρους γὰρ γινώσκομεν*   (13:9)
         in part for we^know
      C *ὅταν δὲ ἔλθῃ τὸ τέλειον, τὸ ἐκ μέρους*   (13:10)
         when but comes the perfect the in part
         καταργηθήσεται.
         will^be^done^away
      D *ὅτε ἤμην νήπιος, ἐλάλουν ὡς νήπιος,*   (13:11)
         when I^was a^child I^spoke as a^child

C' ὅτε   γέγονα   ἀνήρ,   κατήργηκα   τὰ
   when I^became a^man I^**did**^**away**^with the^[ways]^of
τοῦ νηπίου.
the child

B' ἄρτι γινώσκω ἐκ μέρους,   (13:12)
   now **I^know in part**

A' νυνὶ δὲ   μένει   πίστις, ἐλπίς, ἀγάπη,   (13:13)
   now but remain faith   hope **love**
τὰ τρία ταῦτα
the three these

This chiasm forms the S' element of the intermediate level chiasm in (57) which is the Y element of the high level chiasm in (55). The corresponding elements are not only conceptually parallel, but to a certain extent grammatically parallel as well.

A further example of chiasmus in the seventh discourse is found in 14:33b–36, as shown in (62).

(62)   A   Ὡς ἐν   πάσαις ταῖς ἐκκλησίαις τῶν   ἁγίων   (14:33b)
            As in   all   the   churches   of^the   saints,

           B   αἱ γυναῖκες ἐν ταῖς ἐκκλησίαις σιγάτωσαν   (14:34a)
            the **women in** the **churches** let^them^keep^silent

              C   ἀλλὰ ὑποτασσέσθωσαν,   (14:34b)
              but   let^them^be^subordinate

              C'   ἐν οἴκῳ τοὺς ἰδίους ἄνδρας   (14:35a)
              at   home their   own   husbands
ἐπερωτάτωσαν,
let^them^ask

           B'   αἰσχρὸν γάρ ἐστιν γυναικὶ   λαλεῖν   (14:35b)
            shameful for   it^is   for^a^**woman** to^speak
ἐν ἐκκλησίᾳ.
in church.

   A' ἢ   ἀφ' ὑμῶν ὁ   λόγος τοῦ   θεοῦ ἐξῆλθεν,   (14:36)
     or   from you   the   word   of   God   came^out
ἢ   εἰς ὑμᾶς μόνους κατήντησεν;
or   to   you   only   did^it^arrive?

This chiasm is purely conceptual. The point presented in a phrase at the beginning (the A element) is repeated at the end in the A' element with a compound question (or it can be analyzed as two questions).

Finally, the eighth discourse also contains an example of chiasmus in 15:12–13, as shown in (63).

(63) A *Εἰ δὲ Χριστὸς κηρύσσεται ὅτι ἐκ νεκρῶν*   (15:12)
          if but **Christ** is^preached that from the^dead
          ἐγήγερται,
          he^is^**raised**
      B *πῶς λέγουσιν ἐν ὑμῖν τινες ὅτι*
          how do^say among you some that
          ἀνάστασις νεκρῶν οὐκ ἔστιν;
          resurrection of^the^dead not there^is?
      B' *εἰ δὲ ἀνάστασις νεκρῶν οὐκ ἔστιν,*   (15:13)
          if but **resurrection of^the^dead** not there^is
      A' *οὐδὲ Χριστὸς ἐγήγερται·*
          neither **Christ** has^been^**raised**

The ninth and tenth discourses in chapter 16 are very short and do not seem to contain examples of chiasmus. The examples listed here are not exhaustive. Both Lund (1992) and Bailey (1983) list other examples, although the correspondences for some of them seem rather strained; only the most obvious have been listed above. But these are enough examples to show that Paul made ample use of the rhetorical device of chiasm at all levels of the text and that these patterns are best seen from a field perspective.

The value of multiple perspective. No single analytical perspective can shed all the light on a text that a multiple perspective approach such as tagmemics can provide. Every text contains hierarchical structuring, transitions from point to point, and various patterns, often interwoven. Only a multiple perspective approach can bring these different aspects to light. For the biblical exegete, not every structure, transition, or pattern is useful in uncovering meaning. But some of the insights provided by the multiple perspective approach are quite useful for purposes of interpretation.

The particle perspective as provided by constituent structure analysis is especially suited for uncovering the hierarchically embedded relationships within a linear text. For example, a viewpoint that would see a text as merely a concatenation of sentences, with each related primarily to its immediately preceding sentence, would miss the relationship between 1 Cor. 1:14 and 1:17. The danger is in taking verse 17 as the cause of the immediately preceding statement in verse 16 in the following way: "I do not know whether I baptized anyone else for Christ did not send me to baptize." In actuality, verse 17 is the cause of verse 14 in the following way: "I am thankful that I baptized none of you for Christ did not send me to baptize." The chart in table 11 makes it clear that this text is not merely a linear collection of concepts.

The wave perspective can also be used to shed more light on meaning. 1 Cor. 2:13 contains a subtopic transition which is completely missed by a particle analysis such as that shown in table 12. The last clause, *πνευματικοῖς πνευματικὰ συγκρίνοντες,* can be translated in two different ways: either 'interpreting spiritual things in spiritual words' or 'interpreting spiritual things to spiritual people'. The former translation fits well with the preceding *λόγοις . . . ἐν διδακτοῖς πνεύματος* 'in words taught by the Spirit'; the latter with the following *ὁ . . . πνευματικός* 'the spiritual person' in verse 15. It is difficult to decide which translation is better because both fit the context, one the preceding material and the other the following. A wave view allows the interpreter to see that it is not necessary to make a choice. The writer has apparently left the expression ambiguous so that either meaning can be applied at this pivotal point in the text. As one topic subsides, another begins, and thus there is overlap in this clause.

The third perspective also helps to clarify meaning. For example, 1 Cor. 14:33b–36 contains a chiastic pattern, as shown in (62). Fee (1987:697–98) has argued that 33b (*'Ὡς ἐν πάσαις ταῖς ἐκκλησίαις τῶν ἁγίων* 'as in all the churches of the saints') should be taken with the preceding clause in 33a (*οὐ γάρ ἐστιν ἀκαταστασίας ὁ θεὸς ἀλλὰ εἰρήνης* 'for God is not [a God] of disorder but of peace') rather than the following clause in 34a (*αἱ γυναῖκες ἐν ταῖς ἐκκλησίαις σιγάτωσαν* 'let the women keep silent in the churches'). But to do so would destroy the chiastic pattern, a pattern which has often been overlooked from ignoring a field perspective. If 33b is taken with 33a, the A' leg (verse 36) of the chiasm has no conceptual counterpart in an A leg, unless of course one says that the chiasm is built across topics. The fact that such a conceptual chiasm exists argues against Fee's position. But there are other reasons for rejecting his claim. For one thing, his argument is built on the fact that the Western manuscript tradition moves verses 34–35 to a place following verse 40. But the editors of the United Bible Societies' *Greek New Testament* have given this passage a solid B rating for inclusion at this point (Metzger 1971:565). It is most likely that scribes who failed to understand the Greek tradition of women prophets, pointed out in chapter 2 of this study, moved the heart of this admonition about women to the end of the discourse to separate it from the teaching about prophets. It is also worth noting that when verse 33b is taken with 34a, it forms a clause in the preceding dependent slot which begins with *ὡς* 'as' and also begins a paragraph. In two other places in 1 Corinthians where clauses in preceding dependent slots begin with *ὡς,* they also begin paragraphs. The transitional paragraph in 4:18–21 begins with *ὡς;* likewise, the amplification sub-paragraph in 10:15–22 begins with *ὡς.*

Other arguments could be advanced beyond these against Fee's position, but it is not the purpose of this study to disprove his point. These are presented here to illustrate the influence that discourse analysis, especially the study of constituent structures from a multiple perspective, can have on the interpretation and understanding of an ancient text. Each of these three viewpoints (particle, wave, and field) provides a perspective that complements the others and gives the reader a more complete picture.

Conclusions. This chapter has focused on the study of the smaller structures of 1 Corinthians from the triple perspective of tagmemic theory. That theory says that any text can be viewed three ways by examining its hierarchy of units (particle), transitions (wave), and patterned relationships (field).

Beginning with the particle approach, four types of structural paragraphs are found in 1 Corinthians: question-answer paragraphs, question-command paragraphs, chiastically structured paragraphs, and paragraphs with parallel structures. Orthographic paragraphs are of limited value in analyzing a text; however, by comparing them in editions of the Greek text and English translations, a rough approximation of the embedding level of each paragraph can be determined. This has the value of providing a control for the discourse analyst who approaches a text seeking to study the recursively embedded levels of paragraphs. The analysis shows that several devices are used to mark the beginnings of new paragraphs, including vocatives, exclamations, first and second person verbs, and various conjunctions. When Longacre's method of constituent structure analysis (1970; 1980; 1983a; 1989a) was applied to five passages, the following results were found: First, reason, amplification, and motivation paragraphs are at all levels of embedding, while clarification and evidence paragraphs are limited to lower levels. Second, a salience ranking chart shows that present imperatives are on the mainline of hortatory texttype. Present subjunctives when used in appeals are also on the mainline. Farther down in salience level, present indicative verbs mark several roles, including condition, explanation, introduction, and reason. Rhetorical questions are introduced to provide motivation. Still farther down in level, aorist verbs are used to show purpose and result. Finally, quotations are used to provide evidence.

The constituent structure analysis in this study was done on only five selections covering forty-six verses, chosen to illustrate different texttypes. Further analysis is needed to demonstrate that the selections, arbitrarily chosen, are in fact representative of their texttype. Ideally such an analysis should not be limited to either 1 Corinthians or Paul's letters, but should expand across several authors.

This chapter has shown that using the wave perspective three types of unusual transitions are discovered in 1 Corinthians: they can involve a change of topic within one clause, a change of topic while retaining a metaphor, and a change of topic with the corresponding grammatical signals indicating no change at all. Such areas of transition belong to both the preceding and following text, although a particle approach by its very nature assigns it to one or the other.

The field approach focuses on different patterns in 1 Corinthians, especially chiasmus. Not only do six of the discourses show major patterns of chiasmus as chapter 3 indicated, but each of the first eight discourses show chiasmus on a smaller paragraph level as well. There are three types of chiasmus that exist in 1 Corinthians: lexical, grammatical, and conceptual. Some patterns have only a single one of these types, but others show a combination of them.

Each of these three approaches to a text provides a different perspective on that text. Sometimes the same portion of text is under view, but the multiple perspectives give a more complete picture than any one approach. A chiasm can be studied as either a structured paragraph (particle view) or as a pattern of concepts (field view). A transitional paragraph can be assigned to a particular discourse or section of a discourse (particle view) or be seen as belonging to both (wave view). Not only does a multiple perspective approach provide additional linguistic frameworks for analyzing a text, it also sheds additional light on meaning. Thus a multiple perspective provides an analytical tool that no methodology using a single perspective can have.

5

Other Features of Discourse

In this chapter, the results are based on a database of clause structure in 1 Corinthians used to study the questions of peak, participant analysis, clause word order, quotations and their introducers, and the influence of the rhetorical situation on the grammatical structure of stylistic features in 1 Corinthians. Each of these areas of study is important in its own right. They are combined here because they all lend themselves to computer-assisted analysis.

First, the study of peak gives the interpreter a way to determine those parts of the text which the writer viewed as especially important. In narrative texttype, peak marking features are found in such areas as inciting incident, climax, and denouement. The exact significance of peak in non-narrative text has not yet been fully determined, but it is hypothesized that this technique is used to mark important parts of the text. Second, the study of participant tracking in subject slot gives the student of discourse a way to determine any grammatical rules that may lead the writer to use a noun, a pronoun, or simply a verb ending in referring to a given concept. Third, the study of clause-level word order gives the student a way to find the nonemphatic order so that both sentential and discourse motivations for varying the order can be isolated. Fourth, the study of quotations allows the student of a text to discover the usual ways of introducing overt intertextuality. Finally, the study of the relationship of style and rhetorical situation provides a tool for under-standing why variations in grammar occur.

The information in this chapter was compiled using a computer database containing twenty-eight variables for each clause in the book of

1 Corinthians. These variables and their possible values are listed in table 18. The database program used was ANACLAUS, developed specifically for the study of Greek clause structure. It allows the variables to be charted against one another, and against a division of the text into various sections (i.e., chapters, discourses, blocks, etc.). It also allows the production of tables showing the data in various ways for further study.

The database was constructed for this study from a chart of the Greek text of 1 Corinthians developed along the lines presented in (2) in chapter 1. Information was checked against the *Analytical Greek New Testament* (Friberg and Friberg 1981) to insure accuracy.

Table 18
Database categories for studying clause structure

Variable	Values
Chapter and verse	
Sentence location	preceding dependent, independent, following dependent
Clause type	independent, dependent, quote, relative
Relationship of this clause to others	main, subordinate, conditional, embedded noun, adjectival, adverbial, absolute
Independent relationship	I, DI, ID, DID (I = Independent; D = Dependent)
Level of embedding	0, 1, 2, 3, 4, 5
Same subject as previous	yes, no, in a previous clause, in the previous colon, new subject
Complex order description	V, VO, SVO, SVN, SVA, etc.
Order type	V, VO, SVO, VSO, VOS, OV, SOV, OSV, OVS, SV, VS, SO, OS, other
Verb mode/type	indicative, subjunctive, imperative, infinitive, participle, optative, periphrastic, modal
Verb tense	aorist, present, perfect, future, imperfect, pluperfect
Verb voice	active, middle, passive
Number	singular, plural, compound
Verb semantic type	action, motion, sensing, thinking, feeling, speech, equative, depiction, creation
Type of subject	noun, vocative, participle, clause, pronoun, article

Subject semantics	agent (actor), patient (undergoer)
Subject person	first, second, third, first and third
Subject article	no, yes, demonstrative
Type of object	noun, oblique, participle, clause, pronoun, adjective
Object case	accusative, dative, genitive, nominative
Object article	no, yes, demonstrative
Indirect object	dative pronoun, dative, accusative
Negative	positive, negative
Prepositional phrase	location, time, both, other, all
Texttype	narrative, expository, hortatory, procedural, persuasive
Number of words in clause	1, 2, 3, 4, 5, etc.
First clause in colon	yes, no
Introductory words	δέ, καί, γάρ, ὅτι, etc.
Form	statement, question, command

The database program employs the chi-square test to check for the significance of variable relationships. Where the number of occurrences in each cell of a matrix is greater than five items, this test is a valid indicator of the probability of statistical significance (Hoel 1962:244–47). For the purposes of this study, a relationship between variables that the chi-square test shows as having less than a 5% probability of being due to random factors of data is said to be significant. Similarly, a relationship between variables that the chi-square test shows as having less than a 0.5% probability of being due to random factors of data is said to be highly significant.

5.1 Peak

Sometime between the first and third centuries A.D., an unknown writer whom scholars have come to call "Longinus" wrote a treatise on Greek style entitled *On the Sublime* (Fyfe 1932:xvii–xviii). In chapters 23 to 29 of that work, Longinus discusses techniques which lend variety and liveliness to a composition through grammatical changes. Among those changes which he discusses are the expansion of the singular into the plural to convey the idea of multitude (23.2–3), the contraction of the plural into the singular to give an effect of sublimity (chap. 24), the use of the present tense in narrating past time in order to increase vividness (chap. 25), the change of the person addressed from the whole audience to a single individual also to give a vivid effect (chap. 26), the use of the first person for one of the characters to show an outbreak of emotion (chap. 27), and the use of periphrasis or circumlocution to give the work a far richer note (chap. 28–29). His conclusion is that these techniques "all serve to lend emotion and excitement to the style" (*On the Sublime* 29.2)

Recently, linguistic study in discourse has found that techniques such as these are used, not only by the Greeks, but by storytellers around the world in many, if not all, of the world's languages. In the last two decades, Longacre (1981, 1983b, 1985a, 1990b) has studied this phenomenon of grammatical change to increase emotional effects and labeled it PEAK. An extended discussion of the theory of peak is given in chapter 1 of this study. The discussion in this chapter centers on the techniques for discovering the zone or zones of peak grammatical turbulence in 1 Corinthians and the significance of such zones for hortatory texttype.

There are a couple of features, which elsewhere seem to mark peak (cf. Terry 1992:121–22 for the book of James), which do not seem productive in 1 Corinthians. One is the use of vocatives at other places than the beginning of paragraphs. Seven vocatives fall in this category. They are found in 1:11, 7:16 (bis), 7:24, 15:31, and 15:55 (bis). Of these, the one in 1:11 seems to be marking the beginning of the first discourse, the three in chapter 7 are found in the final colons of their paragraphs, and the two in 15:55 occur in a quotation. The one instance of a vocative in 15:31 without another explanation can hardly be said to be determinative of peak. The same can be said of the interjection ἰδού 'behold'. It occurs only once in 1 Corinthians, in 15:51. Even though these two items occur in the same chapter, two cases do not provide much evidence.

Actually, there are two aspects of peak which jump out at the reader who is on the lookout for a zone of grammatical turbulence in 1 Corinthians. First, the fact that chapter 15 is primarily persuasive rather than hortatory in nature is a rather obvious difference from the rest of the book. This is indicated primarily by a noticeable lack of imperatives, which serve as the mainline of hortatory text. Second, the reader may well note the large number of verbless clauses that begin to appear in the text beginning with chapter 12. These factors give an initial impression that the text from chapters 12 to 15 may contain peak material, but that impression must be checked out in a methodical manner to confirm it.

Table 19 lists three variables for each chapter in the book of 1 Corinthians. First, the number of clauses for each of four types of texttype is given for each chapter. Those places where more than fifty occurrences of one texttype are found in a chapter are indicated by bold print. Of special note is the strong hortatory nature of chapters 7 and 14 and the strong persuasive nature of chapter 15.

Table 19
Indicators of peak in 1 Corinthians

| chap. | Texttype | | | | Clause order | | No. of verbless clauses | | |
	hor.	per.	exp.	nar.	VO%	OV%	implied	equative	spread
1	4	28	47	1	68%	32%	1	12	
2	1	32		8	41%	59%		1	
3	17	33	18		40%	60%		7	1
4	72				39%	61%	1	7	1
5	26		8		58%	42%		2	1
6	61				40%	60%		4	
7	132		18		44%	56%		3	1
8	8	31	4		58%	42%		6	
9	18	71	13		39%	61%	1	1	6
10	69	21	4	8	38%	62%		4	1
11	84		15	12	42%	58%		11	3
12	1	54	33		53%	47%		19	9
13		53			57%	43%		4	1
14	131	1			38%	62%		7	
15	10	139	11	14	63%	37%	1	35	7
16	38		15	14	60%	40%		4	

The second variable in table 19 is the clause ordering of verbs and objects across the chapters. Considering all kinds of clauses, objects are slightly more likely to precede verbs in 1 Corinthians than vice versa (by a count of 370 to 331). In seven chapters (1, 5, 8, 12, 13, 15, and 16), however, there are more clauses with objects following the verbs than vice versa. These have been indicated in bold. An application of the chi-square test to this data shows that this distribution is statistically significant, that is, there is less than a 5% probability that it would occur due to random distribution of objects and verbs. Some of this turbulence may be analogous to that found around an inciting incident in narrative, for chapters 1, 5, 8, and 12 all begin multi-chapter discourses; the heavy distribution of VO clauses toward the end of the book, however, would seem to point to a peak area.

The third variable presented in table 19 is the number of verbless clauses. There are three kinds of verbless clauses in 1 Corinthians: implied, equative, and spread. In four cases (in 1:1, 4:6, 9:10, and 15:8) a verb is omitted from a clause, but it can be supplied from the context by implication. The most common situation is that forms of the equative verbs (εἰμί 'be' and γίνομαι 'be, become', often called copulas) may be omitted from equative clauses. This is a well documented fact of Greek grammar (Blass, Debrunner, and Funk 1961:70–71 [127–28]; Robertson 1934:395–96; and Turner 1963:294–98). The remarkable thing about this omission is that chapters 12 and 15 show 19 and 35 instances of this feature, respectively. In fact, chapter 15 has three major spans of text with no verbs (verses 38b–41, 45b–48, and 55–56). No other chapter shows more than 12 instances. The third kind of omission of the verb occurs in clauses where the verb would have been the same as the verb of the previous clause. The verb of the previous clause spreads across the following clause or clauses. Again, chapters 12 and 15 stand out with 9 and 7 instances of verb spreading, respectively.

All of these factors seem to point toward chapters 12, 13, and 15 as showing a marked difference from the rest of the text. From a wave perspective, chapters 12 and 13 may be the peak for the discourses in response to the Corinthians' letter, while chapter 15 may be the peak for the discourses in response to the oral reports. But from a particle perspective, it seems advisable to hypothesize that the region also includes chapter 14 and thus take the zone of grammatical turbulence as covering chapters 12 through 15. This would be confirmed by the high degree of embedded chiasmus found in chapters 12–14 while studying the field perspective. With this in mind, the database of clauses in 1 Corinthians was set to compare grammatical structures in chapters 12 through 15 against the rest of the book. When this was done, the following variables listed in table 18 showed a highly significant difference between the peak area and the rest of the book: sentence location, clause relationship, independent relationship, clause order type, verb mode, verb tense, verb voice, verb semantic type, subject type, subject person, texttype, and statement or question form. This means that for these variables there are such grammatical differences between the peak zone of chapter 12 through 15 and the rest of the book that there is less than 0.5% probability that such differences could be due to random distribution factors of these grammatical features. From this list, the twenty-one most significant factors in causing these differences have been listed in table 20.

This is not to imply that all of these factors are uniformly distributed across the peak zone. The aorist tense is still used in the peak area, but notably less frequently than in nonpeak areas. But toward the end of chapter 15, from verses 38 through 48, there is a small region of very little verb use at all. Only fifteen verbs are used at all in these eleven verses, and only two (13.3%) of them are aorist. The distribution of tense is not uniform.

Table 20
Highly significant peak indicators in 1 Corinthians
for chapters 12–15 as peak

Variable	Peak		Nonpeak	
Persuasive texttype	**55.3%**	(n = 247)	23.2%	(n = 216)
Hortatory texttype	31.8%	(n = 142)	**56.9%**	(n = 530)
Preceding clauses	**18.1%**	(n = 81)	11.0%	(n = 102)
Following clauses	8.7%	(n = 39)	**20.0%**	(n = 186)
Independent clauses	**58.2%**	(n = 260)	51.7%	(n = 481)
Dependent clauses	41.8%	(n = 187)	**48.3%**	(n = 450)
Verbless clauses	**18.6%**	(n = 83)	8.4%	(n = 79)
Conditional clauses	**12.5%**	(n = 56)	7.2%	(n = 67)
VO Clause order	**52.5%**	(n = 96)	45.4%	(n = 235)
OV Clause order	47.5%	(n = 87)	**54.6%**	(n = 283)
OS Clause order*	**56.3%**	(n = 18)	23.1%	(n = 9)
Statements	**76.5%**	(n = 342)	63.1%	(n = 587)
Questions	11.9%	(n = 53)	**15.8%**	(n = 147)
Commands	11.6%	(n = 52)	**21.2%**	(n = 197)
Aorist tense verbs†	20.6%	(n = 75)	**26.6%**	(n = 227)
Passive voice verbs†	**19.8%**	(n = 72)	14.2%	(n = 121)
Noun subjects‡	**61.4%**	(n = 154)	44.5%	(n = 203)
Pronoun subjects‡	23.1%	(n = 58)	**38.2%**	(n = 174)
First-person subjects	19.9%	(n = 89)	**24.2%**	(n = 225)
Second-person subjects	9.8%	(n = 44)	**18.5%**	(n = 172)
Third-person subjects	**69.8%**	(n = 312)	56.3%	(n = 524)

All unmarked percentages are based on 447 clauses in peak text and 931 clauses in nonpeak text.

*These percentages are based on 83 verbless clauses in peak text and 79 verbless clauses in nonpeak text.

†These percentages are based on 364 verbs in peak text and 852 verbs in nonpeak text.

‡These percentages are based on 251 overt subjects in peak text and 456 overt subjects in nonpeak text.

There is also a greater use of passive voice verbs in the peak area than in the letter as a whole. But closer examination reveals that this greater use is limited to chapter 15, where 35.9% of the verbs are in the passive voice, while chapters 12 through 14 show a 10.7% use of passive voice verbs, which is less than the average percentage of passive verbs used in the rest of 1 Corinthians. The point is that peak constitutes a zone of turbulence, but different factors change at different rates.

The question remains as to the significance of peak in the book of 1 Corinthians. Peak can hardly be said to constitute a hortatory climax in a region of text where the primary texttype is persuasive rather than hortatory. Of course, there is a relationship between persuasive and hortatory texttype. Persuasive text tends to influence the reader toward a different belief, while hortatory text tries to get the reader to change a course of action. This distinction is similar to that noted by Stowers in ancient letters of advice: "When advice calls for a specific course of action it is deliberative; when it only seeks to increase adherence to a value or to cultivate a character trait it is epideitic" (1986:107). Just as both texttypes convey advice, so both texttypes rely on motivation to achieve their ends. These similarities between these texttypes may indicate that peak does mark a kind of advice climax here. Since it is in a letter, it could also be called an epistolary climax.

It is also worth noting that this peak area covers two of the discourses, one in response to the Corinthians' letter (chapters 12–14) and one in response to the oral reports (chapter 15). Perhaps there is a peak for each of these response types.

However that may be, it can be said that the peak area in 1 Corinthians does indicate topics about which Paul felt and showed a marked increase in emotion and wanted to convey that emotion to his intended audience. He was deeply concerned about the oneness of the body of Christians as it was endowed with different spiritual gifts. Likewise, he considered the topic of the resurrection to be a matter of first importance (cf. 1 Cor. 15:3).

This is further signified by the fact that these topics are the ones mentioned in the opening thanksgiving in 1:4–9. There Paul mentions that the Corinthians had all speech (both prophecy and speaking in tongues) and all knowledge and were "not lacking in any spiritual gift" (1:5–6). These themes are discussed in full in chapters 12 through 14. He goes on to say that the Corinthians were waiting "for the revealing of the Lord Jesus Christ" who would sustain them as "guiltless in the day of our Lord Jesus Christ" (1:7–8). That day is thoroughly treated in the discussion about the resurrection in chapter 15.

New Testament studies in the Epistles have taken seriously Schubert's proposal that the opening thanksgiving often suggested the purpose of the letter and outlined its key topics (Doty 1973:32–33; Stowers 1986:21–22). There has been some attempt to make the opening thanksgiving of 1 Corinthians fit this pattern, but the efforts fall short. The macrostructures of the ten discourses cover much more material than the few items noted in the thanksgiving.

To be sure, Bailey (1983:157) has tried to make his five-fold analysis of 1 Corinthians fit the thanksgiving. But the weaknesses of his method have already been discussed in chapter 3 of this study. In addition, he tries to identify the discussion of wisdom in 1 Corinthians 1–4 with the "all speech" and "all knowledge" of 1:5 in the thanksgiving. The problem is that wisdom is not mentioned in the thanksgiving and knowledge is not mentioned again until chapter 8 ("all knowledge" not until 13:2). Further, Bailey's (1983:157) identification of guiltless in 1:8 with the discussion of sexual matters in chapters 5–7 falls far short since the Corinthians could hardly be said to be guiltless in sexual matters.

Stowers' (1986:22) identification of knowledge in the thanksgiving with chapters 1–4 and 8 is open to the same kinds of criticism. It is very difficult to identify the Corinthians' "all knowledge" (1:5) with their reliance on man's wisdom which was causing them to boast about men (3:19–21). Similarly, it is difficult to identify it with the knowledge about idols in chapter 8 which all did not have (8:2, 7). Stowers' identification of knowledge with chapters 12–14 seems much better.

All of this is to suggest that the themes of the opening thanksgiving in 1 Corinthians point primarily to the items covered in the peak material of chapters 12–15, not to the whole letter. Perhaps in other New Testament books that have a unified macrostructure, a similar relationship between thanksgiving and peak material holds, but it is masked by the fact that the peak material brings to a climax the discussion of themes that are central to the whole letter. The matter is worthy of further research.

5.2 Participant reference

To date, most of the work on participant reference has been done on narrative texttype. Longacre (1989b:141–57) devotes chapter 6 of his study on the Joseph narrative in Genesis to participant reference. K. Callow (1974:32–37) discusses participants as they relate to cohesion mainly in terms of the Gospel narratives. Grimes (1972:43–50) discusses participants in a number of nonbiblical narratives. But theme-oriented texttypes (i.e., expository, hortatory, and persuasive) differ from sequential event texttypes (narrative and procedural) in that the themeline is more prominent in the former than in the latter.

To be sure, epistolary texts do contain a storyline as well as a themeline. But the storyline in letters has to do with such items as what the writer has been doing, what the writer hears the reader has been doing, letters that the writer has written to the reader, letters that the writer has received from the reader, and plans that the writer has for the future, especially any travel plans that relate to seeing the reader. All of these elements are present in the letter of 1 Corinthians. But an epistolary storyline has few restrictions on temporal ordering compared with a narrative. While letters may be written that are primarily epistolary storyline, letters of advice, such as 1 Corinthians, have a primary themeline and only a secondary storyline.

This primary themeline has a significant effect on participant reference. First, the central participants are the writer and the readers. This is signaled by use of the first-person and second-person grammatical categories, respectively. Second, if the letter is primarily concerned with advice, the majority of subject slots refer not to participants or props, but to key concepts within themes. Finally, unless the topic is fairly unified, the themes (as contained in the subject slots) may change quite often so that there are few long chains of reference to one concept. All three of these features are characteristic of 1 Corinthians.

Greek has several grammatical devices to point to conceptual reference, whether of participants, props, or themes. These include clauses embedded within subject and object slots, noun phrases, nouns (both with an article and without), vocative nouns, participles, pronouns, articles alone, and verb suffixes. In addition, it is also possible to have null reference, where a grammatical trace is missing, but the reference is obviously to a concept which has already been introduced. This is the regular case with the subject of infinitives, which are often missing but are frequently the same as the subject of the main verb in the sentence. With other verb forms, the verb ending provides a minimal trace to help provide reference to the concept in focus. This being the case, all other examples of null reference are found in object slots. Greek will sometimes omit objects which are obligatory in English, but the possibilities of the available concepts occurring with the verb being used serves to limit the reference. The reader knows what concept is being acted upon in the clause because no other concept makes good sense.

Most of these grammatical devices may be used to switch the reference to a new concept, resume reference to a concept already introduced (whether currently under discussion or not), or continue reference to the same concept that has been the primary focus. But there are certain preferred forms for each of these tasks. Table 21 presents the relationships between the subject slot grammatical devices and these tasks.

Table 21

Relationship of grammatical devices and tracking tasks for 1 Corinthians

Grammatical device	Continuation of same subject	Resumption from clause or colon	New or different reference
Clause	3.7% (n = 20)	1.3% (n = 2)	3.2% (n = 22)
Noun or NP	6.3% (n = 34)	25.9% (n = 41)	41.4% (n = 281)
Vocative	0.2% (n = 1)	0.6% (n = 1)	0.9% (n = 6)
Participle	0.6% (n = 3)	0.6% (n = 1)	1.0% (n = 7)
Pronoun	12.4% (n = 67)	20.3% (n = 32)	19.7% (n = 134)
Article	2.6% (n = 14)	1.3% (n = 2)	5.7% (n = 39)
Verb suffix	74.2% (n = 400)	50.0% (n = 79)	28.0% (n = 190)
Totals	539	158	679

These tracking tasks can be defined as follows. The first tracking task is the continuation of the same subject as that used in the previous clause. The second task is the immediate resumption of a subject previously mentioned in a previous clause within the same colon or the immediately preceding colon following the introduction of a different subject. The final task is the introduction of a different subject. This category includes both resumption of subjects which have not been used in the current or preceding colons and subjects which are entirely new.

From table 21 it is possible to see that the three major subject slot devices used to express reference are the noun, the pronoun, and the verb suffix. The frequency of each of these varies markedly depending upon the reference task being carried out. For example, in 74.2% of the cases where the same concept must be referred to, the grammatical device used is the verb suffix. Nouns or noun phrases are used only 6.3% of the time to carry out this task. Pronouns are used in this situation only 12.4% of the time. Where the task is to resume a reference to a concept that has been mentioned in a previous clause in the colon or in the previous colon, pronoun usage increases to 20.3% and noun usage to 25.9%. The usage of 50.0% verb endings to express this resumption does not produce as much ambiguity as might be thought in a language which marks number and person on finite verbs and number and gender on participles. Finally the introduction of a new concept or resumption of a concept not recently referred to is done with nouns in 41.4% of the time. Pronoun usage stays about the same (19.7%), but reliance on verb ending usage alone drops to

28.0%. The chi-square test shows the skewed distribution of grammatical devices and reference tasks to be highly significant.

If the 21 new concepts introduced in subject slots are split out of the last column of table 21 and looked at alone, 19 (86.4%) are introduced by nouns or noun phrases. One is introduced by a participial clause (those baptized on account of *[ὑπέρ]* the dead in 15:29) and one by the indefinite pronoun *τινα* 'someone' (in 5:1). No new concepts are referred to only by verb endings. The primary way in which new concepts are introduced in 1 Corinthians is to position them in object slots (either as direct objects, indirect objects, or objects of prepositions). It is notable that only 21 new concepts are introduced as subjects.

Several other variables are highly significant when compared with the same or a different subject. Table 22 shows how the tracking tasks relate to the three major divisions of a colon or sentence. There is no significant difference as to how the tasks are distributed between preceding dependent clauses and independent clauses, but there is a highly significant difference between the distribution of tracking tasks in these types of clauses and in dependent clauses that follow the independent clause. These following dependent clauses show a much higher frequency (47.1% as compared with 37.5% to 38.3%) of retaining the same subject as previously mentioned. In the same way, different subjects are much more likely to be found in preceding dependent clauses (48.1%) and independent clauses (52.3%) than in following dependent clauses (37.7%).

Table 22
Relationship of tracking tasks and sentence location for 1 Corinthians

Tracking task	Preceding dependent	Independent	Following dependent
Same subject	38.3% (n = 70)	37.5% (n = 364)	47.1% (n = 105)
Resumed	13.6% (n = 25)	10.2% (n = 99)	15.2% (n = 34)
Different	48.1% (n = 88)	52.3% (n = 507)	37.7% (n = 84)

There is a similar situation when the first clause in a colon is compared with the clauses that follow it, as shown in table 23. Once again, following clauses show a much higher rate (48.4% as compared to 25.3%) of retaining the same subject than first clauses in a colon do. First clauses within colons introduce different subjects in 64.9% of the cases, while following clauses introduce different subjects in only 39.0% of the cases. This distribution of tracking tasks is also highly significant statistically.

Since first clauses can occur as either a preceding dependent clause or in an independent one, but not as a following dependent clause, it may be that the distribution shown in table 23 is responsible for the difference in distribution shown in table 22 between the following dependent clause and the other two types.

Table 23

Relationship of tracking tasks and clause location for 1 Corinthians

Tracking task	First clause	Following clauses
Same subject	25.3% (n=140)	48.4% (n=399)
Resumed	9.8% (n=54)	12.6% (n=104)
Different	64.9% (n=358)	39.0% (n=321)

There is also a highly significant difference in tracking tasks when they are distributed across different types of colons or sentences (either statement, question, or command), as shown in table 24. Statements are more likely (41.0% as compared to 34.0% or 36.4%) to continue the same subject as previously than either questions or commands. Questions are more likely (58.0% as compared with 48.7% or 44.9%) to begin a new or different subject than either statements or commands. Commands are more likely (18.6% as compared to 10.3% or 8.0%) to resume a subject which was discussed in a previous clause or the previous colon than either statements or questions.

Table 24

Relationship of tracking tasks and statement or question for 1 Corinthians

Tracking task	Statement	Question	Command
Same subject	41.0% (n=381)	34.0% (n=68)	36.4% (n=90)
Resumed	10.3% (n=96)	8.0% (n=16)	18.6% (n=46)
Different	48.7% (n=452)	58.0% (n=116)	44.9% (n=111)

Texttype is another variable which shows a significant difference in the way that tracking tasks are distributed throughout a text. Table 25 shows that the narrative texttype embedded in 1 Corinthians is significantly different from the non-narrative texttypes. It shows a 54% rate of retaining the same subject, while the most that any non-narrative texttype shows is a 40% retention rate. Conversely, clauses in narrative texttype begin new or different subjects only 33% of the time, while non-narrative texttypes show rates of 47% to 57% for this tracking task. But the significance of table 25 is not limited to the difference between narrative and non-narrative texttypes. Even the differences between the hortatory and persuasive texttypes (which seem to be the most similar) are statistically significant. Expository texttype shows markedly less (33% as compared with 39% or 40%) of the same subject tracking and markedly more (57% as compared with 47% or 51%) of different subject tracking than either hortatory or persuasive texttypes.

Table 25

Relationship of tracking tasks and texttype for 1 Corinthians

Tracking task	Narrative	Hortatory	Persuasive	Expository
Same subject	54% (n = 31)	39% (n = 261)	40% (n = 185)	33% (n = 62)
Resumed	12% (n = 7)	14% (n = 92)	9% (n = 40)	10% (n = 19)
Different	33% (n = 19)	47% (n = 317)	51% (n = 238)	57% (n = 105)

Some of this difference in texttypes, as far as tracking tasks is concerned, may be due to the difference in tracking task distribution as it relates to subject person. Table 26 shows how tracking tasks relate to first-, second-, and third-person subjects. Note that third-person subjects (which characterize expository texttype) show a highly significant difference from either first- or second-person subjects when compared on either the same or different subject tasks. First person (with 58.3%) has more continuance of the same subject than second person (41.7%), which has more continuance of the same subject than third person (31.2%). The use of the first person (with 28.7%) is much less likely to introduce a new or different subject than either second person (with 42.1%) or especially third person (with 59.1%).

Table 26

Relationship of tracking tasks and subject person for 1 Corinthians

Tracking task	First person	Second person	Third person
Same Subject	58.3% (n = 183)	41.7% (n = 90)	31.2% (n = 261)
Resumed	13.0% (n = 41)	16.2% (n = 35)	9.7% (n = 81)
Different	28.7% (n = 90)	42.1% (n = 91)	59.1% (n = 494)

Perhaps this difference accounts for the fact that of the fifty-seven chains of four or more consecutive subject references to the same concept in 1 Corinthians, twenty-two use the first person and fourteen use the second person. These chains are listed in table 27. This table shows both the length of some reference chains and the grammatical devices used to maintain those chains.

The first column in table 27 lists the verses in which the chains begin. The size column gives the number of clauses for each chain. The next column lists the tracking task of the first clause to refer to the subject of the chain. There are four possible beginning types: new, different, colon, and clause. New is the first introduction of a topic to the letter. Different is the use of a topic which has not recently been used as a subject. Colon is resumption of a topic which appeared in a subject slot in the previous colon. Clause is resumption of a topic which appeared in the subject of a previous clause within the same colon. The fourth column gives the person and number of the subject being tracked. Where the person and number is changed within the chain, the change is given after a slash. The next column gives the number of colons over which the chain extends. The final column gives a representation of the grammatical categories that make up the chain. Bold print is used to identify the point or points at which the person and number begin or switch.

The longest same reference chains in 1 Corinthians are found in either the first person or third person. Four chains of the same reference for fifteen or more subject slots occur in 1 Corinthians. It is perhaps significant that two of these four chains occur in the peak section of chapters 12 through 15. That is 50% of the very long chains in 25% of the letter. It is not the presence of such chains that is significant, but their frequency.

The first long chain is found beginning in 4:10 and extending for eighteen subject slots over five different colons. It begins with a first-person plural pronoun (ἡμεῖς 'we') and extends for fourteen more subject slots using first-person verb endings only. Then it narrows the focus by shifting to first-person singular verb endings for three more subject slots.

The second long chain of same subject reference begins in 9:18 and extends across eight colons filling twenty subject slots. This is the longest such chain in the letter. With the exception of the tenth subject slot (filled by the pronoun αὐτός 'self', in context meaning 'myself'), all same-subject tracking is carried forward by first-person singular verb endings.

Table 27
Chains of four or more consecutive references to the same concept

Start	Size	Beginning type	Person/ number	Colons	Grammatical categories
1:12	5	diff.	2s/1s	1	ppppp
1:26	4	diff.	2p/3p	1	vnnn
1:27	5	diff.	3s	1	nenen
1:30	5	diff.	1s	2	peeee
3:18	4	diff.	3s	1	peee
4:3	4	diff.	1s	3	eeee
4:7	9	diff.	2s/2p	6	eeeeeeee
4:10	18	colon	1p/1s	5	peeeeeeeeeeeeeeeee
6:9	5	diff.	2p	5	eeepe
6:11	4	diff.	2p	2	peee
6:19	5	clause	2p	4	eeeee
7:10	4	diff.	3s	1	neee
7:25	4	diff.	1s/4s	1	eece
7:27	4	diff.	2s	3	eeee
7:36	4	clause	3s/3p	3	peee
7:37	6	diff.	3s	1	peeeec
7:39	5	colon	3s	2	eeeee
8:8	4	diff.	1p	2	eeee
8:13	5	diff.	1s	4	eeeee
9:4	5	diff.	1p	2	eeeee
9:12	4	colon	1p	2	eeee
9:16	5	diff.	1s	3	eeeee
9:18	20	diff.	1s	8	eeeeeeeeepeeeeeeeeee
9:26	8	diff.	1s	3	peeeepee
10:1	6	diff.	3p	2	nppppe
10:7	5	diff.	3s/3p	1	neeee
10:12	4	diff.	3s	1	aece
10:23	4	diff.	3s	2	pppp
10:31	4	diff.	2p	1	eeee
11:5	5	diff.	3s	3	neene
11:22	4	colon	2p	2	eeee
11:22	5	diff.	1s	4	eeepe
11:23	5	diff.	3s	1	neeee
11:26	5	diff.	2p	2	eeeee
11:28	6	diff.	3s	2	neeace

Start	Size	Beginning type	Person/ number	Colons	Grammatical categories
11:31	5	diff.	1p	2	eeeee
12:1	5	diff.	2p	2	peeee
12:15	4	new	3s/1s	1	neee
12:16	4	new	3s/1s	1	neee
12:29	7	diff.	3p	7	ppppppp
12:31	15	diff.	1s	4	eeeeeeeeeeeeeee
13:4	16	diff.	3s	3	nneneeeeeeeeeeen
13:11	6	diff.	1s	2	eeeeee
14:6	4	diff.	1s	1	eeee
14:15	4	diff.	1s	2	eeee
14:18	5	diff.	1s	2	eeeee
14:26	6	diff.	2p/3s	1	epeeee
15:3	6	diff.	3s	2	neeeee
15:7	4	colon	3s	2	eeee
15:9	6	diff.	1s	2	ppeeee
15:30	4	diff.	1p/1s	3	peee
15:36	4	diff.	3s	2	ceee
15:42	7	diff.	3s	4	eeeeeen
16:1	4	colon	2p/3s	2	ppee
16:5	4	colon	1s	2	eeee
16:6	5	clause	1s	2	eeeee
16:13	4	diff.	2p	1	eeee

Size is the number of subjects. Bold type in the last column indicates a beginning point or shift in person and number.

Abbreviations used: s singular, p plural, n noun, v vocative, c clause, p pronoun, a article, e verb ending

The last two long chains occur in the peak sections. The third such chain begins in 12:31 and extends across four colons filling fifteen subject slots. It is carried forward entirely by first-person singular verb endings. The fourth long subject chain begins immediately after that in 13:4 and fills sixteen subject slots across three colons. It differs from the others in that it carries the third-person concept ἀγάπη 'love'. The concept of love has already been mentioned in the direct object slot of the three preceding colons. The chain begins with the noun in the first two subject slots, then a verb ending in the next clause, and then the noun in the fourth subject slot. It continues on with just third-person singular verb endings, and concludes in 13:8 with the repeat of the noun in the sixteenth and final subject slot in the chain. It becomes obvious from this that long third-person subject chains are more complex than first-person subject chains.

From table 27 it is possible to see that many of the chains in first person and second person are carried entirely by verb endings. This is the case for fourteen of the twenty-two first-person chains and seven of the fourteen second-person chains. By contrast, only two (in 7:39 and 15:7) of the twenty-one third-person chains are carried entirely by verb endings, and in both of these cases, the first reference in the chain resumes a subject which was previously mentioned by a noun. In 7:39 the noun occurs in the previous colon, and in 15:7 the noun occurs at the beginning of the chain begun in 15:3, which subject is resumed in 15:7.

Perhaps the most unusual third-person chain begins in 15:42 extending across four colons and filling seven (or perhaps eight, if the two bodies are seen as identical) subject slots. Here the ψυχικόν 'soulical' body which dies is contrasted with the spiritual body which will be raised. But the noun σῶμα 'body' is postponed until the end of the chain, and the chain is carried at first by verb endings.

All of the other third-person chains begin with either a noun (in eleven cases), a pronoun (in five cases), a clause (once, in 15:36), or an article (once, in 10:12). This is in sharp contrast to first-person chains (where only six chains begin with pronouns) and second-person chains (where only four chains begin with pronouns and only one with a noun). The last mentioned begins in 1:26 with a vocative noun ἀδελφοί 'brothers', referring to the Corinthians, and continues with three uses of the third person πολλοί 'many'.

The other grammatical device worthy of note for carrying a same subject chain is a series of pronouns. The second-person case begins in 1:12 with the phrase ἕκαστος ὑμῶν 'each of you' and continues for four subject slots with first-person singular pronoun ἐγώ 'I'. The third-person examples are found in 10:23 and in 12:29, repeatedly using the words πάντα 'all things' and πάντες 'all people', respectively.

Finally, the relation between subject tracking tasks and word order within a clause needs to be explored. Table 28 gives the word order within clauses for noun subjects as distributed among tracking tasks. The table has been divided into three general areas: word orders in which the subject precedes the verb, word orders in which the subject follows the verb, and word orders without a verb. The totals for all three of these areas do not show a statistical significance for the distribution, but the difference between the first two areas is statistically significant.

Table 28
Relationship of clause order and tracking
tasks for subject nouns in 1 Corinthians

Clause order	Continuation of same subject	Resumption from clause or colon	Different reference	New reference
SV	6	9	51	1
SVO	3	4	29	1
SOV	3	5	48	4
OSV	0	0	4	0
Totals	(34.3%) 12	(43.9%) 18	(50.4%) 132	(31.6%) 6
Verbal	(48.0%)	(56.3%)	(71.7%)	(46.2%)
VS	7	13	22	3
VSO	3	0	4	3
VOS	0	0	10	1
OVS	3	1	16	0
Totals	(37.1%) 13	(34.1%) 14	(19.8%) 52	(36.8%) 7
Verbal	(52.0%)	(43.7%)	(28.3%)	(53.8%)
SO	5	1	11	3
OS	1	1	21	0
other	4	7	46	3
Totals	(28.6%) 10	(22.0%) 9	(29.8%) 78	(31.6%) 6

The data for new and different reference have been split into separate columns for table 28 because these show quite different results. New references are those topics that are introduced for the first time in the letter at this point. Different references are those that are not new to the letter but are different from those topics used as a subject in the immediately preceding context; they include both topics that have been introduced in an object slot and those that are resumed from a subject slot found at least two colons previously.

Omitting for the moment the SO and OS clauses and just looking at clauses with verbs, 71.7% of the nouns that introduce a different subject than one recently discussed are found in an SV word order, while only 46.2% of the subject nouns that introduce a new topic to the letter are found in this order. There is perhaps a correlation between the fact that a majority of new topics are introduced in an object slot and over half of those introduced in a subject slot follow the verb, but that would require further work in object slot participant tracking which is beyond the scope of this study. It is noteworthy that among those clauses that introduce new topics in the subject slot, only one has the object preceding the subject. Again, in clauses with verbs, the majority of the subjects which continue the same topic (52.0%) are also found in a VS word order, while 48.0% have a SV word order. Conversely, 56.3% of those subjects which resume a recently discussed topic favor an SV word order, while only 43.7% have a VS word order. It seems likely that resumption favors subject fronting, with the probability of fronting increasing as the distance to the previous discussion of the topic increases.

The analysis of participant reference tracking in this study has been limited to items that occur in subject slots. The same kind of analysis needs to be done for items that occur in all kinds of object slots: direct objects, object complements, indirect objects, and objects of prepositions. There is also a need for tracking reference tasks across both subjects and objects. Specifically, when different subjects occur in the text, this study has not distinguished between those that are resumed from a distant subject slot and those which are picked up from an object slot. Such a distinction may or may not prove a useful tool of analysis.

5.3 Clause word order

Greek is a synthetic language rather than analytic; that is, grammatical slots, such as subject and object, are shown by inflectional case endings, rather than by word order. This means that word order in Greek is free to serve other functions, usually on a discourse level. Roberts has noted, "the classical writers make the freest use, for rhetorical effects (such as emphasis, euphony, variety, etc.), of the departure from normal order which, in an inflected language, is usually possible without ambiguity" (1912:178). But this raises the question of what was normal word order in a clause for Koiné Greek.

Although it was possible to form clauses in all six permutations of subject, object, and verb (SVO, SOV, VSO, VOS, OVS, OSV) in Koiné Greek, in actual fact certain constructions were preferable to others. In general, those orders in which the subject preceded the object were used more frequently than those in which the object preceded the subject. Roberts refers to the subject-object order as "natural" and the object-subject order as "unnatural" (1912:178). Evidence from this study will bear that out. This is the same order that Friberg found in his study of word order in the Gospel of Luke (1982:204–6; cf. J. Callow 1983a:13).

When the question arises as to which of the three possible subject-object word orders is normal, there is little consensus among Greek grammarians. Blass has suggested that predicate-subject-object is the normal Greek word order for New Testament narrative, but Debrunner qualifies this by noting that the verb in initial position is "common only with verbs of saying" (Blass, Debrunner, and Funk 1961:248 [472]). Debrunner further suggests that the good number of clauses with verb initial order in Mark are due to Semitic influence in that book (Blass, Debrunner, and Funk 1961:248 [472]). Robertson (1934:417) refers to Blass with approval, broadening the restriction from narrative to prose, but then qualifying his statement to say that spontaneity is the only unalterable Greek rule.

Moulton and Howard (1920:416–17) refer to Wellhausen and Norden as authorities who note that the verb first in a clause is a sure sign of Semitism, but they cite Lagrange and Torrey as experts who oppose this. They also give the results of Kieckers' research that suggests that the normal order for the verb in classical literature was primarily in the middle position, followed by the final position, and last of all in initial position, while the New Testament Gospels vary from this in that initial position is used more than final (Moulton and Howard 1920:417–18). Turner (1963:347) suggests that the normal order of ancient Greek was subject-object-verb, and that the verb initial order is an idiosyncrasy of Biblical Greek through Semitic influence. In this, he refers to Rife (1933:250), who, restricting himself to main declarative clauses with noun subjects and objects, found that classical Greek favored the SOV word order followed closely by the SVO word order. By contrast, he shows that the Greek translation of the first five books of the Old Testament slavishly follows the Hebrew word order, restricting itself to VSO most of the time (Rife 1933:250). Turning to the New Testament, Rife's results are shown in table 29, supplemented by data from the ANACLAUS databases for James and 1 Corinthians.

According to table 29, the primary word order for both narrative and hortatory books is SVO, followed by VSO in the narrative books and SOV in the hortatory books. For object emphasis orders, OVS is preferred to both VOS and OSV for both narrative and hortatory books. Rife's point is to show that the Gospels are not translations of an Aramaic original, but Matthew's Gospel approaches the 65.7% SVO order of Biblical Aramaic from the book of Daniel (1933:251).

The analysis of Greek word order, however, cannot be limited to statistical tabulations of data. As Turner notes, "requirements of emphasis will everywhere upset rules of word-order" (1963:348). Robertson says, "emphasis consists in removing a word from its usual position to an unusual one" (1934:417).

Table 29
Primary word order for main declarative clauses
in selected New Testament books

Book	VSO	SVO	SOV	VOS	OSV	OVS
Matthew	12.5%	62.5%	12.5%	—	—	12.5%
	(n=1)	(n=5)	(n=1)	(n=0)	(n=0)	(n=1)
Mark	16.7%	50.0%	22.2%	—	5.6%	5.6%
	(n=3)	(n=9)	(n=4)	(n=0)	(n=1)	(n=1)
Luke	23.1%	48.7%	20.5%	5.1%	—	2.6%
	(n=9)	(n=19)	(n=8)	(n=2)	(n=0)	(n=1)
John	—	40.0%	30.0%	10.0%	20.0%	—
	(n=0)	(n=4)	(n=3)	(n=1)	(n=2)	(n=0)
Acts	13.3%	68.9%	2.2%	2.2%	2.2%	11.1%
	(n=6)	(n=31)	(n=1)	(n=1)	(n=1)	(n=5)
Narrative	15.8%	56.7%	14.2%	3.3%	3.3%	6.7%
books	(n=19)	(n=68)	(n=17)	(n=4)	(n=4)	(n=8)
Romans	—	40.0%	50.0%	—	—	10.0%
	(n=0)	(n=4)	(n=5)	(n=0)	(n=0)	(n=1)
1 Corinthians	—	52.9%	23.5%	5.9%	5.9%	11.8%
	(n=0)	(n=9)	(n=4)	(n=1)	(n=1)	(n=2)
James	11.1%	44.4%	44.4%	—	—	—
	(n=1)	(n=4)	(n=4)	(n=0)	(n=0)	(n=0)
Hortatory	2.8%	47.2%	36.1%	2.8%	2.8%	8.3%
books	(n=1)	(n=17)	(n=13)	(n=1)	(n=1)	(n=3)

Data are restricted to main declarative clauses with noun subjects and objects. Data for the first six books are taken from Rife 1933:250. Data from Matthew, John, and Romans are restricted to a sampling of the first ten occurrences only.

In the following analysis, it will be shown that the usual word order positions differ from clause to clause according to the syntactic constructions of each clause. The two primary clause orders apart from discourse considerations are SVO and SOV.

In recent years, some progress has been made in identifying factors on a discourse level that cause changes in word order in Greek. Friberg (1982:9–10) has classified these factors into four categories: syntactic, semantic, pragmatic, and stylistic. An example of his syntactic category is the relative clause, which regularly begins with a relative pronoun. Among the semantic factors he lists are emphasis and topicalization. His pragmatic factors include afterthought, interruption, and the hearer's or reader's ability to process the information signal. Finally, he lists variation as a stylistic factor.

To this list, Radney adds the concept of MOTIF, which he defines as "a usually-recurring item (i.e., character, prop, or concept) in a text that contributes in some prominent way to the theme of a larger grammatical unit" (1988:60). J. Callow (1983b:15) sees this as comparable to Friberg's category of general emphasis. Other factors which Radney identifies as influencing word order include relative and interrogative clauses, pronouns, correlative constructions, negation, and the introduction of new subjects (1988:13, 19, 27, 40, and 48).

A factor which neither Friberg nor Radney considers but which Rife (1933) has shown to be very real is the influence of the original order of a translated text. The Hebrew VSO order has markedly affected word order in the translation of the Old Testament into Greek. This in turn produced a word order for biblical Greek which seems to have influenced writers trying to sound scriptural (cf. Moulton and Howard 1920:478). This influence of another language on a synthetic language such as Greek is also seen when the writer is a speaker of Greek as a second language. The word order of a primary language can have an ordering effect on the order of Greek. This means that native speakers of Hebrew would prefer a VSO order (Turner 1963:348), native speakers of Aramaic a SVO order (Rife 1933:251), and native speakers of Latin a SOV order (Wheelock 1960:15) in their use of Greek. The fact that Coptic has a VSO word order (Plumley 1977:143) helps explain why Rife found that the Greek papyri, mostly from Egypt, had a 40% VSO word order (1933:250), which is an unusually high percentage with the exception of translation to Greek from a Hebrew original.

Although Friberg and Radney have done New Testament discourse studies a service by suggesting discourse level factors that help to account for Greek word order, they have both suggested that the underlying unmarked word order for Greek is VSO (Friberg 1982:207; Radney 1988:2; cf. J. Callow 1983a:20–21; 1983b:4, 18). This is less than desirable for several reasons.

First, word order typology is traditionally based upon dominant order rather than underlying order. Greenberg's first universal principle of word order applies to the dominant order of "declarative sentences with nominal subject and object" (1963:61), which is very similar to the restrictions with which Rife (1933) worked. The reason for this restriction is that certain syntactic categories show a different word order. Greenberg's universals 11 and 12 relate to different orders that questions may have (1963:65). Comrie (1981:83) has pointed out that clauses with pronouns may also have a different word order than those with nouns. He also notes that there has been some discussion as to the basic word order of German; the dominant order for main clauses is SVO, while for subordinate clauses it is SOV (Comrie 1981:83). Comrie goes on to point out that "surface structure typologists tend to opt for main clause order as less marked, while transformational-generative grammarians tend to opt for subordinate clause word order as more basic" (1981:83). It is possible to maintain that SOV is the underlying order that is transformed to SVO through a rule that the verb or its auxiliary must come second in a main clause. But even here, the underlying order is dominant in subordinate clauses and the debate is about which dominant order is basic. The word order VSO is not dominant for any syntactic category in Koiné Greek, as the next point shows.

Second, the statistical data seems to be against taking Greek as a verb initial language. This is demonstrated below for 1 Corinthians from the ANACLAUS database, but even Friberg's and Radney's research illustrate it. Of fifty-five clauses in Luke that have noun subjects, simple noun objects, and indicative verbs, only fifteen (27.3%) show VSO word order (Friberg 1982:30, 33–34). In fact, taking all clauses in Luke that show both a single overt subject and a verb, only 481 of 1,179 (40.8%) clauses show the verb initial (Friberg 1982:191). In defining the unmarked case for subject, object, and indirect object orders, Friberg appeals to the greater frequency as defining the unmarked case (1982:204, 207). It is only in defining verb-subject order that Friberg abandons his principle that greater frequency indicates the unmarked case (1982:192). In addition, Cervin (1993:63) has shown that it is the SVO order which is statistically significant in Friberg's data.

Radney too must deal with the fact that not many examples of VSO occur in the book of Hebrews. He gives only two examples (Hebrews 4:2 and 4:4; cf. Radney 1988:11) and comments on "the outlandish rarity of VSO clauses in the data" (Radney 1988:12). One of his examples is a quotation from Genesis (which is highly VSO in order). To be sure, the Hebrew original and Septuagint translation do not have an overt subject (they are VO order). But the preceding clause in Genesis 2:2 is VSO with subject spreading into the clause quoted, and Radney overlooks the possibility of a Biblical Greek word order as mentioned above being used to make the quote sound scriptural.

Third, two major factors given by Friberg for the frequency of the subject preceding the verb in Luke are problematic. The first of these factors is topicalization (Friberg 1982:197–99). J. Callow (1983a:18) notes that Friberg accounts for 31% of fronted subjects using this device. The problem with this is in separating the topic from the subject. To be sure, there is such a thing as object topicalization (cf. Foley and van Valin 1985:355–58). But the unmarked situation is that the subject is the topic of a sentence; even Friberg admits this for his unmarked VSO order (1982:197). If this is the case, in what sense can the subject of a SVO clause be said to be topicalized in a way different than the subject of a VSO clause? Even a VSO clause must have a topic. The problem is so severe that Radney (1988:13) disavows using the term topic to explain subject fronting. He rightly notes, "there is the question of why marked topicalization is necessary at all, since the grammatical subject of a clause should automatically be interpreted as the topic" (Radney 1988:13).

The other problematic factor that Friberg identifies for subject fronting is emphasis. To be sure, there is such a thing as emphasis. When an object is fronted, it is emphasized because this is a less usual position. But if the subject before the verb is the more usual case, in what sense can a subject be emphasized by moving it from the less common to the more common position? If Robertson is correct in saying, "emphasis consists in removing a word from its usual position to an unusual one" (1934:417), the shift of a subject from a position following the verb to one preceding it would serve to deemphasize that subject.

Fourth, the identification of Greek as a dominantly VSO language tends to be an abstract interpretation, since that order is not reflected as the principal word order in any Greek text studied by scholars except for those that are translations of a Hebrew original (cf. the chart in Rife 1933:250). There is the problem that any abstract solution can be interpreted in alternative ways. In addition, if topicalization is allowed as a legitimate reason for fronting a subject, English could be abstractly interpreted as a VSO language in which the subject is fronted whenever it is the topic. Since the subject in English is almost always the topic, this could explain the fact that English shows SVO order in its surface structure. An abstract interpretation such as this is unacceptable for English. By analogy, it should not be acceptable for Greek either.

Finally, Friberg chooses the VSO word order as primary because he states that "attempts to explain the subject following the verb are in vain" (1982:192). Actually, there are several reasons why the subject may follow the verb. It has already been noted that Debrunner points out that many of the cases of the subject following the verb occur with verbs of speaking while others are due to Semitic influence (Blass, Debrunner, and Funk 1961:248 [472]). In fact, the two VSO independent clauses in 1 Corinthians that have both a noun subject and accusative noun object (in 6:16 and 15:45) are quotes from Genesis 2:24 and 2:7, respectively. Both of them have oblique objects in Greek; that is, their objects are objects of the preposition εἰς 'into' which is functioning as a literal translation of the Hebrew direct object marker *et*. This is hardly standard Greek form.

There is, in fact, evidence that Luke's Greek in both the Gospel of Luke and the book of Acts imitates the biblical style of the Greek Old Testament, the Septuagint (LXX). In his commentary on Luke, Morris notes, "From 3:1 on the Gospel is written in a type of Hellenistic Greek which is strongly reminiscent of the Septuagint" (1974:26). In his commentary on the Greek text of Acts, Bruce states, "Luke can use this 'Biblical Greek' as readily as any other writer. It is found most abundantly in those parts of his work where he has a Palestinian or Jewish setting" (1951:28). Turner also notes "the Jewish Greek of some parts of the Gospel and the early chapters of Acts," but he is not sure whether this is due to Luke's skill for writing in "a deliberate LXX style" or whether this was "perhaps Luke's natural speech" (1976:56). This Jewish or Biblical Greek style may account for the relatively high percentage of verb initial clauses which Friberg found in Luke and which Levinsohn (1987:3) also found in Acts. To be sure, there is a possibility that this higher percentage means that narrative and non-narrative texttypes have different underlying or even dominant word orders, but until stylistic factors are accounted for, it would be premature to conclude this. Just as Greek in the Old Testament translation of the Septuagint has produced a narrative style that is more characteristic of Hebrew than of Greek, so imitation of that style may have produced a modified word order in Luke and Acts.

Turning to 1 Corinthians, there are seventeen clauses that have VSO word order. All of them are marked by grammatical features that are usually considered secondary. Four of the VSO clauses use a subjunctive verb (3:4; 12:15, 16; 15:28); two use an imperative verb (10:15 and 11:28); and one has a participle (9:20). In line with the tendency noted above, six of the seventeen are used with verbs of speaking (3:4; 7:10; 12:15, 16; 15:12, 35). In addition, five are used with forms of the equative verbs εἰμί 'be' and γίνομαι 'become' (6:16; 9:20; 12:19; 15:28, 45). Five are used with cognitive verbs (1:21; 7:16 bis; 10:15; 11:28) and one with a depictive verb (1:20). No VSO clauses use the more common action or stative verbs. Two VSO clauses are used in quotes, seven are used in dependent clauses, four are used in questions, and four are used with negatives. At least nine of them have a clause or a quotation as their object. Perhaps more significantly, thirteen of the seventeen VSO clauses occur as the first clause in a colon. This distribution of VSO clauses across many secondary features is hardly what one would expect to find if VSO were in fact the underlying unmarked order.

Further, when all possible cases of the four types of verb-subject order (VS, VSO, VOS, and OVS) are considered, the following items are statistically significant as opposed to the four types of subject-verb order (SV, SVO, SOV, OSV) in 1 Corinthians. VS order is found in 32% of the dependent clauses that precede the independent clause, as opposed to less than 20% of independent clauses. VS order is used in 67% of adverbial clauses in 1 Corinthians, as opposed to only 25% of main clauses. The subjunctive mood is used 41% of the time in VS order, while the indicative mood is used in VS order only 24% of the time. The imperfect tense is found 43% of the time in VS order, while the present is found in VS order less than 18% of the time. The middle and passive voices are used with VS order 30% of the time, while the active is used only 19% of the time with VS order. Verbs that relate to motion are used 43% of the time in VS order, while those that relate to creative activity are used 56% of the time in VS order. By way of contrast, action verbs are used in VS order only 14% of the time and stative verbs are used with VS order less than 13% of the time.

Clauses with compound subjects appear in VS order 56% of the time as opposed to 23% for clauses with singular subjects. Clauses that have mixed first- and third-person subjects are in VS order 67% of the time, while clauses with just third-person subjects are in VS order just 22% of the time. Clauses with pronoun objects occur in VS order 38% of the time and clauses with no object use VS order 26% of the time. These figures contrast with clauses with noun objects, which occur in VS order only 6% of the time. When new information is introduced in a subject slot, the clause is in VS order 53% of the time. This is in contrast with clauses with the same subject as previous clauses, which have VS order only 15% of the time. Previous clause order seems to have some effect on VS ordering. The VS order is found 57% of the time following VSO order and 41% of the time following VS order (that is, in a clause with no object). This tendency has been noted by both Dover (1960:53, 56) and Levinsohn (1987:3). On the other hand, VS order clauses occur following SVO order clauses 19% of the time, after SOV clauses 21% of the time, after SV clauses 16% of the time, after VO clauses 15% of the time, after OV clauses 20% of the time, and after V clauses (those with neither overt subject nor object) 22% of the time.

To be sure, the mere quoting of percentages does not prove that VS order is not unmarked. But these items with high VS order are mostly secondary features. The chi-square test shows that for all of them the difference between these frequent occurrences and the less frequent ones of more primary features has less than a 5% probability of being due to random distribution. For some of them, the percentage of use of VS is so high that these features become factors in explaining why the VS order is used in these cases.

It is beyond the scope of this study to formulate rules as to why a particular order is or is not used in certain situations. This analysis is limited to the influence on word order of the syntactic and semantic variables in the ANACLAUS database for 1 Corinthians. The material presented below suggests, however, that there are good reasons for supposing that a verb-subject order is secondary and thus marked. There is no reason why attempts to find justification for using VS order in Greek should be in vain, since the data above suggest several possible reasons. Friberg's argument that there can be no other explanation is not valid.

If Koiné Greek was not in fact a VSO language, the question remains as to what its unmarked order was. The following data for 1 Corinthians will suggest that for epistolary material the underlying order (if such exists for a synthetic language) was either SVO or SOV, the two dominant orders. It is difficult to decide between the two since there are preferred orders for different situations. It would be as easy to write rules to move from SVO to SOV as from SOV to SVO since each order predominates in mutually exclusive syntactic constructions. It would seem that, for each of several such constructions, there was an unmarked order.

Table 30 lists the distribution of clauses throughout 1 Corinthians into preceding dependent clauses, independent clauses, and following dependent clauses for each of fourteen different types of word order. The category labeled other in the chart represents clauses with missing components; it contains units that English teachers have traditionally labeled as sentence fragments. It is perhaps stretching the definition of the term clause to include these units here, but they function as clauses with implied constituents.

From table 30 it is possible to see that the largest category of Greek clauses are those that contain neither an overt subject nor object but only a verb. The next three orders in terms of frequency are VO, OV, and SV with nearly equal numbers of clauses. The fifth most frequent order is SOV; it is the most frequently used order with all three main constituents present. The sixth most frequent order is SVO. These six categories of clauses, each of which has over a hundred examples in 1 Corinthians, account for more than 78% of the clauses in 1 Corinthians. The other eight categories in descending order of frequency are other (the miscellaneous category), VS, SO,

OVS, OS, OSV, VSO, and VOS. Of the fourteen categories, VSO is next to last in frequency.

When all fourteen categories are used to try to determine significant differences in word order, twenty-four of twenty-six variables show statistically significant differences of some sort. In order to bring the analysis under control, it is useful to restrict the study to those clauses that contain all three major constituents: subject, object, and verb.

Table 30
Word order distribution in 1 Corinthians

Word order type	Preceding dependent	Independent clauses	Following dependent
V	39	164	61
VO	25	131	37
SVO	15	77	16
VSO	5	10	2
VOS	1	10	2
OV	20	136	36
SOV	16	105	12
OSV	0	13	5
OVS	2	21	4
SV	24	135	27
VS	18	39	8
SO	4	32	8
OS	1	26	0
other	13	71	7
Totals	183	970	225

There is a good theoretical reason to do this as well. Table 31 shows that there is a marked difference in the percentage of verb initial clauses that occur with objects and without objects, that is, with transitive and intransitive verbs. This holds true for data from both Luke (primarily a narrative text) and 1 Corinthians (primarily a non-narrative text). For both books, the difference is statistically significant. The fact that clauses without objects are at least 11% more likely to have initial verbs raises serious questions about the validity of determining verb-subject-object order by looking at all clauses with verbs and subjects. In passing, it is worth noting that the difference in verb ordering between Luke and 1 Corinthians is highly significant statistically. Whether this difference is caused by a different dominant word order between narrative and non-narrative text or by Luke's use of a style in imitation of the Greek Old Testament is beyond the scope of this study.

When the data are limited to clauses with all three major constituents, six variables show differences between their features for different word orders that are highly significant: clause type, clause relationship, subject type, object type, object case, and texttype. In the following analysis, SV is a combination of SVO, SOV, and OSV; VS of VSO, VOS, and OVS; VO of SVO, VSO, and VOS; OV of SOV, OSV, and OVS; SO of SVO, SOV, and VSO; and OS of OVS, OSV, and VOS. These combinations are also used in tables 31 and 32.

Table 31
The effect of objects on word order distribution
in Luke and 1 Corinthians

| | Luke | | 1 Corinthians | |
	VS	SV	VS	SV
With objects	31.5%	68.5%	19.9%	80.1%
	(n = 133)	(n = 289)	(n = 36)	(n = 145)
Without objects	42.7%	57.3%	33.3%	66.7%
	(n = 212)	(n = 284)	(n = 45)	(n = 90)
Totals	37.6%	62.4%	25.6%	74.4%
	(n = 345)	(n = 573)	(n = 81)	(n = 235)

The data for Luke are taken from Friberg (1982:30, 191). For comparison purposes with Friberg, the data are limited to third-person indicative verbs.

Analysis of clauses distinguishes four types: independent, dependent, quotations, and relative clauses. Among these, independent clauses show 64.8% in OV order; dependent clauses show 51.7% in OV order; quotations show 68.8% in VO order; and relative clauses show 66.7% in VO order. These are different enough to be highly significant in a VO-OV comparison.

There are seven different kinds of clauses found in the variable labeled clause relationship: main, subordinate, conditional, embedded, adjectival, adverbial, and absolute. The latter two can be omitted from the study of three element clauses since there is only one example of an adverbial clause and only two examples of absolute clauses. Among the remaining five clause types, main, subordinate, and embedded favor an OV order with percentages of 64.1%, 60.7%, and 50.7%, respectively. Conversely, the OV order of conditional and adjectival clauses drop in percentage to 46.4% and 22.2%, respectively; that is, these clause types have more VO clauses than OV clauses. The difference is statistically significant. In addition, none of the conditional clauses has the object fronted before the subject. Only 6.8% of the embedded clauses (i.e., clauses serving in subject or object slots) show this kind of object fronting. The other three kinds of clauses have over 20% of their objects fronted before their subjects. The difference in distribution of object fronting is highly significant. This may indicate that conditional clauses do not allow object fronting.

Table 32 presents the distribution of the six full word orders over the four types of text found in 1 Corinthians. In each case the two most common orders are SOV and SVO. For narrative, hortatory, and persuasive texttypes, the most common order is SOV; for expository it is SVO. The percentage of SVO clauses varies at most 12.5%, which is hardly significant. The occurrence of SOV, however, varies somewhat more—from a high of 53.1% in hortatory to a low of 17.6% in expository. The combination statistics at the bottom of the table show that expository is the only texttype in which more objects are found after the verb than before it. It is also marked by much more object fronting than the other texttypes. This object fronting makes the distributions of subject-object ordering highly significant. The other combinations are not significant.

It is difficult to tell whether the varied distribution by texttype is due to the texttype itself or to other factors based on the types of clauses found within each texttype. To the extent that word ordering may be determined by verb semantics and this factor influenced by topic of discussion, the distribution may vary greatly from discourse to discourse. It is only after several texts of Koiné Greek have been analyzed in this way that the significance of the distribution shown in table 32 will become apparent.

Table 32
Texttype and word order in 1 Corinthians

	Narrative		Expository		Hortatory		Persuasive	
SVO	37.5%	(n=3)	43.1%	(n=22)	30.6%	(n=45)	34.5%	(n=38)
VSO					4.1%	(n=6)	10.0%	(n=11)
VOS			13.7%	(n=7)	2.7%	(n=4)	1.8%	(n=2)
SOV	50.0%	(n=4)	17.6%	(n=9)	53.1%	(n=78)	38.2%	(n=42)
OSV			11.8%	(n=6)	2.7%	(n=4)	7.3%	(n=8)
OVS	12.5%	(n=1)	13.7%	(n=7)	6.8%	(n=10)	8.2%	(n=9)
Total		8		51		147		110
VO	37.5%	(n=3)	56.9%	(n=29)	37.4%	(n=55)	46.4%	(n=51)
OV	62.5%	(n=5)	43.1%	(n=22)	62.6%	(n=92)	53.6%	(n=59)
SV	87.5%	(n=7)	72.5%	(n=37)	86.4%	(n=127)	80.0%	(n=88)
VS	12.5%	(n=1)	27.5%	(n=14)	13.6%	(n=20)	20.0%	(n=22)
SO	87.5%	(n=7)	60.8%	(n=31)	87.8%	(n=129)	82.7%	(n=91)
OS	12.5%	(n=1)	39.2%	(n=20)	12.2%	(n=18)	17.3%	(n=19)

When the data for the clauses with all three constituents are examined, several minor patterns emerge. Participial clauses that have an article functioning as a subject in lieu of a pronoun regularly take an SVO order: of 26 examples in 1 Corinthians, 20 (76.9%) have an SVO order and 6 (23.1%) have an SOV order.

All eleven relative clauses that have a relative pronoun as the subject follow the SVO order. Of the six relative clauses that have relative pronouns as the object, three have OVS order, two have OSV order, and one (15:36) has SOV order; the latter order seems to be influenced by a vocative (ἄφρων 'stupid') followed by a second-person singular pronoun σύ 'you' as subject. In all other cases the relative pronoun comes first in the clause, whether it is subject or object.

There are also five examples of demonstrative adjectives modifying an articular noun subject. In every case but one, the order is SVO and the demonstrative follows the noun; the one exception (11:25) with SOV order is a quote from the words of Jesus in which the demonstrative precedes the noun.

Two other tendencies need to be noted. One is the tendency for pronouns to fill slots next to the verb, whether they are subjects, objects, or indirect objects (cf. Radney 1988:21). The other is for compound objects to come at the end of a clause. These are not hard and fast rules, only tendencies that occur more often than not.

Table 33 combines the important factors from the variables subject type, object type, and object case, with the addition of object article, which has significance for noun objects in the accusative case. Some features listed in table 18 for these variables have been omitted from this chart since there are too few instances of their use to draw conclusions as to the significance of the data.

Table 33 shows the distribution of various word orders within clauses for three types of subjects and six types of objects. For each combination, the six types of clause orders are combined to show the percentages of ordering between two of the three elements: subject (S), object (O), and verb (V). Predicate nominatives (N) and predicate adjectives (A) are presented as types of objects. Where any of these constituent elements are pronouns, they are represented in the table and in the description below using lower case letters.

The clearest pattern that emerges from table 33 is that clauses with predicate adjectives are usually found in SOV order. Callow (1992:69) notes that this is true in Romans as well as in 1 Corinthians. The equative verb, which in this type of Greek construction is sometimes omitted, does not add a lot of semantic content to the clause and thus seems to prefer the last slot. A similar situation occurs with predicate nominative constructions; most of the clauses are in SOV order. Here, however, the predicate nominative with a pronoun subject seems to be an exception to the rule. There are five examples of an sVN (a type of SVO) order. Closer examination reveals that there are other reasons why these particular clauses follow an SVO order. Three of these counter-examples (1:30; 3:11; and 4:17) are relative clauses with the pronoun subject being a relative pronoun; the order for this type of construction is regularly SVO. In addition, two of these cases (1:30 and 12:27) have compound objects, and as noted previously, there is a tendency for compound objects to come last in a clause. The clause in 1:30 contains both a relative pronoun as subject and a compound object. This leaves only one counter-example (11:24) to SOV order and it is a quotation of a reported saying of Jesus. It seems therefore that SOV is the standard order for predicate adjectives and nominatives.

Table 33
Subject and object influences on word order in 1 Corinthians

Object type	Pronouns				Clauses				Nouns			
Subject type →												
Clauses	sVO	13	sOV	1	SVO	1	SOV	—	SVO	3	SOV	—
	VsO	4	OsV	—	VSO	—	OSV	—	VSO	3	OSV	—
	VOs	—	OVs	—	VOS	—	OVS	—	VOS	—	OVS	1
	VO	94%	OV	6%	VO	100%	OV	0%	VO	86%	OV	14%
	SV	78%	VS	22%	SV	100%	VS	0%	SV	43%	VS	57%
	SO	100%	OS	0%	SO	100%	OS	0%	SO	86%	OS	14%
Articular accusative nouns	sVO	7	sOV	7	SVO	1	SOV	—	SVO	13	SOV	6
	VsO	—	OsV	3	VSO	—	OSV	—	VSO	2	OSV	1
	VOs	—	OVs	—	VOS	—	OVS	—	VOS	—	OVS	2
	VO	41%	OV	59%	VO	100%	OV	0%	VO	63%	OV	37%
	SV	100%	VS	0%	SV	100%	VS	0%	SV	83%	VS	17%
	SO	82%	OS	18%	SO	100%	OS	0%	SO	88%	OS	12%
Anarthrous accusative nouns	sVO	6	sOV	11	SVO	—	SOV	2	SVO	8	SOV	13
	VsO	—	OsV	3	VSO	—	OSV	—	VSO	—	OSV	—
	VOs	—	OVs	1	VOS	—	OVS	—	VOS	1	OVS	—
	VO	29%	OV	71%	VO	0%	OV	100%	VO	41%	OV	59%
	SV	95%	VS	5%	SV	100%	VS	0%	SV	95%	VS	5%
	SO	81%	OS	19%	SO	100%	OS	0%	SO	95%	OS	5%
Predicate nominatives	sVN	5	sNV	3	SVN	1	SNV	4	SVN	5	SNV	12
	VsN	1	NsV	2	VSN	—	NSV	—	VSN	—	NSV	—
	VNs	—	NVs	—	VNS	—	NVS	—	VNS	—	NVS	—
	VO	55%	OV	45%	VO	20%	OV	80%	VO	29%	OV	71%
	SV	91%	VS	9%	SV	100%	VS	0%	SV	100%	VS	0%
	SO	82%	OS	18%	SO	100%	OS	0%	SO	100%	OS	0%
Predicate adjectives	sVA	4	sAV	8	SVA	—	SAV	6	SVA	4	SAV	11
	VsA	—	AsV	3	VSA	—	ASV	—	VSA	—	ASV	1
	VAs	—	AVs	—	VAS	—	AVS	2	VAS	—	AVS	2
	VO	27%	OV	73%	VO	0%	OV	100%	VO	22%	OV	78%
	SV	100%	VS	0%	SV	75%	VS	25%	SV	89%	VS	11%
	SO	80%	OS	20%	SO	75%	OS	25%	SO	83%	OS	17%
Pronouns	sVo	4	soV	9	SVo	—	SoV	1	SVo	1	SoV	8
	Vso	—	osV	2	VSo	—	oSV	—	VSo	2	oSV	2
	Vos	—	oVs	2	VoS	—	oVS	1	VoS	7	oVS	10
	VO	24%	OV	76%	VO	0%	OV	100%	VO	33%	OV	67%
	SV	88%	VS	12%	SV	50%	VS	50%	SV	37%	VS	63%
	SO	76%	OS	24%	SO	50%	OS	50%	SO	37%	OS	63%

In contrast with predicate adjectives and nominatives, accusative objects show a mixed pattern. Those without a definite article (i.e., anarthrous) modifying the object show a regular SOV word order. There are eight counter-examples to this when the subject is a noun, but four of these eight have a demonstrative adjective modifying the subject, and as previously noted, this factor seems to favor SVO order. When the accusative noun object is modified by an article, two patterns emerge. For clauses with nouns or embedded clauses as subjects, the preferred order is SVO. The three cases with noun subjects and objects fronted to the beginning of the clauses (i.e., the OSV and OVS clauses) are all found in expository texttype. Table 32 shows that expository texttype has over 25% object fronting.

The situation with pronoun subjects and articular accusative noun objects is not so clear. There are seven examples of both sVO and sOV order, and the larger percentage (59%) for OV clauses is caused by the three OsV clauses. These are definite cases of object fronting and should not be considered in deciding between SVO and SOV since object fronting in either could produce an OSV clause. For the sake of simplicity and consistency, it would be convenient to formulate an underlying SVO order so that all articular accusative noun objects would have the same order. On closer examination, however, the SOV order would seem to be primary. All of the pronoun subject clauses which occur with OV order for articular accusative noun objects are found in main and subordinate clauses; those with VO order occur in conditional, embedded, and adjectival clauses. Further, three of the sVO clauses are relative clauses with a relative pronoun as subject; such clauses always have SVO order. Thus the primary order in this case seems to be SOV. To the extent that noun and clause subjects can be spoken of as being heavier than pronoun subjects, and articular accusative nouns can be spoken of as being heavier than anarthrous accusative nouns in an object slot, it seems that the lighter constructions favor SOV order and the heavier ones favor SVO order.

An examination of the data with clause objects seems to confirm this tendency. Clause objects would be considered heavy constructions and an SVO order would be expected. This is exactly what is found. The major counter-examples to this view are found among those clauses with noun subjects and clause objects. In 1:28 a clause occurs in OVS word order with a compound object, a combination of a substantival articular accusative adjective and an articular participial clause. This would seem to be a heavy object in the sense spoken of above. The clause in question, however, is a clear case of object topicalization, as an examination of (64) shows.

(64)   τὰ ἀγενῆ τοῦ κόσμου   καὶ τὰ ἐξουθενημένα ἐξελέξατο
       the ignoble of   theˆworld and the scorned   chose
       ὁ   θεός
       the God

It is perhaps important that this example of object fronting is also found
in expository texttype.

The other three counter-examples using noun subjects and clause objects
all have VSO word order. But of these, two (12:15 and 12:16) are subjunctive mood in conditional clauses and one (7:10) has a compound subject.
As noted previously, 56% of compound subjects in 1 Corinthians follow
the verb. Further, all three are verbs of speech, and Debrunner has noted
the tendency for subjects to follow verbs of speech (Blass, Debrunner, and
Funk 1961:248 [472]). Since there are good explanations for these counter-
examples, it seems reasonable to conclude that the primary word order for
clauses with embedded clauses as objects is SVO.

Finally, table 33 shows the order for clauses with pronoun objects.
Where both subject and object are pronouns, the primary word order is
SOV. One of the four examples of SVO word order (1:8) is a relative
clause with a relative pronoun as subject. Since the word order in such
clauses is always SVO, this clause should not be considered. In the same
way, three of the object fronted clauses (2:8; 3:17; and 10:30) are relative
clauses with relative pronouns as objects. As noted above, object fronting
is always standard in such cases and these cannot be considered valid
counter-examples.

The two examples of clauses with embedded clause subjects and
pronoun objects are not enough from which to draw significant conclusions. Since by analogy SOV seems to be the predominant order for all
clauses with pronoun objects, and since object fronting seems to result in
a secondary order, it seems logical to conclude that further work in other
Koiné Greek texts will indicate that SOV is the primary order in this case
also.

The most difficult of the combinations is that of clauses with noun
subjects and pronoun objects. This is the only combination that results in
all six possible word orders. There are several factors that must be considered as contributing to this wide distribution of forms. Four of the eight
clauses with SOV forms (7:19 bis and 10:19 bis) are actually predicate
nominative clauses with pronoun objects in the nominative case, and it has
already been established that SOV is the primary word order for predicate
nominative clauses. Also, three of the OVS clauses (2:7; 2:9; and 6:18) are
relative clauses with a relative pronoun as object, and this is a standard
order for such a case. A fourth (12:28) begins with the relative pronoun

οὕς 'whom' used as a demonstrative pronoun meaning 'these' (Arndt and Gingrich 1957:589); in such a construction, the relative pronoun regularly comes first. In addition, three of the OVS clauses (3:5 bis and 9:18) have the interrogative pronouns τί 'what' and τίς 'what' in the object slot; such questions regularly have fronted objects. Four of the VOS clauses (7:15; 16:19 bis; and 16:20) contain verbs of speech, which tend to take initial position in a clause. When these factors are considered and the clauses listed above are eliminated from consideration, the primary word order seems to be the SOV order that would be expected by analogy with pronoun and clause subjects. At least the SOV order has the most examples unexplained by syntactic considerations.

Furthermore, there are good semantic factors to explain the object fronting in the three remaining clauses with OVS order. The OVS clause in 4:1, shown in (65), is a good example of object topicalization as the topic of Christian workers is resumed after being mentioned in 3:22.

(65) Οὕτως ἡμᾶς λογιζέσθω   ἄνθρωπος ὡς ὑπηρέτας Χριστοῦ
      Thus   us   let^consider men   as attendants of^Christ
      καὶ οἰκονόμους μυστηρίων   θεοῦ.
      and stewards   of^[the]^mysteries of^God

The OVS clause in 7:17, shown in (66), is a good example of object emphasis when the distributive pronoun is used.

(66) ἕκαστον ὡς κέκληκεν ὁ θεός
      each   as has^called the God

Last, the OVS clause in 12:11, shown in (67), is a good example of summation, as the previous items listed are brought together.

(67) πάντα δὲ ταῦτα ἐνεργεῖ τὸ ἓν καὶ τὸ αὐτὸ πνεῦμα
      all   but these works   the one and the same spirit

In all these cases, the subject is God or the Spirit of God. Since God can be assumed to be the ultimate actor, the mention of God can be placed in the final slot in the sentence without doing damage to the sense. In fact, it is quite common when God is the actor with a passive verb simply to omit any mention of Him (Nida and Taber 1974:114). He can be inferred from the context.

In summary, there is not a single dominant word order for all clauses of Koiné Greek. Rather, the primary and preferred word order seems to be dependent upon the syntactic construction of the clause. SOV is the primary word order for predicate adjective and predicate nominative clauses, as well as for clauses with anarthrous accusative direct objects and pronoun direct objects. It also seems to be the preferred order when the clause contains an articular direct object and a subject pronoun.

SVO is the primary word order for clauses with embedded clauses as objects and for clauses with articular accusative direct objects and without pronoun subjects. In some sense, these clauses have heavy objects that tend to come at the end of a clause.

At this point, it is impossible to tell whether SOV or SVO should be considered the primary underlying word order for Koiné Greek. Since Friberg has shown in relating his data to universals that "Greek is largely consistent with our expectations of the behavior of a VO language" (1982:334), it might be better to favor SVO. But the search for an underlying word order is beyond the scope of this study.

The point here is that each of these orders in the constructions listed above should be considered unmarked. The way to produce emphasis is to move a constituent from its normal word order. Since these orders are the most common, they should be considered normal, and thus orders that differ from these are emphatic and also marked, in some sense. But it is only after syntactic considerations have been given that discourse roles such as those presented in (65) through (67) can have any real significance in marking a text.

Finally, no attempt has been made in this study to search for word order differences between foregrounded and backgrounded text. Some languages mark the main line with a different word order; Angwak is an SVO language of Africa that marks the storyline in narrative text with SOV word order (Longacre 1990b:87). Longacre (1993, personal communication) has suggested that something similar happens in Greek, perhaps even marking narrative storyline with the VSO order that several investigators claim to be primary. This suggestion certainly merits further investigation.

5.4 Quotations

Methods of introducing quotations in 1 Corinthians. A further area of study in discourse analysis is the examination of quotations and the ways in which they are introduced into the text. Table 34 lists the locations of the certain direct quotations in 1 Corinthians together with their introducers and sources. There may be other quotations as well. It has already been suggested in chapter 2 of this study that some of the statements from the Corinthians' letter to Paul are echoed in 1 Corinthians. Possible locations for these quotations from the Corinthians' letter include 6:12, 13;

7:1; 8:1, 4, 5–6, 8; and 11:2 (Hurd 1983:68). None of these locations, however, are marked with quotation introducers to indicate that they are in fact quotations. It seems best to omit them from the study in favor of only those quotations that are certain.

Table 34
Quotation introduction in 1 Corinthians

Passage	Introduction	Source of quote
1:12	λέγει 'says'	some Corinthians
1:12	none	some Corinthians
1:12	none	some Corinthians
1:12	none	some Corinthians
1:19	γέγραπται 'it has been written'	Old Testament
1:31	γέγραπται 'it has been written'	Old Testament
2:9	γέγραπται 'it has been written'	Old Testament
2:16	γάρ 'for'	Old Testament
3:4	λέγη τις 'someone says'	some Corinthians
3:4	ἕτερος δέ 'and another'	some Corinthians
3:19	γέγραπται 'it has been written'	Old Testament
3:20	καὶ πάλιν 'and again'	Old Testament
4:6	τό 'the [saying]'	known saying
5:13	none	Old Testament
6:16	γάρ φησίν 'for it says'	Old Testament
9:9	γέγραπται 'it has been written'	Old Testament
10:7	γέγραπται 'it has been written'	Old Testament
10:26	γάρ 'for'	Old Testament
10:28	τις εἴπῃ 'someone should say'	hypothetical speech
11:24	εἶπεν 'he said'	Jesus
11:25	λέγων 'saying'	Jesus
12:3	λέγει 'says'	hypothetical speech
12:3	δύναται εἰπεῖν 'can say'	hypothetical speech
12:15	εἴπῃ 'should say'	hypothetical speech
12:16	εἴπῃ 'should say'	hypothetical speech
12:21	δύναται εἰπεῖν 'can say'	hypothetical speech
12:21	ἤ πάλιν 'or again'	hypothetical speech
14:21	γέγραπται 'it has been written'	Old Testament
14:25	ἀπαγγέλλων ὅτι 'proclaiming that'	hypothetical speech
15:25	merged into sentence	Old Testament
15:27	γάρ 'for'	Old Testament

Passage	Introduction	Source of quote
15:32	none	Old Testament
15:33	none	Menander
15:35	ἐρεῖ τις 'someone will say'	hypothetical speech
15:45	γέγραπται 'it has been written'	Old Testament
15:54	ὁ γεγραμμένος 'the thing written'	Old Testament
15:55	none	Old Testament

In addition, the book of 1 Corinthians contains indirect quotations. For example, 9:10 looks like a quotation from the Old Testament. It is introduced with ἐγράφη ὅτι 'it is written that', using the same root word for write that is discussed below as regularly introducing Old Testament quotations. Further, although ὅτι 'that' is regularly used with indirect discourse, it can also function like modern quotation marks in introducing a direct quotation (Robertson 1934:1027–28; Turner 1963:326; and Blass, Debrunner, and Funk 1961:246–47 [470]). But the words that follow are not found in any Old Testament, classical, or apocryphal passage and must be a paraphrase or logical inference from Deut. 25:4, quoted in the previous verse (cf. Fee 1987:409).

Another example of indirect discourse is found in 15:12 (πῶς λέγουσιν ἐν ὑμῖν τινες ὅτι ἀνάστασις νεκρῶν οὐκ ἔστιν; 'how do some among you say that there is not a resurrection of the dead?'). Here Paul is paraphrasing the report that has come to him about what some are teaching. The indirect quotation is introduced by λέγουσιν .. ὅτι 'they say .. that'. This is little different from introductions of direct quotation, on which this study focuses.

Eighteen of the thirty-seven quotations listed in table 34 are from the Old Testament. Among these, eight are introduced using the word γέγραπται 'it has been written'. This is the perfect passive indicative form of γράφω 'I write'. The perfect passive participle of the same word (γεγραμμένος 'having been written') is used once (in 15:54) as an introductory word.

The second most used introductory word for Old Testament quotations is γάρ 'for'. Three times (2:16; 10:26; and 15:27) it is used alone and once (6:16) with φησίν 'it says'. In addition, three times (5:13; 15:32; and 15:55) an Old Testament scripture is quoted without any introduction. The last of these flows right from the quotation of Isaiah 25:8 in 15:54 into the quotation of Hosea 13:14 in 15:55. It is possible to view the introduction to 15:54 as introducing both passages. Further, the quotation in 15:25 is merged into the sentence without an introduction. The final example of an introductory phrase for a quotation is καὶ πάλιν 'and again' found in 3:20.

This quotation follows immediately after a quotation in 3:19, which explains the use of the word πάλιν 'again'.

The second largest class of quotations are those that represent hypothetical speech. The hypothetical speakers range from a host at a party (10:28) to a person speaking under the influence of a spirit (12:3) to body parts such as the foot (12:15), ear (12:16), eye (12:21), and head (12:21) to a stranger entering the assembly (14:25) to an opponent of Paul's (15:35). The first and last of these speakers are introduced by the indefinite pronoun τις 'someone'.

Five of these nine cases are introduced using a form of εἶπον, the second aorist form of the verb λέγω 'I say'; in addition, one case (12:3) uses the present tense of this verb and one (15:35) the future tense. Two other forms are used to introduce hypothetical speech: ἀπαγγέλλων ὅτι 'proclaiming that' in 14:25 and ἢ πάλιν 'or again' in 12:21. As mentioned above, here once more πάλιν 'again' is used to introduce the second quotation in a row.

The third group of quotations are those cases in 1:12 and 3:4 where Paul is reproducing the reported speech of the Corinthians. Here different Corinthians are saying different things and so lists of sayings are given. Both lists are introduced with a form of the word λέγω 'I say'. The first list has no introductory words for the second through the fourth items in the list; the quotations simply follow immediately after one another. The second list is shortened to include only two quotations, so the second is introduced with ἕτερος δέ 'and another' with reference to another speaker.

Two quotations found in 11:23–25 are taken from the sayings of Jesus at the institution of the Lord's Supper. Both quotations before Jesus gave his disciples the bread and the cup are introduced with a form of the word λέγω 'I say'.

There are two other quotations in 1 Corinthians. There is a saying in 4:6 which Paul quotes as if the Corinthians are familiar with it. He introduces this saying simply with the neuter article τό 'the'. The other familiar quotation (in 15:33) is one from Menander's *Thais*, "Bad company ruins good morals" (RSV); this had become a popular saying by the time 1 Corinthians was written (cf. Fee 1987:773) and has no introduction at all.

Thus there are several techniques used to introduce quotations in 1 Corinthians. When a quotation comes from the Old Testament scriptures, a written source, it is most often introduced by a perfect passive form of γράφω 'I write'. When a quotation comes from a spoken source, either reported or hypothetical, it is most often introduced by a form of λέγω 'I say'. Written sources are also introduced by the word γάρ 'for' when the quotation is providing support or further explanation. Where two quotations are given together, the second may be introduced by πάλιν 'again' or by ἕτερος 'another'. Finally, familiar sayings, either scriptural or otherwise, may be quoted with no introduction at all. This gives substance to the idea that certain passages may be quotations from the Corinthians' letter, even though they have no introduction as quotations. The Corinthians would certainly have been familiar with their own letter.

Old Testament quotations and synoptic traditions. Turning from the introductions to the quotations to the form of the quotations themselves, the book contains seventeen quotations from the Old Testament. Table 35 lists the Old Testament quotations in 1 Corinthians together with the category codes assigned by Archer and Chirichigno (1983:2–147 passim). The letter A represents a quotation that is substantially the same in the Masoretic Hebrew Text, the Greek Septuagint, and the Greek New Testament. This ranking may be given even if a few minor variations exist between these, in which case a superscript d is added. The letter B represents quotations that follow the Septuagint where it deviates somewhat from the Masoretic Text, but not so much as to change the meaning of the passage. Again, the superscripted d indicates minor variations. The letter C represents quotations that follow the Masoretic Text more closely than the Septuagint, where these two differ. The letter D represents quotations that follow the Septuagint where it has a significantly different reading than the Masoretic Text. Where the quotation from the Septuagint has been modified to more closely reflect the Masoretic Text, a superscript a is added to the D. The letter E represents quotations that show significant differences from both the Masoretic Text and the Septuagint. Table 35 shows that all but three of the quotations agree with the Septuagint. The quotations in 2:16 and 3:19 agree more closely with the Masoretic Text. The quotation in 2:9 is described by Archer and Chirichigno as "a noteworthy example of a conflate quotation from various passages written in a paraphrastic manner" (1983:xxx).

The passage in 1 Cor. 11:23–25 is not strictly speaking a quotation; however, it is interesting in that it contains a close parallel to the synoptic tradition found in Matthew, Mark, and Luke. There are 68 words in the three verses. Omitting the 11 words of introduction, the parallel passage contains 57 words. Of these, 17 (or 29.8%) are found wholly or partly in all three synoptic Gospels. In addition, 38 (or 66.7%) are found wholly or partly in Luke. This would seem to indicate that the synoptic tradition as regards the Last Supper had a high degree of uniformity when 1 Corinthians was written (These statistics were compiled using Aland 1970:284).

Table 35
Old Testament quotations in 1 Corinthians

	Passage	Reference	Code
1	1:19	Isa. 29:14	B[d]
2	1:31	Jer. 9:24	A
3	2:9	Isa. 64:4	E
4	2:16	Isa. 40:13	C
5	3:19	Job 5:13	C
6	3:20	Ps. 94:11	A[d]
7	5:13	Deut. 17:7	A
8	6:16	Gen. 2:24	A
9	9:9	Deut. 25:4	A–
10	10:7	Ex. 32:6	A
11	10:26	Ps. 24:1	A
12	14:21	Is. 28:11–12	D, B[d]
13	15:25	Ps. 110:1	A[d]*
14	15:27	Ps. 8:6	A
15	15:32	Isa. 22:13	A
16	15:45	Gen. 2:7	A
17	15:54	Isa. 25:8	A[d]
18	15:55	Hos. 13:14	D[a]

* not listed in Archer and Chirichigno

5.5 The influence of the rhetorical situation

As discussed in the second chapter of this study, most scholars hold that 1 Corinthians was written as a single letter. Some, however, on the basis of supposed differences in style, have wanted to divide the letter in several parts. Even Hurd (1983:82), who argues for the unity of the letter, suggests that there are differences in style between some of the sections in response to oral reports and some of the sections in response to the Corinthians' letter.

Two questions are raised for the discourse analyst studying 1 Corinthians. First, does this difference in style between different parts of the letter based upon different types of material to which Paul was responding actually exist, or is it merely a subjective assessment? To clarify the question, Hurd characterizes some sections written in response to the Corinthians' letter as having a "calm" tone (1983:74), while others written in response to oral reports as having a tone that is "aroused, even angry" (1983:82). Such subjective assessments as tone are hardly quantifiable. As Habel so aptly put it, "Differences in literary style are sometimes easier to feel than to define" (1971:18). But is there a way to define stylistic differences in terms of discourse grammar so that a quantitative result can be achieved? This definition would seem not only to be possible but desirable. Admittedly, the word style as commonly used means so many things that it comes to mean nothing in particular and has little scientific validity. When Biblical scholars refer to style, however, they are often speaking of a combination of frequently occurring grammatical features that are also the subject of inquiry in discourse analysis. The answer to the question of which features are important in defining stylistic differences in 1 Corinthians can be found by searching the clause database for such grammatical features to see if a statistically significant difference exists between these two types of materials based on differences in type of response.

Second, if such a stylistic difference actually exists, does discourse theory provide an explanation for this difference other than a difference of time of writing? More to the point, does a stylistic difference necessarily imply a difference in origin? Traditionally, literary criticism in Biblical studies has given an affirmative answer to this latter question (cf. Habel 1971). But can a single writer use more than one style in the same letter for different purposes? This section attempts to answer this question also.

In the first section of this chapter, an area of peak was discovered in 1 Corinthians that showed stylistic differences from the rest of the letter. Is it also possible that the same kind of stylistic differences exist between those discourses which were written in response to oral reports which Paul received and those written in response to the Corinthians' letter? When this question is applied to the clause structure database, the following variables from table 18 show a highly significant difference between the two types of materials: clause relationship, verb mode, verb voice, semantic type, subject semantics, texttype, words per clause, statement or question, and same subject as previous. In addition, the following variables show a significant difference between the two types of materials: sentence location (i.e., preceding dependent, independent, or following dependent), clause type, verb tense, subject type, prepositional phrases, and clause order type. This is based on the response to oral reports being contained in 1:10–6:20; 11:2–34; and 15:1–58, while the response to the Corinthians' letter is contained in 7:1–11:1; 12:1–14:40; and 16:1–12.

Some of these are interrelated. For example, verb voice and subject semantics are closely correlated. Also, the significant feature in sentence location is that the parts of the letter in response to the Corinthians' letter contain a greater percentage of preceding dependent clauses than do those parts in response to the oral reports. This seems to be due to the fact that these parts also contain more conditional sentences, which regularly place the condition in the preceding dependent clause slot.

Table 36 lists those features that best illustrate the stylistic differences between the two types of response material. It shows that those parts of 1 Corinthians which are in response to the Corinthians' questions in their letter are generally more hortatory in nature, as evidenced by more command clauses and more imperative and subjunctive verbs. The discourses in these parts are also more direct and argumentative, as evidenced by a larger percentage of conditional clauses and more active voice and present tense verbs.

Table 36

Significant style differences between sections of 1 Corinthians written in response to oral reports and the Corinthians' letter

Category	Oral report		Corinthians' letter	
Narrative texttype	5.6%	(n = 35)	3.1%	(n = 22)
Persuasive texttype	37.1%	(n = 232)	32.4%	(n = 231)
Hortatory texttype	43.7%	(n = 273)	53.6%	(n = 383)
Conditional clauses	6.4%	(n = 40)	11.5%	(n = 82)
Clauses in commands	11.4%	(n = 71)	23.5%	(n = 168)
Clauses in statements	73.4%	(n = 459)	61.8%	(n = 441)
Clauses in quotations	6.2%	(n = 39)	2.9%	(n = 21)
Longer clauses (10 or more words)	9.0%	(n = 56)	4.8%	(n = 34)
Verbless clauses	14.6%	(n = 91)	9.1%	(n = 65)
Noun subjects	29.8%	(n = 186)	22.1%	(n = 158)
Different subjects	49.9%	(n = 312)	44.7%	(n = 319)
Aorist tense verbs	28.5%	(n = 152)	21.7%	(n = 141)
Present tense verbs	54.3%	(n = 290)	64.3%	(n = 417)
Indicative verbs	66.7%	(n = 356)	56.2%	(n = 365)
Subjunctive verbs	9.6%	(n = 51)	15.1%	(n = 98)
Imperative verbs	5.1%	(n = 27)	9.7%	(n = 63)
Active voice verbs	68.3%	(n = 365)	81.2%	(n = 527)
Passive voice verbs	21.0%	(n = 112)	11.2%	(n = 73)

Percentages are based on 625 clauses and 534 verbs in the discourses responding to oral reports and 714 clauses and 649 verbs in the discourses responding to the Corinthians' letter.

The discourses in response to the oral reports that Paul had received are more tentative and less direct, as evidenced by more statements, longer clauses, and more use of the passive voice. These discourses contain more persuasive material, as Paul tries to modify the Corinthians' belief and value systems underlying their behavior rather than just command their obedience. Consequently, they also contain more narrative material in order to illustrate his points. This accounts, to a certain extent, for the increased use of the aorist tense in these discourses, since the aorist tense is the mainline for narrative texttype. These parts of the text also see a greater frequency of noun usage, as Paul changes his subject more often. This is further evidence of the more tentative approach of these discourses.

Several of these features that show such differences are also found in table 20, indicating a difference between peak and nonpeak areas of the text. These features include persuasive and hortatory texttypes, verbless and conditional clauses, statements, commands, aorist tense and passive voice verbs, and noun subjects. Is it possible that the same feature can be used with different frequencies in blocks of text that are in response to oral reports or a letter and then be used at still different frequencies when the writer comes to the peak of the text that he wants to emphasize? The answer is yes. Table 37 illustrates this for two of the shared features, conditional clauses and passive voice.

The parts of the text written in response to the Corinthians' letter contain more conditional clauses in nonpeak areas than those parts written in response to oral reports (9.3% conditional clauses as compared with 5.5%). But when Paul reaches the peak, the percentage of use increases in both kinds of response material (15.0% conditional clauses as compared with 8.6%). Both peak and response type are influencing the 15.0% figure.

There is a different situation with the use of the passive voice. More passives (16.1% as compared to 11.5%) are used in nonpeak areas of the responses to oral reports than to the letter. But in the peak material, passive use increases dramatically in the discourse responding to the oral report (rising to 35.9% use in chapter 15), while it remains about the same in the peak discourse responding to the Corinthians' letter (at 10.7% use in chapters 12 to 14). Actually, the latter figure represents a small drop, but 0.8% is hardly significant.

Table 37
Relationship of peak and rhetorical influence in 1 Corinthians

	Conditionals (percent of clauses)			Passives (percent of verbs)		
	Total	Peak	Nonpeak	Total	Peak	Nonpeak
Total		12.5% (n = 56)	7.2% (n = 67)		19.8% (n = 72)	14.2% (n = 121)
Oral report	6.4% (n = 40)	8.6% (n = 15)	5.5% (n = 25)	21.0% (n = 112)	35.9% (n = 47)	16.1% (n = 65)
Letter	11.5% (n = 82)	15.0% (n = 41)	9.3% (n = 41)	11.2% (n = 73)	10.7% (n = 25)	11.5% (n = 48)
Introduction and conclusion	2.6% (n = 1)		2.6% (n = 1)	24.2% (n = 8)		24.2% (n = 8)

Percentages are based on 451 clauses and 403 verbs in the nonpeak response to oral reports, 174 clauses and 131 verbs in the peak response to oral reports, 441 clauses and 416 verbs in the nonpeak response to the Corinthians' letter, 273 clauses and 233 verbs in the peak response to the Corinthians' letter, and 39 clauses and 33 verbs in the introduction and conclusion.

The introduction and conclusion have been presented separately in this table since the former contains the thanksgiving in expository texttype and the latter contains parting admonitions in primarily hortatory texttype. These are predictable in the epistolary genre and should not be included when comparing two types of responses in two parts of a letter.

To turn to the second major question of this section, is there an explanation other than a different author or at least time of writing that would account for such a marked difference of style between these two types of responses? The answer is yes. The rhetorical situation is different in the two cases: in one case Paul has been asked for advice, even for a ruling; in the other case Paul is talking about matters which they may well have wished he never knew about. These different circumstances provide motivation for the stylistic differences that Hurd perceived in the text (1983:82). In answering their letter, Paul could afford to be direct; it would have been expected of him. A ruling from an authority calls for the use of commands. But in addressing troublesome situations, which they did not feel free to write to him about, more caution was required. The situation called for an indirectness and tentativeness that is reflected in the grammar.

All of this means that in trying to account for questions of stylistic difference more than one factor must be taken into account. Different authors, of course, will often use different characteristic styles. In addition, a person's characteristic style can change over time. But the same person will often use several different styles of writing depending upon the purpose of his work. This choice of style is primarily based upon the texttype that is required by the purpose. That purpose can be molded in many situations by the rhetorical situation. Thus, rhetorical situation can determine style and can account for significant differences between passages.

Where a language allows variation of expression, different people tend to utilize different grammatical forms in different ratios. This has traditionally been used as a tool for determining commonalty of authorship. To what extent is variation in style an indication of a different rhetorical situation rather than a different author? Computer aided analysis should allow this question to be studied with more precision than ever before.

6

Discourse Analysis as a
Study of Constraints

The preceding analysis is not complete by any measure. There are other aspects of discourse which could be studied in 1 Corinthians, even linguistic aspects such as the tracking of participants in object slots, the use of conjunctions for cohesion, the use of pronouns for cohesion, the use of lexical chaining, and the distribution frequency of vocabulary, to name but a few. Adding these aspects to the various aspects of discourse studied here may make an analysis with discourse linguistics look like a study of a hodgepodge of items, but there is a unifying thread that runs through them all—their constraining influence.

It is well known that grammar on the sentence level provides constraints that facilitate understanding. English, for example, uses word order to indicate the subject and object of a clause. For standard declarative sentences, the grammar constrains the order of elements into an SVO pattern. When the sentence "John taught Bill" is encountered, it is obvious that John is the one doing the teaching while Bill is the one receiving it. The person who says "Taught Bill John" will not be understood much of the time, for the hearer has no way to know, since the constraints of the shared syntax are missing, whether the speaker means that Bill taught John or that John taught Bill. Thus the person who desires to be understood is constrained by sentence level grammar to produce a clause in SVO order.

In much the same way, discourse grammar also constrains the speaker or writer in a language. If a person wishes to tell a story in English, normally he or she will use the past tense, since that is the mainline tense for

165

narrative texttype. A storyteller in Koiné Greek used the aorist for the same reason. A person is not at liberty to change the rules of discourse grammar arbitrarily and still be understood. If the storyteller decides to use a future tense, the narrative will be understood as some sort of prophecy. If a story is told using a perfect tense, the listener will not know how to interpret the story. This is why the constraint against using this tense is so strong that the storyteller cannot sustain the perfect tense without deliberately thinking about how to form each sentence.

If there is a difference between constraints imposed by sentence grammar and discourse grammar, it is one of degree. Because paraphrase is possible, the same idea can generally be expressed in more than one way. Constraints at the discourse level are generally looser than at the sentence level; that looseness, however, should not be misunderstood as a lack of constraints. The rule of thumb is well expressed by Kenneth Pike (1993:63), who quotes Goodman's (1978:x) maxim, "radical relativism under rigorous restraints." There are various ways to express an idea, especially on the discourse level, but all of them are under the constraints of a person's grammar.

An author, whether speaking or writing, is constrained by the rhetorical situation. While there are many ways to express an idea, not all of them may be appropriate for a given situation. This explains why Paul adopted a more direct style to answer the Corinthians' questions from their letter than he used in addressing matters of which he had only heard reports.

An author is also constrained by the frame structures in his or her mind and those in the minds of the audience, or at least by the way that the author conceives of the audience's frame structures. More or less background information will be provided in the text depending upon what the author thinks that the audience already knows. Thus, to understand the book of 1 Corinthians, the modern reader must learn something about Greek culture and society in order to build frame structures that correspond in some degree to those of the original readers.

The author is further constrained by the idea or ideas which may be described as macrostructures (or theses) and meta-structures (or themes). A text which is continually cluttered with extraneous ideas will not be easily understood; it will lack the coherence that the audience expects. There are many ways in which these central ideas can be presented, but only a finite number of rhetorical patterns can be used to arrange them. It is this finite number of patterns that constrains the presentation and ordering of material in a discourse. These patterns are, to a certain extent, culturally determined. While chiasmus may be perfectly acceptable in a given society, such as it was in the ancient Hebrew and Greek worlds, it may not be a pattern which is readily used in other societies. This helps to explain why some passages are misunderstood in the modern western world, where the average reader does not expect to find chiasmus in ancient documents and probably does not recognize it when it is encountered. It also helps to explain why western readers, expecting a linearly organized text, often miss the cyclic and chiastic patterns of organization in 1 Corinthians, such as those shown in table 4.

The author is constrained by the types of relationships which a given language permits between paragraphs. In a similar way, the available conjunctions which indicate those relationships and transitions between ideas further constrain the way an author can structure a text. The discourse grammar of a language may permit or forbid paragraphs to be deeply embedded for a given texttype.

Even where peak areas dictate a change in the grammatical devices used, the available choices are constrained. In a narrative Greek text, one may find the aorist replaced on the storyline by the present or the imperfect in the span of text containing the peak, but one will not find the future or the perfect. A non-narrative text may show an increase in the use of the passive voice or conditional sentences, such as is found in 1 Corinthians 12–15, but that increase will be relative; there will not be an absolute switch to these devices.

A well-told narrative constrains the number of characters that can be introduced at any one time. A non-narrative text such as 1 Corinthians, on the other hand, permits many more subtopics to be introduced and may show rapid switching between them. But even here, there is a constraint on the way in which new ideas can be introduced.

Greek word order is perhaps unique in the many ways that it allows a clause to be ordered. As this study has shown for non-narrative texttypes, there is also an unmarked order, summarized in table 38, from which the author must vary to highlight a semantic category such as contrast. There is some indication from the significant differences between Luke and 1 Corinthians that the unmarked order may vary from texttype to texttype, showing that discourse grammar constrains it.

The ways in which quotations can be introduced are also constrained by discourse considerations. Obviously a text originally spoken is more likely to be introduced by "says" (λέγω in Greek), while one originally written is more likely to be introduced by "writes" (γράφω in Greek). But there are an additional limited number of devices by which any quoted text can be introduced, as this study of 1 Corinthians shows. Again, the author is constrained in the use of these devices.

Table 38
Non-narrative unmarked Greek word order

Subject Type

Object Type	Pronouns	Clauses	Nouns
Clauses	sV(O)	(S)V(O)	SV(O)
Articular Accusative Nouns	sOV	(S)VO	SVO
Anarthrous Accusative Nouns	sOV	(S)OV	SOV
Predicate Nominatives	sNV	(S)NV	SNV
Predicate Adjectives	sAV	(S)AV	SAV
Pronouns	soV	(S)oV	SoV

Finally, as an interpretive principle, meaning is constrained by discourse grammar. Sentences, like words, may have different meanings in different contexts. It is the surrounding discourse which limits the meaning of a sentence to that which the author had in mind at the time of composition.

The study of discourse, and especially discourse grammar rules, is in its infancy as it applies to the interpretation of the New Testament. This study of 1 Corinthians demonstrates that discourse grammar rules can be discovered and that, with an understanding of these rules and the constraints which they impose, a clearer understanding is possible of that most famous of Books.

Appendix A
Texttype in 1 Corinthians

Passage	Texttype	Passage	Texttype
1:1–1:9	expository	9:24–10:1	hortatory
1:10–1:10	hortatory	10:1–10:4	narrative
1:11–1:12	expository	10:4–10:4	expository
1:13–1:15	persuasive	10:5–10:5	narrative
1:16–1:16	narrative	10:6–10:6	expository
1:16–1:17	expository	10:7–10:15	hortatory
1:18–1:25	persuasive	10:16–10:22	persuasive
1:26–1:31	expository	10:23–11:7	hortatory
2:1–2:4	narrative	11:8 –11:9	expository
2:5–2:5	hortatory	11:10–11:10	hortatory
2:6–3:9	persuasive	11:11–11:12	expository
3:10–3:10	expository	11:13–11:22	hortatory
3:10–3:10	hortatory	11:23–11:23	expository
3:11–3:15	expository	11:23–11:25	narrative
3:16–3:17	persuasive	11:26–11:26	expository
3:18–4:21	hortatory	11:27–11:34	hortatory
5:1–5:2	expository	12:1–12:11	expository
5:2–5:7	hortatory	12:12–12:30	persuasive
5:7–5:7	expository	12:31–12:31	hortatory
5:8–5:11	hortatory	12:31–13:13	persuasive
5:12–5:13	expository	14:1–14:1	hortatory
5:13–7:13	hortatory	14:1–14:1	persuasive
7:14–7:14	expository	14:2–14:40	hortatory
7:15–7:21	hortatory	15:1–15:2	persuasive
7:22–7:22	expository	15:3–15:8	narrative
7:23–7:32	hortatory	15:9–15:11	expository
7:32–7:34	expository	15:12–15:32	persuasive
7:35–7:40	hortatory	15:33–15:34	hortatory
7:40–7:40	expository	15:35–15:57	persuasive
7:40–8:1	hortatory	15:58–16:4	hortatory
8:1–8:1	expository	16:5–16:9	narrative
8:2–8:2	hortatory	16:10–16:11	hortatory
8:3–8:3	expository	16:12–16:12	expository
8:4–8:8	persuasive	16:13–16:16	hortatory
8:9–8:9	hortatory	16:17–16:18	expository
8:10–9:9	persuasive	16:18–16:18	hortatory
9:9–9:9	hortatory	16:19–16:20	expository
9:9–9:15	persuasive	16:20–16:20	hortatory
9:16–9:18	expository	16:21–16:21	expository
9:19–9:23	persuasive	16:22–16:22	hortatory

Appendix B
Greek Constituent Structure Displays for 1 Corinthians

Table 11G
Constituent display of 1 Corinthians 1:10–17
Mixed texttypes

Point 1: (H) Motivation paragraph
   Thesis: (H) Reason paragraph
     Thesis: **10** Παρακαλῶ δὲ ὑμᾶς, ἀδελφοί, διὰ τοῦ ὀνόματος
                τοῦ κυρίου ἡμῶν Ἰησοῦ Χριστοῦ, ἵνα τὸ αὐτὸ
                λέγητε πάντες καὶ μὴ ᾖ ἐν ὑμῖν σχίσματα, ἦτε δὲ
                κατηρτισμένοι ἐν τῷ αὐτῷ νοῒ καὶ ἐν τῇ αὐτῇ
                γνώμῃ.
   Reason: (E) Amplification paragraph
     Thesis: **11** ἐδηλώθη γάρ μοι περὶ ὑμῶν, ἀδελφοί
               μου, ὑπὸ τῶν Χλόης ὅτι ἔριδες ἐν ὑμῖν
               εἰσιν.
     Amplification: **12** λέγω δὲ τοῦτο, ὅτι ἕκαστος ὑμῶν λέγει,
               Ἐγὼ μέν εἰμι Παύλου, Ἐγὼ δὲ Ἀπολλῶ,
               Ἐγὼ δὲ Κηφᾶ, Ἐγὼ δὲ Χρισποῦ.
Motivation: (P) Comment paragraph
   Thesis: (P) Coordinate paragraph
     Thesis$_1$:   **13** μεμέρισται ὁ Χριστός;
     Thesis$_2$:   μὴ Παῦλος ἐσταυρώθη ὑπὲρ ὑμῶν,
     Thesis$_n$:   ἢ εἰς τὸ ὄνομα Παύλου ἐβαπτίσθητε;
   Comment: (P) Reason paragraph
     Thesis: (P) Clarification paragraph
         Thesis: **14** εὐχαριστῶ [τῷ θεῷ] ὅτι οὐδένα
                    ὑμῶν ἐβάπτισα εἰ μὴ Κρίσπον
                    καὶ Γάϊον, **15** ἵνα μή τις εἴπῃ
                    ὅτι εἰς τὸ ἐμὸν ὄνομα
                    ἐβαπτίσθητε.
         Clarification: (N) Antithetical paragraph
           Thesis: **16** ἐβάπτισα δὲ καὶ τὸν
                    Στεφανᾶ οἶκον·
           Antithesis: λοιπὸν οὐκ οἶδα εἴ τινα
                    ἄλλον ἐβάπτισα.
     Reason: **17** οὐ γὰρ ἀπέστειλέν με Χριστὸς βαπτίζειν
               ἀλλὰ εὐαγγελίζεσθαι, οὐκ ἐν σοφίᾳ
               λόγου, ἵνα μὴ κενωθῇ ὁ σταυρὸς τοῦ
               Χριστοῦ.

Key: E expository, H hortatory, N narrative, and P persuasive.

Table 12G
Constituent display of 1 Corinthians 2:6–16
Persuasive texttype

Point X: (P) Amplification paragraph
  Thesis: **6** Σοφίαν δὲ λαλοῦμεν ἐν τοῖς τελείοις, σοφίαν δὲ οὐ
                    τοῦ αἰῶνος τούτου οὐδὲ τῶν ἀρχόντων τοῦ αἰῶνος
                    τούτου τῶν καταργουμένων·
  Amplification: (P) Amplification paragraph
    Thesis: (P) Reason paragraph
      Thesis: **7** ἀλλὰ λαλοῦμεν θεοῦ σοφίαν ἐν μυστηρίῳ,
                    τὴν ἀποκεκρυμμένην, ἣν προώρισεν ὁ θεὸς
                    πρὸ τῶν αἰώνων εἰς δόξαν ἡμῶν, **8** ἣν
                    οὐδεὶς τῶν ἀρχόντων τοῦ αἰῶνος τούτου
                    ἔγνωκεν·
      Reason: (P) Evidence paragraph
        Thesis: εἰ γὰρ ἔγνωσαν, οὐκ ἂν τὸν κύριον τῆς
                    δόξης ἐσταύρωσαν.
        Evidence: **9** ἀλλὰ καθὼς γέγραπται
                    ῍Α ὀφθαλμὸς οὐκ εἶδεν καὶ οὖς
                    οὐκ ἤκουσεν
                    καὶ ἐπὶ καρδίαν ἀνθρώπου οὐκ
                    ἀνέβη,
                    ἃ ἡτοίμασεν ὁ θεὸς τοῖς ἀγαπῶσιν
                    αὐτόν.
  Amplification: (P) Amplification paragraph
    Thesis: (P) Clarification paragraph
      Thesis: **10** ἡμῖν δὲ ἀπεκάλυψεν ὁ θεὸς διὰ τοῦ
                    πνεύματος·
      Clarification: (P) Amplification paragraph
        Thesis: τὸ γὰρ πνεῦμα πάντα ἐραυνᾷ, καὶ
                    τὰ βάθη τοῦ θεοῦ.
      Amplification: Rhetorical (P) Evidence paragraph
        Evidence: **11** τίς γὰρ οἶδεν ἀνθρώπων
                    τὰ τοῦ ἀνθρώπου εἰ μὴ τὸ
                    πνεῦμα τοῦ ἀνθρώπου τὸ
                    ἐν αὐτῷ;
        Thesis: οὕτως καὶ τὰ τοῦ θεοῦ οὐδεὶς
                    ἔγνωκεν εἰ μὴ τὸ πνεῦμα τοῦ
                    θεοῦ.

Amplification: Chiastic (P) Antithetical paragraph
Thesis A₁: 12 ἡμεῖς δὲ οὐ τὸ πνεῦμα τοῦ κόσμου
ἐλάβομεν ἀλλὰ τὸ πνεῦμα τὸ ἐκ
τοῦ θεοῦ, ἵνα εἰδῶμεν τὰ ὑπὸ τοῦ
θεοῦ χαρισθέντα ἡμῖν· 13 ἃ καὶ
λαλοῦμεν οὐκ ἐν διδακτοῖς
ἀνθρωπίνης σοφίας λόγοις ἀλλ᾽
ἐν διδακτοῖς πνεύματος,
πνευματικοῖς πνευματικὰ
συγκρίνοντες.

Antithesis B: 14 ψυχικὸς δὲ ἄνθρωπος οὐ
δέχεται τὰ τοῦ πνεύματος τοῦ
θεοῦ, μωρία γὰρ αὐτῷ ἐστιν,
καὶ οὐ δύναται γνῶναι, ὅτι
πνευματικῶς ἀνακρίνεται·

Thesis A₂: (P) Evidence paragraph
Thesis: 15 ὁ δὲ πνευματικὸς ἀνακρίνει
[τὰ] πάντα, αὐτὸς δὲ ὑπ᾽
οὐδενὸς ἀνακρίνεται.

Evidence: (P) Comment paragraph
Thesis: 16 τίς γὰρ ἔγνω νοῦν κυρίου,
ὃς συμβιβάσει αὐτόν;
Comment: ἡμεῖς δὲ νοῦν Χριστοῦ
ἔχομεν.

Note: The punctuation of 2:7–8 follows the corrected third edition of the UBS *Greek New Testament*.

Table 13G
Constituent display of 1 Corinthians 3:10–15
Primarily expository texttype

Point X: (P) Illustration paragraph
   Thesis: verse 5
   Illustration: (P) Coordinate paragraph
      Thesis$_1$: verses 6–9
      Thesis$_2$: verses 10–15 analyzed below

Thesis$_2$: (E) Amplification paragraph
   Thesis: (E) Comment paragraph
      Thesis: **10** Κατὰ τὴν χάριν τοῦ θεοῦ τὴν δοθεῖσάν μοι ὡς
          σοφὸς ἀρχιτέκτων θεμέλιον ἔθηκα, ἄλλος δὲ
          ἐποικοδομεῖ.
      Comment: (H) Reason paragraph*
         Thesis: ἕκαστος δὲ βλεπέτω πῶς ἐποικοδομεῖ·
         Reason: **11** θεμέλιον γὰρ ἄλλον οὐδεὶς δύναται θεῖναι
              παρὰ τὸν κείμενον, ὅς ἐστιν Ἰησοῦς Χριστός.
   Amplification: (E) Reason paragraph
      Thesis: **12** εἰ δέ τις ἐποικοδομεῖ ἐπὶ τὸν θεμέλιον χρυσόν,
         ἄργυρον, λίθους τιμίους, ξύλα, χόρτον, καλάμην,
         13 ἑκάστου τὸ ἔργον φανερὸν γενήσεται, ἡ γὰρ
         ἡμέρα δηλώσει·
      Reason: (E) Amplification paragraph
         Thesis: ὅτι ἐν πυρὶ ἀποκαλύπτεται, καὶ ἑκάστου τὸ ἔργον
            ὁποῖόν ἐστιν τὸ πῦρ [αὐτὸ] δοκιμάσει.
      Amplification: (E) Antithetical paragraph
         Thesis: **14** εἴ τινος τὸ ἔργον μενεῖ ὃ
              ἐποικοδόμησεν, μισθὸν λήμψεται·
         Antithesis: **15** εἴ τινος τὸ ἔργον κατακαήσεται,
              ζημιωθήσεται, αὐτὸς δὲ σωθήσεται,
              οὕτως δὲ ὡς διὰ πυρός.

*This paragraph functions as a hortatory aside.

Table 14G
Constituent display of 1 Corinthians 6:12–20
Hortatory texttype

Point N: (H) Reason paragraph
  Reason: (H) Antithetical paragraph
    Introduction: (H) Coordinate paragraph
      Thesis₁: **12** Πάντα μοι ἔξεστιν, ἀλλ᾽ οὐ πάντα συμφέρει.
      Thesis₂: πάντα μοι ἔξεστιν, ἀλλ᾽ οὐκ ἐγὼ
               ἐξουσιασθήσομαι ὑπό τινος.
    Antithesis: (H) Antithetical paragraph
      Thesis: **13** τὰ βρώματα τῇ κοιλίᾳ, καὶ ἡ κοιλία τοῖς
                βρώμασιν·
      Antithesis: ὁ δὲ θεὸς καὶ ταύτην καὶ ταῦτα καταργήσει.
  Thesis: (H) Comment paragraph
    Thesis: τὸ δὲ σῶμα οὐ τῇ πορνείᾳ ἀλλὰ τῷ κυρίῳ, καὶ
          ὁ κύριος τῷ σώματι·
    Comment:**14** ὁ δὲ θεὸς καὶ τὸν κύριον ἤγειρεν καὶ ἡμᾶς
           ἐξεγερεῖ διὰ τῆς δυνάμεως αὐτοῦ.
Thesis: (H) Motivation paragraph
  Motivation: (H) Result paragraph
    Thesis: **15** οὐκ οἴδατε ὅτι τὰ σώματα ὑμῶν μέλη
             Χριστοῦ ἐστιν;
    Result: Rhetorical (H) Clarification paragraph
      Thesis: ἄρας οὖν τὰ μέλη τοῦ Χριστοῦ ποιήσω
             πόρνης μέλη;
      Clarification: (H) Reason paragraph
        Thesis: μὴ γένοιτο.
        Reason: (H) Antithetical paragraph
          Thesis: (H) Evidence paragraph
            Thesis: **16** [ἢ] οὐκ οἴδατε ὅτι ὁ
                    κολλώμενος τῇ πόρνῃ ἓν
                    σῶμά ἐστιν;
            Evidence: Ἔσονται γάρ, φησίν οἱ
                    δύο εἰς σάρκα μίαν.
            Antithesis: **17** ὁ δὲ κολλώμενος τῷ
                    κυρίῳ ἓν πνεῦμά ἐστιν.

Thesis: (H) Motivation paragraph
  Thesis: (H) Reason paragraph
    Thesis: **18** φεύγετε τὴν πορνείαν·
    Reason: πᾶν ἁμάρτημα ὃ ἐὰν ποιήσῃ
        ἄνθρωπος ἐκτὸς τοῦ σώματός ἐστιν, ὁ
        δὲ πορνεύων εἰς τὸ ἴδιον σῶμα
        ἁμαρτάνει.
  Motivation: (H) Result paragraph
    Thesis: Rhetorical (H) Amplification paragraph
      Amplification: **19** ἢ οὐκ οἴδατε ὅτι τὸ
              σῶμα ὑμῶν ναὸς τοῦ ἐν
              ὑμῖν ἁγίου πνεύματός
              ἐστιν, οὗ ἔχετε ἀπὸ
              θεοῦ, καὶ οὐκ ἐστὲ
              ἑαυτῶν;
      Thesis: **20** ἠγοράσθητε γὰρ τιμῆς·
      Result: δοξάσατε δὴ τὸν θεὸν ἐν τῷ σώματι ὑμῶν.

Table 15G
Constituent display of 1 Corinthians 10:23–11:1
Hortatory texttype

Point N: (H) Generalization paragraph
   Introduction: (H) Coordinate paragraph
      Thesis₁: 23   Πάντα ἔξεστιν, ἀλλ' οὐ πάντα συμφέρει.
      Thesis₂: πάντα ἔξεστιν, ἀλλ' οὐ πάντα οἰκοδομεῖ.
   Generalization: Chiastic (H) Coordinate paragraph
      Thesis A₁: 24   μηδεὶς τὸ ἑαυτοῦ ζητείτω ἀλλὰ τὸ τοῦ ἑτέρου.
      Thesis: (H) Coordinate paragraph
      Thesis B₁: 25   Πᾶν τὸ ἐν μακέλλῳ πωλούμενον ἐσθίετε μηδὲν
                  ἀνακρίνοντες διὰ τὴν συνείδησιν, τοῦ κυρίου
                  γὰρ ἡ γῆ καὶ τὸ πλήρωμα αὐτῆς.
      Thesis B₂: (H) Antithetical paragraph
         Thesis: 27   εἴ τις καλεῖ ὑμᾶς τῶν ἀπίστων καὶ θέλετε
                  πορεύεσθαι, πᾶν τὸ παρατιθέμενον ὑμῖν
                  ἐσθίετε μηδὲν ἀνακρίνοντες διὰ τὴν
                  συνείδησιν.
        Antithesis: (H) Reason paragraph
         Thesis: 28   ἐὰν δέ τις ὑμῖν εἴπῃ, Τοῦτο
                  ἱερόθυτόν ἐστιν, μὴ ἐσθίετε δι'
                  ἐκεῖνον τὸν μηνύσαντα καὶ τὴν
                  συνείδησιν— 29 συνείδησιν δὲ λέγω
                  οὐχὶ τὴν ἑαυτοῦ ἀλλὰ τὴν τοῦ ἑτέρου.
        Reason:(H) Coordinate paragraph
           Thesis₁: ἱνατί γὰρ ἡ ἐλευθερία μου
                  κρίνεται ὑπὸ ἄλλης συνειδήσεως;
           Thesis₂: 30   εἰ ἐγὼ χάριτι μετέχω, τί
                  βλασφημοῦμαι ὑπὲρ οὗ ἐγὼ
                  εὐχαριστῶ;
   Thesis A₂: (H) Comment paragraph
      Thesis: (H) Amplification paragraph
         Thesis: 31   εἴτε οὖν ἐσθίετε εἴτε πίνετε εἴτε τι
                  ποιεῖτε, πάντα εἰς δόξαν θεοῦ
                  ποιεῖτε.

Amplification: **32** ἀπρόσκοποι καὶ Ἰουδαίοις
γίνεσθε καὶ Ἕλλησιν καὶ
τῇ ἐκκλησίᾳ τοῦ θεοῦ,
33 καθὼς κἀγὼ πάντα
πᾶσιν ἀρέσκω, μὴ ζητῶν τὸ
ἐμαυτοῦ σύμφορον ἀλλὰ τὸ
τῶν πολλῶν, ἵνα σωθῶσιν.
Comment: **11:1** μιμηταί μου γίνεσθε, καθὼς κἀγὼ Χριστοῦ.

Note: Thesis A₂ is chiastically coordinate with Thesis A₁.

References

Aeschylus. 1926a. Eumenides. In Hugh Lloyd-Jones (ed.), Aeschylus 2: Agamemnon; libation-bearers; Eumenides; fragments. Herbert Weir Smyth, tr. Loeb Classical Library. Cambridge, Mass.: Harvard University Press.

————. 1926b. Agamemnon. In Hugh Lloyd-Jones (ed.), Aeschylus 2: Agamemnon; libation-bearers; Eumenides; fragments. Herbert Weir Smyth, tr. Loeb Classical Library. Cambridge, Mass.: Harvard University Press.

Aland, Kurt, ed. 1970. Synopsis of the four gospels. Stuttgart: United Bible Societies.

————, H. Bachmann, and W. A. Slaby, eds. 1978. Vollständige konkordanz zum Griechischen Neuen Testament 2: Spezialübersichten. Berlin: Walter de Gruyter.

————, Matthew Black, Carlo M. Martini, Bruce M. Metzger, and Allen Wikgren, eds. 1975. The Greek New Testament. 3rd ed. New York: United Bible Societies.

————, ————, ————, ————, and ————, eds. 1983. The Greek New Testament. 3rd ed. corrected. New York: United Bible Societies.

Alford, Henry. 1983. The New Testament for English readers. Grand Rapids, Mich.: Baker Book House.

Apuleius, [Lucius]. 1915. The golden ass: Being the metamorphoses of Lucius Apuleius. W. Adlington, tr. S. Gaselee, rev. Loeb Classical Library. Cambridge, Mass.: Harvard University Press.

Archer, Gleason L. and Gregory Chirichigno. 1983. Old Testament quotations in the New Testament. Chicago: Moody Press.

181

Aristides, P. Aelius. 1981. Sacred tales. In P. Aelius Aristides, The complete works 2: Orations 17–53. Charles A. Behr, tr. Leiden, The Netherlands: E. J. Brill.

Aristophanes. 1924. Wasps. In Aristophanes 1: The Archarnians; the knights; the clouds; the wasps. Benjamin Bickley Rogers, tr. Loeb Classical Library. Cambridge, Mass.: Harvard University Press.

Aristotle. 1936. On the soul; parva naturalia; on breath. W. S. Hett, tr. Loeb Classical Library. Cambridge, Mass.: Harvard University Press.

Arndt, William F. and F. Wilbur Gingrich. 1957. A Greek-English lexicon of the New Testament and other early Christian literature. Chicago: The University of Chicago Press.

Athenaeus. 1937. Deipnosophists 6. Charles Burton Gulick, tr. Loeb Classical Library. Cambridge, Mass.: Harvard University Press.

Athenagoras the Athenian. 1979. On the resurrection of the dead. In A. Cleveland Coxe (ed.), Ante-Nicene fathers 2: Fathers of the second century, by Alexander Roberts and James Donaldson. B. P. Pratten, tr. Grand Rapids, Mich.: William B. Eerdmans.

Bailey, Kenneth E. 1983. The structure of 1 Corinthians and Paul's theological method with special reference to 4:17. Novum Testamentum 25:152–81.

Barrett, Charles Kingsley. 1964. Christianity at Corinth. Bulletin of the John Rylands Library 46:269–97. Manchester, England: The John Rylands Library.

———. 1965. Things sacrificed to idols. New Testament Studies 11:138–53.

———. 1968. A commentary on the first epistle to the Corinthians. In Henry Chadwick (ed.), Harper's New Testament commentaries. New York: Harper & Row.

———. 1973. A commentary on the second epistle to the Corinthians. In Henry Chadwick (ed.), Harper's New Testament commentaries. New York: Harper & Row.

Beekman, John, John Callow, and Michael Kopesec. 1981. The semantic structure of written communication. 5th ed. Dallas: Summer Institute of Linguistics.

Black, David Alan, ed. 1992. Linguistics and New Testament interpretation: Essays on discourse analysis. Nashville: Broadman Press.

Blass, Friedrich, Albert Debrunner, and Robert W. Funk. 1961. A Greek grammar of the New Testament and other early Christian literature. Chicago: The University of Chicago Press.

Bloomfield, Leonard. 1933. Language. New York: Holt, Rinehart, and Winston.

Boers, Hendrikus. 1980. Discourse structure and macro-structure in the interpretation of texts: John 4:1–42 as an example. In Paul J. Achtemeier (ed.), Society of Biblical Literature 1980 seminar papers, 159–82. Chico, Calif.: Scholars Press.

Booth, Steven Craig. 1991. A discourse analysis of selected peak marking features in the gospel of John. Ph.D. dissertation. Southwestern Baptist Theological Seminary.

Brown, Gillian and George Yule. 1983. Discourse analysis. Cambridge: Cambridge University Press.

Bruce, Frederick Fyvie. 1951. The Acts of the Apostles: The Greek text with introduction and commentary. Grand Rapids, Mich.: William B. Eerdmans.

———. 1971. 1 & 2 Corinthians. In Matthew Black (ed.), The new century Bible commentary. Grand Rapids, Mich.: William B. Eerdmans.

Burquest, Don and Immanuel Christian. 1982. Rhetorical questions in First Corinthians and Galatians. Notes on Translation 89 (June): 2–47.

Callow, John. 1983a. Word order in New Testament Greek 1. Selected Technical Articles Related to Translation 7:3–50.

———. 1983b. Word order in New Testament Greek 2. Selected Technical Articles Related to Translation 8:3–32.

———. 1992. Constituent order in copula clauses: A partial study. In David Alan Black (ed.), Linguistics and New Testament interpretation, 68–89. Nashville: Broadman Press.

Callow, Kathleen. 1974. Discourse considerations in translating the Word of God. Grand Rapids, Mich.: Zondervan Publishing House.

Calvin, John. 1948. Calvin's commentaries 39: Commentary on the epistles of Paul the apostle to the Corinthians 1. John Pringle, tr. Grand Rapids, Mich.: William B. Eerdmans.

Cervin, Richard S. 1993. A critique of Timothy Friberg's dissertation: New Testament Greek word order in light of discourse considerations. Journal of Translation and Textlinguistics 6:56–85.

Charolles, M. 1983. Coherence as a principle in the interpretation of discourse. Text 3:71–97.

Chomsky, Noam. 1957. Syntactic structures. The Hague: Mouton.

Cicero, [Marcus Tullius]. 1927. In defense of Cluentius. In The speeches. H. Grose Hodge, tr. Loeb Classical Library. Cambridge, Mass.: Harvard University Press.

Clendenen, Ewell Ray. 1987. Discourse strategies in Jeremiah 10:1–16. Journal of Biblical Literature 106:401–8.

———. 1989. The interpretation of biblical Hebrew hortatory texts: A textlinguistic approach to the book of Malachi. Ph.D. dissertation. University of Texas at Arlington.

Comrie, Bernard. 1981. Language universals and linguistic typology. Chicago: University of Chicago Press.

Conzelmann, Hans. 1975. A commentary on the first epistle to the Corinthians. James W. Leitch, tr. Hermeneia commentary series. Philadelphia: Fortress Press.

Craig, Clarence T. 1953. The first epistle to the Corinthians. In George Arthur Buttrick (ed.), The interpreter's Bible 10. New York: Abingdon Press.

de Beaugrande, Robert-Alain and Wolfgang Ulrich Dressler. 1981. Introduction to text linguistics. New York: Longman.

Demetrius. 1932. On style. In Aristotle, The poetics; Longinus, On the sublime; Demetrius, On style. W. Rhys Roberts, tr. Loeb Classical Library. Cambridge, Mass.: Harvard University Press.

Dio Chrysostom. 1940. Orationes. In Dio Chrysostom 3. J. W. Cohoon and H. Lamar Crosby, trs. Loeb Classical Library. Cambridge, Mass.: Harvard University Press.

————. 1946. Orationes. In Dio Chrysostom 4. H. Lamar Crosby, tr. Loeb Classical Library. Cambridge, Mass.: Harvard University Press.

Diodorus. 1946. Diodorus of Sicily 4. C. H. Oldfather, tr. Loeb Classical Library. Cambridge, Mass.: Harvard University Press.

Dionysius of Halicarnassus. 1937. The Roman antiquities 1. Earnest Cary, tr. Loeb Classical Library. Cambridge, Mass.: Harvard University Press.

Doty, William G. 1973. Letters in primitive Christianity. Guides to Biblical Scholarship series. Philadelphia: Fortress Press.

Dover, K. J. 1960. Greek word order. Cambridge: Cambridge University Press.

Edwards, Thomas Charles. 1885. A commentary on the first epistle to the Corinthians. London: Hodder and Stoughton; Hamilton, Adams & Co.

Eitrem, S. and L. Amundsen. 1936. Papyri Osloenses. Oslo: Det Norske Videnskaps-Akademi.

Euripides. 1912. Ion. In Euripides 4. Arthur S. Way, tr. Loeb Classical Library. Cambridge, Mass.: Harvard University Press.

Faw, Chalmer E. 1952. On the writing of First Thessalonians. Journal of Biblical Literature 71:217–25.

Fee, Gordon D. 1987. Commentary on the first epistle to the Corinthians. In Frederick Fyvie Bruce (ed.), The new international commentary on the New Testament. Grand Rapids, Mich.: William B. Eerdmans.

Feine, Paul, Johannes Behm, and Werner Georg Kümmel. 1966. Introduction to the New Testament. 14th rev. ed. A. J. Mattill, Jr., tr. New York: Abingdon Press.

Fillmore, Charles J. 1981. Pragmatics and the description of discourse. In Peter Cole (ed.), Radical pragmatics, 143–66. New York: Academic Press.

Findlay, G. G. 1979. St. Paul's first epistle to the Corinthians. In W. Robertson Nicoll (ed.), The expositor's Greek Testament 2. Grand Rapids, Mich.: William B. Eerdmans.

Fleming, Ilah. 1988. Communication analysis: A stratificational approach 2. Dallas: Summer Institute of Linguistics.

Foley, William A. and Robert D. van Valin, Jr. 1985. Information packaging in the clause. In Timothy Shopen (ed.), Language typology and syntactic description 1: Clause structure, 282–364. Cambridge, England: Cambridge University Press.

Friberg, Barbara and Timothy Friberg. 1981. Analytical Greek New Testament: Greek text analysis. Grand Rapids, Mich.: Baker Book House.

Friberg, Timothy. 1978. The discourse structure of the Greek text of Galatians. M.A. thesis. University of Minnesota.

––––––. 1982. New Testament Greek word order in light of discourse considerations. Ph.D. dissertation. University of Minnesota.

Fries, Charles Carpenter. 1952. The structure of English: An introduction to the construction of English sentences. New York: Harcourt, Brace and Co.

Fyfe, W. Hamilton. 1932. Introduction. In Aristole, The poetics; Longinus, On the sublime; Demetrius, On style. Loeb Classical Library. Cambridge, Mass.: Harvard University Press.

Gaius. 1988. The institutes of Gaius. W. M. Gordon and O. F. Robinson, trs. Ithaca, New York: Cornell University Press.

Garland, David E., ed. 1983. First Corinthians [thematic issue]. Review and Expositor 80:313–425.

Goodenough, Erwin Ramsdell. 1964. Jewish symbols in the Greco-Roman period 11. New York: Pantheon Books.

Goodman, Nelson. 1978. Ways of worldmaking. Indianapolis: Hockett Publishing.

Greenberg, Joseph H. 1963. Some universals of grammar with particular reference to the order of meaningful elements. In Joseph H. Greenberg (ed.), Universals of language, 58–90. Cambridge, Mass.: MIT Press.

Grenfell, B. P. and A. S. Hunt, eds. 1916. The Oxyrhynchus Papyri 12. London: Oxford Press.

Grimes, Joseph E. 1972. The thread of discourse. Janua Linguarum 207. The Hague: Mouton.

Grosheide, Fredrick Willen. 1955. Commentary on the first epistle to the Corinthians. In N. B. Stonehouse (ed.), The new international commentary on the New Testament. Grand Rapids, Mich.: William B. Eerdmans.

Guthrie, Donald. 1970. New Testament introduction. 3rd ed. Downers Grove, Illinois: InterVarsity Press.

Habel, Norman. 1971. Literary criticism of the Old Testament. Guides to Biblical Scholarship series. Philadelphia: Fortress Press.

Haberlandt, Karl and Geoffrey Bingham. 1982. The role of scripts in the comprehension and retention of texts. In Teun A. van Dijk and Janos S. Petofi (eds.), New developments in cognitive models of discourse processing. Special issue of Text 2:29–46.

Halliday, M. A. K. and R. Hasan. 1976. Cohesion in English. London: Longmans.

Hauck, Friedrich and Siegfried Schulz. 1968. πόρνη κτλ. In Gerhard Kittel (ed.), Theological dictionary of the New Testament 6:579–95. Geoffrey W. Bromiley, tr. Grand Rapids, Mich.: William B. Eerdmans.

Héring, Jean. 1962. The first epistle of Saint Paul to the Corinthians. P. J. Allcock and A. W. Heathcole, trs. London: The Epworth Press.

Herodotus. 1924. Herodotus 2. A. D. Godley, tr. Loeb Classical Library. Cambridge, Mass.: Harvard University Press.

Hoel, Paul G. 1962. Introduction to mathematical statistics. 3rd ed. New York: John Wiley & Sons.

Hoopert, Daniel Arthur. 1981. The discourse structure of 1 Corinthians 1–4. M.A. thesis. University of Texas at Arlington.

Hopper, Paul J. and Sandra A. Thompson. 1980. Transitivity in grammar and discourse. Language 56(2):251–99.

Hurd, John Coolidge, Jr. 1983. The origin of 1 Corinthians. 2nd ed. Macon, Georgia: Mercer University Press.

Hymes, Dell. 1986. The general epistle of James. International Journal of the Sociology of Language 62:75–103.

Josephus. 1930. Josephus 4: Jewish antiquities: Books 1–4. H. St. J. Thackeray, tr. Loeb Classical Library. Cambridge, Mass.: Harvard University Press.

Kittel, Gerhard, ed. 1965. Theological dictionary of the New Testament. Grand Rapids, Mich.: William B. Eerdmans.

Kubo, Sakae. 1975. A reader's Greek-English lexicon of the New Testament and a beginner's guide for the translation of New Testament Greek. Andrews University Monographs 4. Grand Rapids, Mich.: Zondervan Publishing House.

Larson, Mildred L. 1984. Meaning-based translation: A guide to cross-language equivalence. Lanham, Mass.: University Press of America.

Lenski, Richard C. H. 1946. The interpretation of St. Paul's first and second epistle to the Corinthians. Columbus, Ohio: Wartburg Press.

Levinsohn, Stephen H. 1987. Textual connections in Acts. Society of Biblical Literature Monograph Series. Atlanta: Scholars Press.

———. 1992. Discourse features of New Testament Greek. Dallas: Summer Institute of Linguistics.

Liddell, Henry George, Robert Scott, Henry Stuart Jones, and Roderick McKenzie. 1968. A Greek-English lexicon: With a supplement. 9th ed. Oxford: Clarendon Press.

Lightfoot, John. 1979. A commentary on the New Testament from the Talmud and Hebraica. Grand Rapids, Mich.: Baker Book House.

Longacre, Robert E. 1968. Philippine languages: Discourse, paragraph and sentence structure 1. Summer Institute of Linguistics Publications in Linguistics and Related Fields 21. Santa Ana, Calif.

————. 1970. Sentence structure as a statement calculus. Language 46(4):783–815.

————. 1979a. The discourse structure of the flood narrative. Journal of the American Academy of Religion 47 (Supplement B):89–133.

————. 1979b. The paragraph as a grammatical unit. In Talmy Givón (ed.), Discourse and syntax, 115–34. Syntax and Semantics series 12. New York: Academic Press.

————. 1980. An apparatus for the identification of paragraph types. Notes on Linguistics 15:5–22.

————. 1981. A spectrum and profile approach to discourse analysis. Text 1(4):337–59.

————. 1983a. Exhortation and mitigation in First John. Selected Technical Articles Related to Translation 9:3–44.

————. 1983b. The grammar of discourse. New York: Plenum Press.

————. 1985a. Discourse peak as a zone of turbulence. In J. Wirth (ed.), Beyond the sentence, 81–92. Ann Arbor, Mich.: Karome.

————. 1985b. Tagmemics. Word 36:137–77.

————. 1989a. Joseph: A story of divine providence. Winona Lake, Ind.: Eisenbrauns.

————. 1989b. Two hypotheses regarding text generation and analysis. Discourse Processes 12:413–60.

————. 1990a. Class notes from lecture entitled 'Macrostructures'. Discourse Grammar. April 12, 1990. University of Texas at Arlington.

————. 1990b. Storyline concerns and word order typology in East and West Africa. Studies in African Linguistics, Supplement 10:1–181.

————. 1990c. Introduction. Occasional Papers in Translation and Textlinguistics 4(1–2):1–17.

Longinus. 1932. On the sublime. In Aristole, The Poetics; Longinus, On the Sublime; Demetrius, On Style. W. Hamilton Fyfe, tr. Loeb Classical Library. Cambridge, Mass.: Harvard University Press.

Louw, Johannes P. 1982. Semantics of New Testament Greek. The Society of Biblical Literature Semeia Studies. Philadelphia: Fortress Press.

————, Eugene A. Nida, Rondal B. Smith, and Karen A. Munson. 1988. Greek-English lexicon of the New Testament: Based on semantic domains. New York: United Bible Societies.

Lund, Nils W. 1992. Chiasmus in the New Testament. Chapel Hill: University of North Carolina Press. Reprint from 1942, Peabody, Mass.: Hendrickson Publishers.

Mann, William C. and Sandra A. Thompson. 1988. Rhetorical structure theory: Towards a functional theory of text organization. Text 8(3):243–81.

Martin, Ralph P. 1986. New Testament foundations: A guide for Christian students 2: The Acts; The letters; The Apocalypse. rev. ed. Grand Rapids, Mich.: William B. Eerdmans.

Matsumura, Takashi. 1983. A semantic structure analysis of 1 Corinthians 5–7. M.A. thesis. University of Texas at Arlington.

Menander. 1930. The peevish man. In The principal fragments. Francis G. Allinson, tr. Loeb Classical Library. Cambridge, Mass.: Harvard University Press.

Metzger, Bruce M. 1971. A textual commentary on the Greek New Testament. New York: United Bible Societies.

Miehle, Helen Louise. 1981. Theme in Greek hortatory discourse: van Dijk and Beekman-Callow approaches applied to 1 John. Ph.D. dissertation. University of Texas at Arlington.

Miller, James R. and Walter Kintsch. 1981. Knowledge-based aspects of prose comprehension and readability. Text 1:215–32.

Minsky, M. 1980. A framework for representing knowledge. In Dieter Metzing (ed.), Frame conceptions and text understanding, 1–25. Berlin: de Gruyter.

Morgan-Wynne, John. 1983. Introduction to 1 Corinthians. The Southwestern Journal of Theology 26:4–15.

Morris, Leon. 1958. The first epistle of Paul to the Corinthians. In R. V. G. Tasker (ed.), The Tyndale New Testament commentaries 7. Grand Rapids, Mich.: William B. Eerdmans.

————. 1974. The gospel according to St. Luke. In R. V. G. Tasker (ed.), The Tyndale New Testament commentaries 3. Grand Rapids, Mich.: William B. Eerdmans.

Moulton, James Hope. 1908. Prolegomena. In James Moulton Hope (ed.), A grammar of New Testament Greek 1. Edinburgh: T.& T. Clark.

———— and Wilbert Francis Howard. 1920. Accidence and word formation. In James Hope Moulton (ed.), A grammar of New Testament Greek 2. Edinburgh: T. & T. Clark.

Moulton, W. F., A. S. Geden, and H. K. Moulton. 1963. A concordance to the Greek Testament. 4th ed. Edinburgh: T. & T. Clark.

Nestle, Eberhard, Erwin Nestle, and Kurt Aland. 1957. Novum Testamentum Graece. 23rd ed. Stuttgart, Germany: Privileg. Wurtt. Bibelanstalt.

————, ————, ————, Matthew Black, Carlo M. Martini, Bruce M. Metzger, Allen Wikgren, and Barbara Aland. 1979. Nestle-Aland Novum Testamentum Graece. 26th ed. Stuttgart, Germany: Deutsche Bibelstiftung.

Nida, Eugene A. 1984. Signs, sense, translation. Cape Town: Bible Society of South Africa.

————. 1992. Lexical semantics of the Greek New Testament: A supplement to the Greek-English lexicon of the New Testament based on semantic domains. Atlanta: Scholars Press.

————, J. P. Louw, A. H. Snyman, and J. v. W. Cronje. 1983. Style and discourse: With special reference to the text of the Greek New Testament. Cape Town: Bible Society of South Africa.

———— and Charles R. Taber. 1974. The theory and practice of translation. Helps for Translators 8. Leiden, Netherlands: E. J. Brill.

Niebuhr, H. Richard. 1951. Christ and culture. New York: Harper & Brothers.

Nock, Arthur Darby. 1964. Early Gentile Christianity and its Hellenistic background. New York: Harper & Row.

Oates, J. F., A. E. Samuel, and C. B. Welles. 1967. Yale papyri in the Beinecke rare book and manuscript library. New Haven: Yale University Press.

Oepke, Albrecht. 1965. κατακαλύπτω κτλ. In Gerhard Kittel (ed.), Theological dictionary of the New Testament 3:561–63. Geoffrey W. Bromiley, tr. Grand Rapids, Mich.: William B. Eerdmans.

Orr, William F. and James Arthur Walther. 1976. 1 Corinthians. In William Foxwell Albright and David Noel Freedman (eds.), The Anchor Bible 32. Garden City, New York: Doubleday & Company.

Osburn, Carroll D. 1976. That which is perfect. In Carl Brecheen (ed.), Freedom in Christ, 139–71. Abilene, Tex.: Abilene Christian College Bookstore.

Pausanias. 1918. Descriptions of Greece 1. W. H. S. Jones, tr. Loeb Classical Library. Cambridge, Mass.: Harvard University Press.

Philo. 1937. De specialibus legibus. In Philo. 7. F. H. Colson, tr. Loeb Classical Library. Cambridge, Mass.: Harvard University Press.

Pike, Kenneth L. 1967. Language in relation to a unified theory of the structure of human behavior. 2nd ed. The Hague: Mouton.

————. 1982. Linguistic concepts: An introduction to Tagmemics. Lincoln: University of Nebraska Press.

————. 1987. Teaching in His image: The structure of the Sermon on the Mount. Arts & Letters 1:3–11.

————. 1993. Talk, thought, and thing: The emic road toward conscious knowledge. Dallas: Summer Institute of Linguistics.

———— and Evelyn G. Pike. 1983. Text and tagmeme. Norwood, NJ: Ablex Publishing.

Plato. 1937. The republic 1. Paul Shorey, tr. Loeb Classical Library. Cambridge, Mass.: Harvard University Press.

Plutarch. 1928. Advice to bride and groom. In Moralia 2. Frank Cole Babbitt, tr. Loeb Classical Library. Cambridge, Mass.: Harvard University Press.

————. 1931. Sayings of Spartans: Charillus. In Moralia 3. Frank Cole Babbitt, tr. Loeb Classical Library. Cambridge, Mass.: Harvard University Press.

————. 1936a. The Roman questions. In Moralia 4. Frank Cole Babbitt, tr. Loeb Classical Library. Cambridge, Mass.: Harvard University Press.

————. 1936b. Isis and Osiris. In Moralia 5. Frank Cole Babbitt, tr. Loeb Classical Library. Cambridge, Mass.: Harvard University Press.

————. 1936c. Obsolescence of oracles. In Moralia 5. Frank Cole Babbitt, tr. Loeb Classical Library. Cambridge, Mass.: Harvard University Press.

————. 1936d. Oracles at Delphi. In Moralia 5. Frank Cole Babbitt, tr. Loeb Classical Library. Cambridge, Mass.: Harvard University Press.

Plumley, J. Martin. 1977. Limitations of Coptic (Sahidic) in representing Greek. In Bruce M. Metzger (ed.), The early versions of the New Testament: Their origin, transmission, and limitations, 141–52. Oxford: Clarendon Press.

Radney, J. Randolph. 1988. Some factors that influence fronting in Koiné clauses. Occasional Papers in Translation and Textlinguistics 2(3):1–79.

Ramsey, William M. 1960. The cities of St. Paul. Grand Rapids, Mich.: Baker Book House.

Richardson, Peter. 1980. Judgment, immorality, and sexual ethics in 1 Corinthians 6. In Paul J. Achtemeier (ed.), Society of Biblical Literature 1980 seminar papers, 337–57. Chico, Calif.: Scholars Press.

Rife, J. Merle. 1933. The mechanics of translation Greek. Journal of Biblical Literature 52:244–52.

Roberts, W. Rhys. 1912. A point of Greek and Latin word-order. The Classical Review 26:177–79.

Robertson, A. T. 1934. A grammar of the Greek New Testament. Nashville: Broadman Press.

Robertson, Archibald and Alfred Plummer. 1914. A critical and exegetical commentary on the first epistle of St. Paul to the Corinthians. In Samuel Rolles Driver, Alfred Plummer, and Charles Augustus Briggs (eds.), The international critical commentary on the holy scriptures of the Old and New Testaments. 2nd ed. Edinburgh: T. & T. Clark.

Schmithals, Walter. [1956] 1971. Gnosticism in Corinth. John E. Steely, tr. Reprint, New York: Abingdon Press.

Scranton, Robert L. 1980. Corinth. In The New Encyclopaedia Britannica, 1980 ed.

Seneca, [Lucius Annaeus]. 1935. On Benefits. In Moral essays 3. John W. Basore, tr. Loeb Classical Library. Cambridge, Mass.: Harvard University Press.

Smith, Dennis E. 1977. The Egyptian cults at Corinth. Harvard Theological Review 70:201–31.

Sophocles. 1913. Electra. In Sophocles 2: Ajax, Electra, Trachiniae, Philoctetes. F. Storr, tr. Loeb Classical Library. Cambridge, Mass.: Harvard University Press.

Stowers, Stanley K. 1986. Letter writing in Greco-Roman antiquity. Library of Early Christianity. Philadelphia: The Westminister Press.

Strabo. 1927. The geography of Strabo 4. Horace Leonard Jones, tr. Loeb Classical Library. Cambridge, Mass.: Harvard University Press.

Strack, H. L. and P. Billerbeck. 1922ff. Kommentar zum NT ans Talmud und Midrasch 2. München: Beck.

Tatian. 1979. Address of Tatian to the Greeks. In A. Cleveland Coxe (ed.), Ante-Nicene fathers 2: Fathers of the second century. J. E. Ryland, tr. Grand Rapids, Mich.: William B. Eerdmans.

Terry, Ralph Bruce. 1992. Some aspects of the discourse structure of James. Journal of Translation and Textlinguistics 5(2):106–25.

Thayer, Joseph Henry. 1979. The new Thayer's Greek-English lexicon of the New Testament. Corrected edition from 1889. Lafayette, Ind.: AP&A.

Turner, Nigel. 1963. Syntax. In James Hope Moulton (ed.), A grammar of New Testament Greek 3. Edinburgh: T. & T. Clark.

———. 1976. Style. In James Hope Moulton (ed.), A grammar of New Testament Greek 4. Edinburgh: T. & T. Clark.

van Dijk, Teun A. 1972. Some aspects of text grammars. The Hague: Mouton.

———. 1977. Text and context. New York: Longman House.

———. 1981. Semantic macro-structures and knowledge frames in discourse comprehension. Text 1:3–32.

Virgil. 1935. Aeneid. In Virgil 1: Eclogues, Georgics, Aeneid 1–6. H. Rushton Fairclough, tr. rev. ed. Loeb Classical Library. Cambridge, Mass.: Harvard University Press.

Wheelock, Frederic M. 1960. Latin: An introductory course based on ancient authors. 2nd ed. College Outline Series. New York: Barnes & Noble.

Willis, Wendell Lee. 1985. Idol meat in Corinth: The Pauline argument in
1 Corinthians 8 and 10. Society of Biblical Literature Dissertation Series
68. Chico, California: Scholars Press.

Young, Richard E., Alton L. Becker, and Kenneth L. Pike. 1970. Rhetoric:
Discovery and change. New York: Harcourt, Brace & World.

Youngman, Scott. 1987. Stratificational analysis of a hortatory text:
1 Corinthians 8.1–11.1. M.A. thesis. University of Texas at Arlington.

Ziesler, John A. 1986. Which is the best Commentary? III. 1 Corinthians.
The Expository Times 97:263–67.

Zinserling, Verena. 1973. Women in Greece and Rome. L. A. Jones, tr.
New York: Abner Schram.

Summer Institute of Linguistics and
The University of Texas at Arlington
Publications in Linguistics

10. **Verb studies in five New Guinea languages,** ed. by Alan Pence. 1964.
15. **Bolivian Indian tribes: Classification, bibliography and map of present language distribution,** by Harold Key and Mary R. Key. 1967.
18. **Tzotzil grammar,** by Marion M. Cowan. 1969.
19. **Aztec studies 1: Phonological and grammatical studies in modern Nahuatl dialects,** ed. by Dow F. Robinson. 1969.
20. **The phonology of Capanahua and its grammatical basis,** by Eugene E. Loos. 1969.
21. **Philippine languages: Discourse, paragraph and sentence structure,** by Robert E. Longacre. 1970.
22. **Aztec studies 2: Sierra Nahuat word structure,** by Dow F. Robinson. 1970.
23. **Tagmemic and matrix linguistics applied to selected African languages,** by Kenneth L. Pike. 1970.
24. **The grammar of Lamani,** by Ronald L. Trail. 1970.
25. **A linguistic sketch of Jicaltepec Mixtec,** by C. Henry Bradley. 1970.
26. **Major grammatical patterns of Western Bukidnon Manobo,** by Richard E. Elkins. 1970.
27. **Central Bontoc: Sentence, paragraph and discourse,** by Lawrence A. Reid. 1970.
28. **Identification of participants in discourse: A study of aspects of form and meaning in Nomatsiguenga,** by Mary Ruth Wise. 1971.
29. **Tupi studies 1,** ed. by David Bendor-Samuel. 1971.
30. **L'énoncé Toura (Côte d'Ivoire),** by Thomas Bearth. 1971.
33. **Two studies on the Lacandones of Mexico,** by Phillip Baer and William R. Merrifield. 1971.
36. **Tagmeme sequences in the English noun phrase,** by Peter H. Fries. 1970.
37. **Hierarchical structures in Guajajara,** by David Bendor-Samuel. 1972.
38. **Dialect intelligibility testing,** by Eugene H. Casad. 1974.
39. **Preliminary grammar of Auca,** by M. Catherine Peeke. 1973.
40.1. **Clause, sentence, and discourse patterns in selected languages of Nepal 1: General approach,** ed. by Austin Hale. 1973.
40.2. **Clause, sentence, and discourse patterns in selected languages of Nepal 2: Clause,** ed. by Austin Hale and David Watters. 1973.
40.3. **Clause, sentence, and discourse patterns in selected languages of Nepal 3: Texts,** ed. by Austin Hale. 1973.
40.4. **Clause, sentence, and discourse patterns in selected languages of Nepal 4: Word lists,** ed. by Austin Hale. 1973.
41.1. **Patterns in clause, sentence, and discourse in selected languages of India and Nepal 1: Sentence and discourse,** ed. by Ronald L. Trail. 1973.
41.2. **Patterns in clause, sentence, and discourse in selected languages of India and Nepal 2: Clause,** ed. by Ronald L. Trail. 1973.
41.3. **Patterns in clause, sentence, and discourse in selected languages of India and Nepal 3: Texts,** ed. by Ronald L. Trail. 1973.
41.4. **Patterns in clause, sentence, and discourse in selected languages of India and Nepal 4: Word lists,** ed. by Ronald L. Trail. 1973.

42. A generative syntax of Peñoles Mixtec, by John P. Daly. 1973.
43. Daga grammar: From morpheme to discourse, by Elizabeth Murane. 1974.
44. A hierarchical sketch of Mixe as spoken in San José El Paraíso, by Julia D. Van Haitsma and Willard Van Haitsma. 1976.
45. Network grammars, ed. by Joseph E. Grimes. 1975.
46. A description of Hiligaynon syntax, by Elmer Wolfenden. 1975.
47. A grammar of Izi, an Igbo language, by Paul E. Meier, Inge Meier, and John T. Bendor-Samuel. 1975.
48. Semantic relationships of Gahuku verbs, by Ellis W. Deibler. 1976.
49. Sememic and grammatical structures in Gurung, by Warren W. Glover. 1974.
50. Clause structure: Surface structure and deep structure roles, by Shin Ja Joo Hwang. 1975.
51. Papers on discourse, ed. by Joseph E. Grimes. 1978.
52.1. Discourse grammar: Studies in indigenous languages of Colombia, Panama, and Ecuador 1, ed. by Robert E. Longacre and Frances Woods. 1976.
52.2. Discourse grammar: Studies in indigenous languages of Colombia, Panama, and Ecuador 2, ed. by Robert E. Longacre and Frances Woods. 1977.
52.3. Discourse grammar: Studies in indigenous languages of Colombia, Panama, and Ecuador 3, ed. by Robert E. Longacre and Frances Woods. 1977.
53. Grammatical analysis, by Kenneth L. Pike and Evelyn G. Pike. 1977.
54. Studies in Otomanguean phonology, ed. by William R. Merrifield. 1977.
55. Two studies in Middle American comparative linguistics, by David Oltrogge and Calvin R. Rensch. 1977.
56.1. An overview of Uto-Aztecan grammar: Studies in Uto-Aztecan grammar 1, by Ronald W. Langacker. 1977.
56.2. Modern Aztec grammatical sketches: Studies in Uto-Aztecan grammar 2, ed. by Ronald W. Langacker. 1979.
56.3. Uto-Aztecan grammatical sketches: Studies in Uto-Aztecan grammar 3, ed. by Ronald W. Langacker. 1982.
56.4. Southern Uto-Aztecan grammatical sketches: Studies in Uto-Aztecan grammar 4, ed. by Ronald W. Langacker. 1984.
57. The deep structure of the sentence in Sara-Ngambay dialogues, including a description of phrase, clause, and paragraph, by James Edward Thayer. 1978.
58.1. Discourse studies in Mesoamerican languages 1: Discussion, ed. by Linda K. Jones. 1979.
58.2. Discourse studies in Mesoamerican languages 2: Texts, ed. by Linda K. Jones. 1979.
59. The functions of reported speech in discourse, by Mildred L. Larson. 1978.
60. A grammatical description of the Engenni language, by Elaine Thomas. 1978.
61. Predicate and argument in Rengao grammar, by Kenneth J. Gregerson. 1979.
62. Nung grammar, by Janice E. Saul and Nancy F. Wilson. 1980.
63. Discourse grammar in Gaⁿdang, by Michael R. Walrod. 1979.
64. A framework for discourse analysis, by Wilbur N. Pickering. 1980.
65. A generative grammar of Afar, by Loren F. Bliese. 1981.
66. Phonology and morphology of Axininca Campa, by David L. Payne. 1981.
67. Pragmatic aspects of English text structure, by Larry B. Jones. 1983.
68. Syntactic change and syntactic reconstruction: A tagmemic approach, by John R. Costello. 1983.

69. **Affix positions and cooccurrences: The PARADIGM program,** by Joseph E. Grimes. 1983.
70. **Babine & Carrier phonology: A historically oriented study,** by Gillian L. Story. 1984.
71. **Workbook for historical linguistics,** by Winfred P. Lehmann. 1984.
72. **Senoufo phonology, discourse to syllable (a prosodic approach),** by Elizabeth Mills. 1984.
73. **Pragmatics in non-Western perspective,** ed. by George Huttar and Kenneth J. Gregerson. 1986.
74. **English phonetic transcription,** by Charles-James N. Bailey. 1985.
75. **Sentence initial devices,** ed. by Joseph E. Grimes. 1986.
76. **Hixkaryana and linguistic typology,** by Desmond C. Derbyshire. 1985.
77. **Discourse features of Korean narration,** by Shin Ja Joo Hwang. 1987.
78. **Tense/aspect and the development of auxiliaries in Kru languages,** by Lynelle Marchese. 1986.
79. **Modes in Dényá discourse,** by Samson Negbo Abangma. 1987.
80. **Current trends and issues in Hispanic linguistics,** ed. by Lenard Studerus. 1987.
81. **Aspects of Western Subanon formal speech,** by William C. Hall. 1987.
82. **Dinka vowel system,** by Job Malou. 1988.
83. **Studies in the syntax of Mixtecan languages 1,** ed. by C. Henry Bradley and Barbara E. Hollenbach. 1988.
84. **Insights into Tagalog: Reduplication, infixation, and stress from nonlinear phonology,** by Koleen M. French. 1988.
85. **The verbal piece in Ebira,** by John R. Adive. 1989.
86. **Comparative Kadai: Linguistic studies beyond Tai,** ed. by Jerold A. Edmondson and David B. Solnit. 1988.
87. **An etymological dictionary of the Chinantec languages: Studies in Chinantec languages 1,** by Calvin R. Rensch. 1989.
88. **Lealao Chinantec syntax: Studies in Chinantec languages 2,** by James E. Rupp. 1989.
89. **Comaltepec Chinantec syntax: Studies in Chinantec languages 3,** by Judi Lynn Anderson. 1989.
90. **Studies in the syntax of Mixtecan languages 2,** ed. by C. Henry Bradley and Barbara E. Hollenbach. 1990.
91. **Language maintenance in Melanesia: Sociolinguistics and social networks in New Caledonia,** by Stephen J. Schooling. 1990.
92. **Comanche dictionary and grammar,** ed. by Lila W. Robinson and James Armagost. 1990.
93. **Development and diversity: Language variation across time and space (A Festschrift for Charles-James N. Bailey),** ed. by Jerold A. Edmondson, Crawford Feagin, and Peter Mühlhäusler. 1990.
94. **Ika syntax: Studies in the languages of Colombia 1,** by Paul S. Frank. 1990.
95. **Syllables, tone, and verb paradigms: Studies in Chinantec languages 4,** ed. by William R. Merrifield and Calvin R. Rensch. 1990.
96. **Survey on a shoestring: A manual for small-scale language surveys,** by Frank Blair. 1990.
97. **Can literacy lead to development? A case study in literacy, adult education, and economic development in India,** by Uwe Gustafsson. 1991.

98. **The structure of Thai narrative,** by Somsonge Burusphat. 1991.
99. **Tense and aspect in eight languages of Cameroon,** ed. by Stephen C. Anderson and Bernard Comrie. 1991.
100. **A reference grammar of Southeastern Tepehuan,** by Thomas L. Willett. 1991.
101. **Barasano syntax: Studies in the languages of Colombia 2,** by Wendell Jones and Paula Jones. 1991.
102. **Tone in five languages of Cameroon,** ed. by Stephen C. Anderson. 1991.
103. **An autosegmental approach to Shilluk phonology,** by Leoma G. Gilley. 1992.
104. **Sentence repetition testing for studies of community bilingualism,** by Carla F. Radloff. 1991.
105. **Studies in the syntax of Mixtecan languages 3,** ed. by C. Henry Bradley and Barbara E. Hollenbach. 1991.
106. **Tepetotutla Chinantec syntax: Studies in Chinantec languages 5,** by David Westley. 1991.
107. **Language in context: Essays for Robert E. Longacre,** ed. by Shin Ja J. Hwang and William R. Merrifield. 1992.
108. **Phonological studies in four languages of Maluku,** ed. by Donald A. Burquest and Wyn D. Laidig. 1992.
109. **Switch reference in Koasati discourse,** by David Rising. 1992.
110. **Windows on bilingualism,** by Eugene Casad. 1992.
111. **Studies in the syntax of Mixtecan languages 4,** ed. by C. Henry Bradley and Barbara E. Hollenbach. 1992.
112. **Retuarã syntax: Studies in the languages of Colombia 3,** by Clay Strom. 1992.
113. **A pragmatic analysis of Norwegian modal particles,** by Erik E. Andvik. 1992.
114. **Proto Witotoan,** by Richard P. Aschmann. 1993.
115. **The function of verb prefixes in Southwestern Otomí,** by Henrietta Andrews. 1993.
116. **The French imparfait and passé simple in discourse,** by Sharon Rebecca Rand. 1993.
117. **Beyond the bilingual classroom: Literacy acquisition among Peruvian Amazon communities,** by Barbara Trudell. 1993.
118. **Epena Pedee syntax: Studies in the languages of Colombia 4,** by Phillip Lee Harms. 1994.
119. **Discourse features of ten languages of West-Central Africa,** ed. by Stephen H. Levensohn. 1994.
120. **A discourse analysis of First Corinthians,** by Ralph Bruce Terry. 1995
121. **The Doyayo language: Selected studies,** by Elisabeth Wiering and Marinus Wiering. 1994.

For further information or a catalog of SIL publications write to:

International Academic Bookstore
Summer Institute of Linguistics
7500 W. Camp Wisdom Road
Dallas, TX 75236